THE **WEIRD** ACCORDION TO AL

For Declan-Haven and Harris-Theodore,
my little weirdoes.

Nathan Rabin

For my dad.

Felipe Sobreiro

CONTENTS

INTRODUCTION BY
"WEIRD AL"
YANKOVIC

Hey, how ya doin'? Al here.

Now, it's entirely possible you may not be able to relate to this, but... believe me, it's pretty darn cool to read a book about yourself. And that's especially true when the book is written by someone as talented, funny and insightful as Nathan Rabin.

A few years ago, I personally selected Nathan to write Weird Al: The Book – a lovely piece of literature which would have *easily* topped the *New York Times* bestseller list if only it had just been way, way, *way* more popular. Undaunted, Nathan chose to write this follow-up completely on his own volition. So it seems that, for him at least, Weird Al books are analogous to Lay's potato chips: you can't have just one.

Knowing from experience that Nathan has a blatant disregard (some would say contempt) for the rules of the English language (somewhat ironic for a guy who's ostensibly a professional writer, no?), I offered to proofread this book, and he happily accepted. I should point out here that I strictly limited myself to correcting the *thousands upon thousands* of punctuation, spelling and grammatical errors. At no point did I make any attempt whatsoever to alter the actual content or message of Nathan's work – not his slobbering, fawning adoration of me, or even his repeated and highly unfortunate insistence that "Hitler had some good ideas." *Those opinions are strictly his own.*

Anyway, I found *The Weird Accordion to Al* very enlightening – I honestly had absolutely no idea how incredibly awesome I was until I read this book. And I'm sure that you'll enjoy it too, particularly if you appreciate words like "ineffable" (*used 5 times*) and "oeuvre" (*used 23 times*).

Well, that's it for now. Keep in touch, and I look forward to reading the book that Nathan Rabin someday writes about *you*!

xo,
Al Yankovic

"WEIRD AL" YANKOVIC (1983)

1.
RICKY

About eight years ago, I received a direct message on Twitter from my childhood hero "Weird Al" Yankovic that changed my life. Al wrote that, of all the writers in the world, he had chosen me to tell his story and write his coffee table book.

After making sure the offer was not an elaborate hoax, my future wife and I jumped up and down and squealed with delight. Have you ever genuinely squealed with delight? I mean, really, really squealed, with whole-soul, whole-body, utterly non-ironic delight? It feels great. It also feels great when someone you grew up idolizing wants to be your collaborator.

The problem was that I was already contracted to write a book at the time, a detached sociological tome about the surprising commonalities between fans of Phish and Insane Clown Posse, and that project was going terribly.

I had spent a year and tens of thousands of dollars chasing this crazy project aboard the Kid Rock Chillin' the Most and Jam Cruises, through the parking lots of dozens of Phish shows and my first Gathering of the Juggalos, yet I somehow felt farther away from finishing the book than when I began.

And then this offer came along. I couldn't believe it. I kept pinching myself. "Weird Al" Yankovic himself wanted me to write his book. Nathan from the group home. Nathan, the man whose personal idiosyncrasies and appalling grammar were a source of quiet horror to everyone cursed to work alongside him. Nathan the guy whose first book flopped, and whose second book flopped and whose third book was a giant question mark (to the point where it actually ended up being his fourth book). That was the guy this consummate winner wanted to write his book.

Part of me wanted to demur and explain that everything I touched failed, but a childhood of perpetual suffering had

blessed and cursed me with a ferocious sense of ambition that made this an offer I could not refuse. I was a geek. What geek could possibly say no to "Weird Al" Yankovic? I also happened to be the head writer of The A.V. Club at the time, so I had to ask my boss if I could write the book.

I assured him that I would not let the fact that I was writing two books simultaneously, both requiring a fair amount of travel, affect my work for the site, knowing deep down that I could not live up to that promise. I had taken on too much, and I would suffer the consequences of my overreaching ambition. But I was also blessed to live out my childhood dreams as an adult hurtling towards a nervous breakdown.

As part of the gig, I was now professionally obligated to not just listen to "Weird Al" Yankovic but to listen to all of his music. To listen to every single song the man ever released commercially. I'm not sure any professional obligation ever thrilled anyone the way the universe's angry insistence that I listen to all of "Weird Al" Yankovic's music thrilled me.

Being professionally obligated to listen to the music of "Weird Al" Yankovic helped me retain what was left of my sanity when I was deeply depressed and wrestling with anxiety. At a time when I was feeling rootless and alienated, overwhelmed and alone, these songs felt like home.

When I learned that Yankovic would be releasing a career-spanning 15-disc box set many years later, I figured it would be the perfect time to revisit Yankovic's work, this time on a song-by-song basis chronicling Al's complete discography in chronological order.

At this point you might be saying, "Gee, Nathan, it sounds like you're just trying to escape the inexorable horror of the present by escaping into an idealized past while simultaneously trying to recapture earlier professional triumphs," to which I can only reply, "Yes. And?"

Al's music soothed me. It comforted me. It amused and diverted me. Al's music plays that role in many peoples' lives. It connects them, on an almost Proustian level, to the overwhelming emotions of their childhood, when music seemed like magic and performers of Al's caliber like magicians. Al's music is nitro for the burning-hot engine of our childhood imaginations.

Al's story made sense in a way that my own did not. It had a clean, clear arc. It was the tale of a geek triumphant. I just had to tell the tale in a way that did justice to Al's incredible accomplishments, from his demo-like first professional recordings to a 2017 box set that won Al his fifth Grammy.

"My Bologna" might have kicked off Al's career as a recording artist when Capitol released a bare-bones recording as a single on Christmas Eve, 1979. But "Ricky," Al's first music video, officially began his career as an album artist.

With "Ricky," Al left the comfy but confining ghetto of the novelty music world for the more challenging and competitive pop realm.

"Ricky" was bold and calculating in its efforts to win over an audience for whom being an all-time champion of The Dr.

Demento Show's Funny Five meant nothing. Al wrote "Yoda" before his self-titled debut but didn't release it until 1985, so "Ricky" was the first of Al's multi-media mashups where he used the melody of a pop hit to chronicle a ubiquitous pop culture phenomenon.

"Ricky" hit MTV late in the first term of Ronald Reagan, a movie star but also a creature of television, as illustrated by his stock footage cameo in Al's "Christmas at Ground Zero" music video. It was as a television anthology host that the former Democrat first started making inroads into Republican politics. Reagan was the smiling, friendly embodiment of our country's cozy, black-and-white 1950s past. The same could be said of I Love Lucy.

Yankovic came of age comedically during the waning days of the monoculture. This was a time before pop culture fractured into a million weird niches.

Everybody knew *I Love Lucy*, one of the most successful and beloved television shows in history. Everyone also knew Toni Basil's "Mickey," whether they wanted to or not.

Television was, and remains, an integral component of who we are as a people. Al's first two specially themed compilations covered television (*The TV Album*) and food (*The Food Album*). For Al and the hyper-consumerist sensibility he was both parodying and embodying, television was as essential to human life as food or air.

This brings us to "Ricky." The song is a spoof, but there's nothing mean-spirited about it. Al wasn't making fun of *I Love Lucy;* on the contrary, the song is a loving homage. As with his Tonio K. pastiches "Happy Birthday" and "I Was Only Kidding," the source of the humor is fundamentally the same as its inspiration. "Ricky" is not making jokes at *I Love Lucy*'s expense; it's making jokes in an *I Love Lucy* vein, about *I Love Lucy.*

Al wasn't taking the piss out of "Mickey" or *I Love Lucy.* He was lovingly addressing the surprising overlap between the hit pop song and the classic sitcom.

What the young Al (in his very first time up at bat, MTV-wise) and his team of geeky dreamers lacked in money, they made up for in ingenuity. Every moment of the "Ricky" video was planned out methodically in advance to look as much like its inspiration as possible on a tiny budget. That verisimilitude would prove to be an oft-overlooked element of Al's longevity. No matter how ridiculous his subject matter, Al attacks it with a meticulousness that never calls attention to itself.

This realism extended to a disconcertingly suave Al doing the unthinkable and shaving off his signature mustache to play Ricky Ricardo. Musically, Al's parodies and pastiches are madcap mutations that combine his creative DNA with that of everyone from Bruno Mars to Sparks.

That's true visually as well. In his post-"Ricky" videos, Al struck a strangely palatable compromise, making videos where he inhabited the larger-than-life persona of the artist he was parodying while simultaneously remaining himself.

On "Ricky," however, Al deliberately eschews all his visual trademarks to play Ricky Ricardo. His wild mop of kinky hair is tamed into a slick pompadour. His signature mustache and glasses are gone. His wardrobe has been upgraded from colorful goofball to upscale nightclub debonair.

The "Ricky" music video finds Yankovic taking on the dual roles of Ricky Ricardo and "Weird Al" Yankovic in sequences that alternate between performance footage of Al and the band (that, remarkably, continues to tour and record with him decades later) and Al as Ricky opposite Tress MacNeille as Lucy.

Al has always made the most of his resources. In "Ricky" he benefited from the visual aesthetic of old sitcoms being claustrophobic and stage-bound. The use of black and white is true to *I Love Lucy* and the era it is lovingly spoofing/honoring, but it also helps hide the video's cheapness.

The "Ricky" video proves you don't need money to be visually dynamic. Black and white sets the video apart, as does the gimmick of having Al-as-Ricky run into the room where Al and his band are performing the song while in pursuit of Lucy.

"Ricky" is a loving homage to *I Love Lucy* that finds a Cuban-accented Al crooning of both his wild desire and his eternal frustration with his daffy spouse. It's a song whose affection for its source material comes through in every note. But even in this cozy, nostalgic homage to our halcyon black and white past, there's a note of New Wave anti-consumer prickliness when MacNeille-as-Lucy reminds her hubby in one of the many meta lines dotting Al's discography, "Every day's a rerun and the laughter's always canned."

That line serves as a reminder that even the best, most beloved shows are consumer products designed to sell soap ads as much as they are to entertain or, god forbid, educate.

The video ends with Al-as-Ricky playing the accordion for the first time instead of Ricky's trademark bongos. As the video ends, Al laughs Ricky Ricardo's signature laugh. But what, really, is he laughing at? Existence? The pain buried deep within his soul? His implicit understanding that he is a fictional character devoid of agency – a fraud, a lie, a shadow on the wind? Is it a howl of existential rage disguised as a chipper guffaw? No, I'm pretty sure it's just a reference to Desi Arnaz's distinctive laugh. Not everything has to be so dramatic.

2.
GOTTA BOOGIE

When Yankovic began his recording career with silly songs about less-than-ideal public transportation, unhealthily obsessive processed meat consumption and inconvenient mucus, he had no idea that four decades later he would be a multi-Grammy-winning musical legend looking back with pride on a career full of milestone *later* songs about eating excessively, weighing an excessive amount and Luddite customs.

"Gotta Boogie" is unabashed juvenilia from the *Dr. Demento Show* period of Yankovic's career as well as Al's only real disco song. The accordion still takes center stage, but the sound is fuller and busier, if also more irritatingly, intentionally repetitive.

"Gotta Boogie" is partly commentary on the simplistic musical structure of disco. Al begins the song by repeating the title over and over, in an affected parody of a swinger's confident swagger that recalls the stylized delivery of fellow *Dr. Demento Show* favorite Frank Zappa on his single "Dancin' Fool."

Al only stops repeating the chorus to deliver the song's punchline: "Gotta boogie on my finger and I can't shake it off."

"Gotta Boogie" is the first song Al released to address romance, or sex, even indirectly. Even in this embryonic stage, Al's vision of sex and romance was that both were gross, and a waste of everyone's time. In this case, the song's narrator prides himself on being a disco maniac, but when a woman asks him why he dances with his hand behind his back, he reveals that it's because he's got an ugly glob of snot stuck on his finger and he can't get it off.

So even when a creepy Casanova is being social and romantic, he's still hiding something gross while also singing very specifically about that grossness. He's getting into all matter of homophone trouble when he asks women, "Wanna boogie?" and, judging from their disgusted replies, they clearly imagine that he's offering them the mucus on his finger and not an opportunity to dance with him, although both seem like extremely unappealing options.

3.
I LOVE ROCKY ROAD

Al has a disc jockey or A&R man's feel for identifying songs that weren't just big hits, but ubiquitous, unmissable classics in the making.

Of course, Al wasn't taking a chance on random pop songs: he was spoofing songs whose commercial *bona fides* had already been proven.

Yankovic's parodies were unusually, unexpectedly successful, in part because he was building on the sturdy foundation of the tried and true. The first songs Yankovic parodied (The Knack's "My Sharona," Queen's "Another One Bites the Dust," Toni Basil's "Mickey," Joan Jett's "I Love Rock 'n' Roll") for official release are not mere pop songs. They're anthems, future oldies-station staples, perfect pop singles.

When Runaways alumnus Jett first recorded "I Love Rock 'n' Roll," it was with two alumni of an even more famous punk band: Paul Cook and Steve Jones of the Sex Pistols. She had even more success re-recording it with her band the Blackhearts but if the song has an unexpected punk pedigree, Al takes it into a characteristically wholesome direction.

The comic conceit of "I Love Rocky Road" is similar to that of "My Bologna." Yankovic replaced the raw, sexual energy of the original with an obsessive fixation on food. "I Love Rocky Road" depicts overeating taken to pathological, even psychotic extremes, as an unusually pure expression of the American compulsion to over-consume to the point where it stops being pleasurable and becomes punishing.

The demented overeater of "My Bologna" consumes until he throws up, and then begins the process all over again. The life of the obsessive singing "I Love Rocky Road" monomaniacally revolves around dessert consumption.

Like "My Bologna," "I Love Rocky Road" uses the language of addiction when its protagonist boasts, "They tell me ice cream junkies are all the same/All the soda jerkers know my name/When their supply is gone/Then I'll be movin' on."

On "I Love Rocky Road," the accordion constitutes much of the joke. There's a world of difference between androgynous Joan Jett swaggering around with a phallic electric guitar and a geek with a wild mop of curly hair working up a sweat trying to tame the wild beast that is his accordion. "Oh, make it talk!" Yankovic screams midway through an accordion solo in a sly parody of electric-guitar-solo worship.

The music video for "I Love Rocky Road," even more so than "Ricky," is an adorably homemade endeavor. The song is full of references to Yankovic's earlier work, including an *I Love Lucy* pin and appearances from Dr. Demento and "Musical Mike" Kieffer.

Who is "Musical Mike" Kieffer, the uninitiated might ask? Well, he's a man with a curious gift: using only his hands and a craftsman's obsessive devotion to his art, Kieffer could make flatulent noises that have a vaguely percussive feel about them. Early on, Yankovic felt that the percussive fart noises Kieffer specialized in added to the grand gestalt of his own insouciant body of work. What a bittersweet moment it must have been when Yankovic discovered that, in order to realize his creative destiny, he no longer needed fart sounds!

Where Jett is understated and cool, Yankovic is wild-eyed and manic, hollering his obsession with chocolate-based, marshmallow-loaded frozen dessert treats from the mountains. When "I Love Rocky Road" hit the pop charts, he was already returning to what you would imagine would be the limited realm of food and overeating-based musical comedy.

Astonishingly, Al had only just begun. To a world that might take Yankovic to task for making too many songs about food, Yankovic had a rejoinder as sassy as it was prescient. To these doubters, Al sneered and told a skeptical world, "Eat it!"

That they did. They ate it up but good.

4.
BUCKINGHAM BLUES

Al's career is unique. One of the ways Al's career differs from everyone else's involves the central role permission plays in determining which songs he's able to release commercially.

"Buckingham Blues," for example, started out as a parody of John Mellencamp's little ditty 'bout Jack and Diane, two American kids growing up in the heartland. Only instead of chronicling the poignantly small-time existence of American teens in mid-America, the song would have documented the antithetical existences of Prince Charles and Princess Di.

That parody did not happen, but the endlessly resourceful Al took the song in a different direction by making it a blues song rather than a parody. "Buckingham Blues" consequently represents an unusually pure representation of a curious, ubiquitous and strangely deathless comedic sub-genre I have taken to calling "The Comically Incongruous White Folks Blues."

The Comically Incongruous White Folks Blues song understands that blues is an inherently African American art form rooted in a specifically African American set of struggles.

The Comically Incongruous White Folks Blues reverses the racial angle by making the subject and/or singer of the blues not only white but a comically over-the-top representation of white culture. The core conceit is that exemplars of unexamined white privilege have no right to sing the blues, particularly to black people, yet feel compelled to do so anyway.

The Comically Incongruous White Folks Blues is at once a cheeky act of ironic cultural appropriation and a meta-commentary on cultural appropriation. They're a way for white people to perform black music while exaggerating rather than denying their whiteness. These songs both reflect and satirize our confusion, uncertainty and awkwardness regarding race and class.

They're meditations on whiteness more than they are on the blues. No one, with the possible exception of Nicolas Sparks, is whiter than Prince Charles. How white is Prince Charles? If you look up "white dude" in the dictionary, it's accompanied by a picture of Prince Charles. Then again, if you look up "inbred" you will also find an unflattering photograph of the British royal's pasty face and horse mouth. It goes beyond that: if you look up "erectile dysfunction," "micro-penis," "pedophilia," "oozing boil," "dying from syphilis" and literally dozens of disgusting, stomach-turning words and phrases, you'll find the same awful photograph of Prince Charles.

What I'm saying is that the dude who writes the dictionary has a bizarre, slanderous grudge against Prince Charles. Thankfully, the narrator of "Buckingham Blues" has more sympathy for the couple he calls "Chuck and Diane," whom he goes on to describe as a "couple British kids from the Palace of Buckingham."

The comedy comes from the incongruous juxtaposition of an art form that's all about howling despair and subject matter that's all stiff-upper-lip propriety. But it also comes from the song's distinctly American, working-class take on a distinctly British, upper-class world – like when Al observes, "They don't serve no Twinkies with their afternoon tea/Never had a dinner made by Chef Boyardee."

For the young Al of the early 1980s, everything was about the joy and agony and absurdity of capitalism. The singer of "Buckingham Blues" is obviously not a royal subject, nor a gentleman with a sense of propriety. He's a man who clearly processes the lives of the British royal family through the tabloids. In that respect, the royals are as much a product of the supermarket as Oscar Meyer bologna, Twinkies, Chef Boyardee and Rocky Road ice cream.

Yankovic's career spans eras. He started releasing singles officially around the same time Hip Hop did. The Sugar Hill Gang's "Rapper's Delight" was released on September 16th, 1979. "My Bologna" came out just a few months later.

Like Hip Hop, the genre that has given Al some of his biggest, least likely hits, like "Amish Paradise" and "White & Nerdy," Al has gone farther than anyone imagined possible. In the late nineties and aughts, Yankovic revived his career in a big way with "It's All About the Pentiums" and "White & Nerdy," songs that pioneered nerdcore (or Comically Incongruous White Folks Rap, as I like to call it). Whether he's riffing on blues or more contemporary, popular forms of black music, when it comes to being white and nerdy, "Weird Al" Yankovic is an O.G. in the game.

5.
HAPPY BIRTHDAY

"Happy Birthday" has the distinction of being the first pastiche Weird Al officially released. But it also has the distinction of being an homage to one of the most obscure artists Yankovic would ever honor with a tribute, as well as one of the most overlooked.

In his late 1970s prime, Tonio K. specialized in making songs that sound goofy and upbeat but are actually unrelentingly dark. He was a New Wave-era jester in the mold of Elvis Costello, an incorrigible smartass forever enjoying a deeply satisfying inside joke at the universe's expense.

"The Funky Western Civilization" is the closest K. came to a hit and the high watermark of his peppy brand of psychotic dance pop. Over maddeningly insistent "Roadrunner"-style guitars and cheerful horns, K. depicts contemporary society as a toxic mess of depravity, violence, debasement and despair before admonishing listeners to celebrate our impending doom with the titular dance.

Introducing the most nihilistic dance yet, Tonio K. sneers, "They put Hitler in the driver's seat and looked the other way/Now they've got poison in the water and the whole world in a trance/But just because we're hypnotized, that don't mean we can't dance."

Like "The Funky Western Civilization," "Happy Birthday" begins on a deceptively celebratory note, with the maddeningly simple chorus of "Happy Birthday, Happy Birthday to you" repeated twice followed by a cheerful admonition: "Well, it's time to celebrate your birthday, it happens every year/We'll eat a lot of broccoli and drink a lot of beer."

Then things take a turn. The narrator tells the cursed birthday boy or girl that they should be happy to have something to eat, because "a million people every day are starving in the street." This opens the floodgates of misery with "Your daddy's in the gutter with the wretched and the poor."

Because Al is inhabiting a character inspired by Tonio K, there are multiple levels of distance and irony separating Al from the words he's delivering. Yankovic's self-titled album is the punkest in Al's oeuvre, in part because it is so thoroughly rooted in the New Wave of its time, which was essentially Punk Rock with glasses with a keyboard, or better yet, keytar. But the parody king's commitment to character and comedy precluded making overt political statements.

On "Happy Birthday," Al tries on the angry, nihilistic persona of Tonio K. for a song and finds it fits surprisingly well. He then had the wonderful luxury of being able to go back to being "Weird Al" Yankovic, as well as a Rock and Roll Hall of Fame worth of other famous pop stars.

6.
STOP DRAGGIN' MY CAR AROUND

When Al quickly and cheaply recorded "Stop Draggin' My Car Around" with producer/guitar god Rick Derringer for his 1983 self-titled debut, he was no longer a geek with an accordion entertaining his fellow students or the nerds on *The Dr. Demento Show*. Al was a professional musician with a band, a proven professional for a producer and a whole album to prove himself to a skeptical music industry.

In that respect, "Stop Draggin' My Car Around" is fascinating as the first of what would become dozens of parody songs that would live and die as album tracks, never subjected to the scrutiny of songs groomed to do righteous battle on the pop charts, radio and MTV.

If these album-only parodies aren't under the same commercial pressure as singles, the expectations are nevertheless higher than they are for originals. Al only parodies hit songs and it's easier to get a mainstream audience interested in a parody of a hit Tom Petty and Stevie Nicks duet than "Mr. Frump in the Iron Lung."

"Stop Draggin' My Car Around" undercuts the atmospheric gloom of "Stop Draggin' My Heart Around" and Stevie Nicks' hyper-emotional delivery through the skillful application of Mike Kieffer's signature percussive flatulent wizardry.

There's something about the somber, sincere ache of Petty and Nicks' duet that makes Kieffer's strange specialty feel like a righteous blast of vulgarity instead of merely vulgar.

"Stop Draggin' My Car Around" is a song about a car, a rock perennial. But this a "Weird Al" Yankovic car song, so the usual tone of defiant pride is replaced by shame over the singer's inability to keep the lemon of the title out of the avaricious claws of the tow-truck industry.

Over an irreverent accordion and fart-noise-fueled simulation of Stevie Nicks and Tom Petty & the Heartbreaker's New Wave romantic melodrama, Al shares several tales of being unexpectedly and unhappily separated by fate's random cruelty from his decrepit automobile.

By the time "Stop Draggin' My Car Around" came out, Yankovic had developed such an indelible visual aesthetic that when the song's narrator sings, "Took my baby to the local disco, I was jumpin' like a maniac" we don't just imagine a generic swinger out on the dance floor. We imagine Al with his crazy curls, glasses, Hawaiian shirt and his geek glasses boogying up a storm.

The first non-single parody Al ever released is an eminently worthy addition to the overflowing canon of songs about sub-par automobiles.

Honestly, the singer here might have been better off riding the bus, and we will soon discover what a nightmare that form of transportation can be.

7.
MY BOLOGNA

Yankovic spent many of the happiest hours of his teen years as part of the coterie of kooks who gravitated around Dr. Demento's eponymous show. These were characters out of vaudeville (sometimes literally, in the case of Benny Bell of "Shaving Cream" fame) but Yankovic felt at home among the misfits. He was a young man with a very old sense of humor and an affinity for Borsht Belt humor.

The young Yankovic nursed a decidedly Jewish obsession with food. He was enamored of its comic possibilities, because Yankovic understood how funny so many words related to food sound. *Spam, bologna*; you almost don't need jokes. The words are funny in and of themselves.

The comic possibilities posed by the word "bologna" had already been proven by the world-famous Oscar Meyer jingle, that sadistic ear worm that tricked children into not only wrongly desiring this sub-par meat product but knowing how to spell it as well.

Like so much of Yankovic's early music, "My Bologna" is a tale of obsession, only with food standing in for romance and sex. The Knack's "My Sharona," which inspired Al's first official release, isn't just an extremely sexual song: it's sexual in a gross, jailbait, "Gosh, maybe people should stop releasing songs about the hotness of the underage," very 1970s kind of way.

Al might have been performing a parody, a juvenile goof based on someone else's ubiquitous smash. But he was always unique, always a character, always an original even when spoofing someone else's song.

The "Weird Al" Yankovic of "My Bologna" and his self-titled debut album was younger, crazier and rawer than the version that would win America's hearts.

To put it in *The Simpsons* terms, it's the difference between the Klasky-Csupo years and the Film Roman Era, when everything is smoother, rounder, more pleasing and palatable.

The Al of "My Bologna" is at once immediately recognizable as the preeminent jester of pop music and a little off-model.

The lyrics to "My Bologna" are comically obsessive, and obsessively comic, in breaking down every step in the bologna-sandwich-consumption process, from the making of toast to the careful application of mustard, to staving off disaster by ensuring that the bologna never runs out.

Yankovic embraced the fertile comic territory of mindless consumption as one of his earliest and most fruitful themes. In Al's angry-nerd world, the joys of consumerism replace the sensual pleasure of sex and romance. Many of Al's early songs are about both consumerism *and* consumption.

In "My Bologna" the urge to consume isn't just unhealthy, but downright pathological. The narrator doesn't just love to eat bologna; he manically insists, "Such a tasty snack/I always eat too much and throw up, but I'll soon be back." This is no mere bologna aficionado. No, we are dealing with someone who overeats to such an extent that they throw up, then begin the process again.

"My Bologna" finds in the need to consume until you purge a savage metaphor for the way consumer culture encourages us to over-consume to an unhealthy, even dangerous degree. Though "My Bologna" is primitive, rudimentary stuff in many ways – the musical equivalent of a high school yearbook photo, revealing and embarrassing at the same time – a lot of the hallmarks of Yankovic's aesthetic are already in evidence.

It's no coincidence that Yankovic's bologna in the song has a first name, and it's O-S-C-A-R, nor that it has a second name, which is "M-E-Y-E-R." Yankovic is referencing the bologna suppliers who conquered the airwaves with a legendarily

catchy jingle that began with the words "my bologna." From the beginning, TV and commercials and advertisements and consumer culture were at the core of Al's take on American life.

It's not easy for a mustachioed, bespectacled geek with an accordion to convince a label that he's a viable commercial entity. So it helps if the song he's peddling advertises a consumer product and sounds like a commercial itself.

Like Al, "My Bologna" has endured. Forty years after its release as a solo single and thirty-six after it became a full-band number on Al's debut album, it experienced a renewed surge in popularity when it was used in the Netflix '80s nostalgia favorite *Stranger Things* and appeared on its soundtrack.

Like Al, *Stranger Things* cares about getting the details right. If you were a spooky geek in the 1980s, as I was, Al wasn't just someone you listened to compulsively: he was someone you worshiped, someone you patterned yourself after, someone you wanted to be when you grew up – even if you understood that was setting the bar impossibly high.

8.
THE CHECK'S IN THE MAIL

With "The Check's in the Mail," Al began to take advantage of having a virtuoso guitarist and multi-instrumentalist like Rick Derringer as his producer and collaborator. In terms of musical sophistication, the song is light years removed from the primitive early recordings of "My Bologna" and "Another One Rides the Bus."

"The Check's in the Mail" boldly asks why a song can't just be an endless series of clichés and catchphrases slickly joined together to form an all-inclusive spiel of total inauthenticity.

Like the Beatles at their most twee, "The Check's in the Mail" has a Dance Hall feel that hearkens back to the music of the 1930s and '40s. Peppy ukulele and banjo from Jon "Bermuda"

Schwartz's accomplished musician brother Richard Bennett contributes to the sense of vaudevillian exuberance, as does a percussive breakdown that sounds like the drums stepping out to tap-dance.

"The Check's in the Mail" takes its title from a popular cliché that's also a popular lie. "The Check's in the Mail" is so innately associated with dishonesty that it seems heretical to employ it if a check genuinely has been sent out.

"The check's in the mail" is only the beginning of the song's loving catalog of glib clichés, a litany of the hackneyed things liars say.

The narrator begins the song simultaneously trying to blow off, compliment and soothe someone who has clearly had enough of their shenanigans. The narrator is a would-be star-maker, a schmoozing aficionado full of insincere compliments who grows increasingly desperate as his empty words are met with anger.

In "The Check's in the Mail" only a verse separates the narrator breezily assuring a would-be protégé, "Baby, won't you sign on the dotted line/I'm gonna make your dreams come true!" from "You say you hate my guts, you wanna take me to court/And you got yourself a lawyer with a three-piece suit?" By the end of the song, the singer is so befuddled he's getting his platitudes mixed up and proposing, "Why don't you leave a message with my girl/I'll have lunch with your machine."

"The Check's in the Mail" is about our infernal capacity to use words to conceal meaning rather than to express it. Yet there is an underlying ambivalence. The song is fundamentally concerned with the meaninglessness of clichés, yet it's also about how soothing they can be in their familiarity.

The song's infectious joy lies in the pleasure Al takes in playing the ultimate show-business phony. "The Check's in the Mail" is sneakily satirical in chronicling how easy and fun it is to abuse the English language, and its glittering catalog of clichés, to use a whole lot of words to say nothing much at all.

9.
ANOTHER ONE RIDES THE BUS

It's hard to overstate the importance of Dr. Demento in Al's career. He was more than just a mentor. He was like a second father to the pop parodist, a guru who adopted the guise of professional jester but who, like Al, was freakishly smart.

In an analog realm where DJs actually spun records and were compensated both with salaries and sweet, sweet payola (not to mention the occasional smooch from a foxy lady or marijuana cigarette), Demento was a human Wikipedia. He was (and remains) a man who seemed to know everything when it came to novelty performers. Demento wasn't just a man; he was a world unto himself. It was that world that "Weird Al" Yankovic fell in love with as a boy.

As a ten-year-old, I was similarly addicted to the radio. Pop music was my world. As a child, albums like Michael Jackson's *Thriller*, Huey Lewis & the News' *Sports* and *Dare to Be Stupid* bewitched me.

I adored the radio and lived for the countdowns, both in the form of Casey Kasem's Top 40 rundown and in the funhouse mirror version found on *The Dr. Demento Show* and its trademark "Funny Five" countdown.

The "Funny Five" was the first world Al conquered, the first place where an only child from Lynwood, California who called himself "Weird Al" Yankovic could loom large as something approaching a god. Al had found his tribe. Oddballs. Nuts. Goofs. Outcasts. People whose obsessions veered far from the norm, for whom Allan Sherman was bigger than Elvis Presley.

When Yankovic began releasing music professionally – first through the titans at Capitol and then through Placebo, a makeshift label Yankovic formed to release his *Another One*

Rides the Bus EP – his recording career was an extension of his contributions to Dr. Demento's show.

To make the association even stronger, "Another One Rides the Bus," the single that properly launched Al's career, was famously recorded live in the KMET control room for *The Dr. Demento Show* with Jon "Bermuda" Schwartz banging away percussively on an accordion case in preparation for his later role as Al's drummer. Dr. Demento lent Al the money to manufacture a thousand copies of the *Another One Rides the Bus* EP to sell on consignment at record stores.

In that respect, "Another One Rides the Bus" represents the high watermark of Al and his mentor's relationship, and the beginning of the end. After "Another One Rides the Bus" and particularly "Eat It" from Yankovic's follow-up LP, Yankovic would belong to the world, not just the *Dr. Demento Show*.

Part of the goofball appeal of "Another One Rides the Bus" lies in hearing one accordion player and a kid beating an accordion case recreate the big, swaggering, full-body sound of Queen, a band full of virtuosos.

Queen were rock stars. They flew in private planes. Al's put-upon schlemiel gets the worst of public transportation, an institution of life among the poor that's no paradise even under the best of circumstances. "Another One Rides the Bus" contains one of Al's darkest, most transgressive lines when his aggravated bus-rider whines of his predicament, "I haven't been in a crowd like this since I went to see the Who."

A little over a year before *Another One Rides the Bus'* 1981 release a notorious stampede at a Who show resulted in eleven fatalities. This casts "Another One Rides the Bus" in a much darker light. Comparing a singularly unpleasant bus ride to a real-life tragedy like the fatal Who stampede is as tasteless and wrong as it is morbidly funny.

Yankovic and Mercury are both mustachioed showmen. That's where the similarities end. "Another One Bites the Dust" is a screamingly effeminate macho anthem, a strange, seemingly contradictory sub-genre Queen completely owned. "Another One Bites the Dust" makes mastery seem effortless. But particularly in his early days, Al's aesthetic involved exerting as much effort as possible.

Queen were consummate pop artists: beautiful, charismatic men who also happened to be dazzlingly accomplished musicians. Al and his newfound percussionist could never hope to match them on the level of virtuosity or polish so, in true punk tradition, they made up for it with screaming and snotty intensity. Who needs musicianship when you have deafening volume?

That rawness was enhanced by having the official release of "Another One Rides the Bus" be the live recording from *The Dr. Demento Show* instead of something recorded and then finessed in a studio by Rick Derringer.

There was, and remains, a magic to the live *Dr. Demento Show* recording of "Another One Rides the Bus." Even when Al and Jon "Bermuda" Schwartz had a guitar god of a producer in Derringer and a modest budget to make a long-playing album, they held onto a three-year-old recording of "Another One Rides the Bus" made under the loving eye of Al's mentor instead of re-recording it in a more professional setting.

The enraged Al of "Another One Rides the Bus" knows that he has to scream to be heard by a cold, apathetic world and industry. Forty years later, that feral howl of nerd rage continues to resonate.

10.
I'LL BE MELLOW WHEN I'M DEAD

"Weird Al" Yankovic was only twenty-three when he released a debut LP that easily could have been the beginning, end and entirety of his recording career rather than an audacious opening salvo.

Making parodies of pop songs was not something artists based careers around. It was something goofy morning radio DJs did to amuse listeners. It was the domain of flash-in-the-pan novelty acts lucky to have one song that penetrates the public consciousness.

By the time Yankovic made the leap to LPs, it was nearly the mid-1980s. But Yankovic's sensibility had been honed in the Southern Los Angeles of the late 1970s and early '80s. As the satirical novels, movies and albums of the time convey, it was an era of expanding/raising consciousness and intense generational narcissism, as the focus shifted from external matters like politics to an internal obsession with purging the human soul, body and spirit of imperfections. Spiritual and quasi-spiritual hustles like Scientology and EST flourished as lost souls sought out new paradigm-shattering ways of living, but mostly just succeeded in being insufferable.

"I'll Be Mellow When I'm Dead" takes aim at what the cynic singing the song sneeringly dubs "cosmic cowboys," whose New Age beliefs have replaced the stodgy dogma of old with something stupider and even more self-absorbed.

The song is a veritable catalog of 1970s and 1980s New Age clichés. In rapid succession, it rejects karma, hipness, Jacuzzis *and* redwood hot tubs, incense, jogging, Joni Mitchell, organic food *and* health food, Perrier, sushi, vegetarianism, designer jeans, astrology, psychology and casualness. I think that's the full extent of it.

Earlier in my career, I threw around the word "dated" a lot as a pejorative because I had a young writer's inherent distrust of things that were not clearly made for me. Now much of what fascinates me about older art is how thoroughly it embodies the tenor of the times that created it.

What I find most interesting about "I'll Be Mellow When I'm Dead" now is how unabashedly, shamelessly '80s it is. It might just be the single most '80s song Al ever recorded, even if the slightly dusty lifestyle satire found in it reflects the easy satirical targets of the late '70s as well.

"I'll Be Mellow When I'm Dead" is fascinating partially because it's such a product of the Reagan era, but also for the ways it feels off. Al is nearly as famous for being one of pop culture's most high-profile vegetarians as he is for making 70 percent of his early songs about food.

So it's jarring hearing the singer of "I'll Be Mellow When I'm Dead" boast of his desire to devour a mass of dead, fried cow flesh like a Big Mac or a Jumbo Jack from Jack in the Box while also condemning vegetarianism as just another self-absorbed New Age fad.

"Weird Al" Yankovic is different from Al's later albums in other ways as well. Other than *Even Worse*, it's the only full-

length album he's released that does not have a polka parody on it, and of the twelve songs, only five are parodies. Of the seven originals, only one is a pastiche/homage.

Yankovic figured out exactly who he was and what he wanted his career to look like early. Yet on *"Weird Al" Yankovic* and songs like "I'll Be Mellow When I'm Dead" he was still a work in progress.

11.
SUCH A GROOVY GUY

In the music of "Weird Al" Yankovic, genuine love is generally reserved for consumer products and/or random pop culture ephemera. Romantic relationships can't hope to match the intensity of passions for televisions so large they block out the sun, Mr. Popeil's wonder gizmos or aluminum foil.

When Al sings about romantic relationships, it's invariably from the perspective of someone who is deluded at best and a danger to themselves and society at worst.

The singer of "Such a Groovy Guy" is one of Al's rancid Romeos, a man who loves himself enough to compensate for the world's richly merited contempt for him. But before we learn *exactly* what makes this particular gent such an alarming fellow, he's considerate enough to tell us about himself.

The song's sleaziness is musical as well as lyrical. Al delivers this narcissist's myopic tale of delusional self-love in a hiccuping rockabilly sneer that's part Sid Vicious, part feral Elvis Presley.

Everything about this creep's self-absorption is outsized. When he sees himself in the mirror he's not just impressed; he's moved to kneel down and pray. The singer claims his conception of himself as God's gift to humanity is shared by others. "They tell me I'm the greatest and it's hard to disagree" he insists, but all of the available evidence suggests otherwise.

The deranged egotist mistakes sadism and a predilection for BDSM for romance when he proposes, "Oh, and then I might decide to tie you up with dental floss/I'll make you wear a harness and I'll show you who's the boss."

The sex play gets pretty involved for a "Weird Al" Yankovic song but Al was rawer in this incarnation than he was after he'd become the clown prince of MTV.

Al is, above all, a traditionalist. He has a vaudevillian's unshakeable beliefs that there are certain words that are inherently funny. Bologna. Seltzer. Spatula. Dental floss. Dental floss is just plain funny, whether employed in the service of bondage or not. Al is a curator of funny words, the more random the better. On *"Weird Al" Yankovic* he understood that the key to creating ephemeral tomfoolery that will stand the test of time lies in the details – musical, lyrical and otherwise.

By the end of "Such a Groovy Guy," the groovy guy in question has received his comeuppance. His offer of dental-floss-themed sex play and pudding-pouring/electrode-based torture is rejected, and he is unceremoniously dumped. Yet even this unmistakable rejection cannot permeate his impregnable wall of self-delusion.

There are no groovy guys among the would-be womanizers in Al's music, just creeps with strange ideas about the world in general and romance in particular. In its own modest, ramshackle way, "Such a Groovy Guy" provides a rough template for songs that depict romance as something close to a pathology.

As outrageous as "Such a Groovy Guy" is, there are elements of it inspired by real life. When I asked Al about the song when I interviewed him for The A.V. Club, he clarified that it was "written for a woman that I was dating at the time, and it was about her old boyfriend, who… [Laughs.] I'm a little leery to give away too many details here, because I'm not sure he knows the song's about him. But basically, he had done all sorts of kind of horrible things to her, and then when she broke up with him, he couldn't understand it and, this is a quote, "I'm such a groovy guy! Why would you break up with me?" So that song, I wrote it for her basically, just to amuse her."

So, while Al exaggerated for comic effect the awfulness of Los Angeles phonies, he was also drawing from personal experience and reflecting on the free-floating insanity that is as much a part of Southern Californian life as the weather.

"Such a Groovy Guy" does not end *"Weird Al" Yankovic*. It actually ends in a more perverse, non-commercial way, with "Mr. Frump in the Iron Lung," a neo-vaudevillian number that makes more extensive use of an accordion's air release valve than any other song in recent memory.

"Weird Al" Yankovic has an odds and sods quality to it. It's a solid debut cobbled together from a re-recording of a single recorded for another label in a different decade ("My Bologna"), four songs from an EP funded with money borrowed from Dr. Demento, a whole lot of accordion and some artfully employed fart noises.

"Weird Al" Yankovic is raw compared to Al's later releases yet it represented a massive leap forward. Al hadn't entirely escaped the novelty and one-hit wonder tag (although by the end of the album, he'd scored several modest hits) but he'd illustrated that he could make an entire album that he could be proud of, with the core of a band that performs and records with him today.

"Weird Al" Yankovic marked an ending and a beginning. In the tradition of debuts, it marked the end of years of working and dreaming about making the leap from aspiring musician to the real thing. Yet Al's journey had only just begun. His follow-up to *"Weird Al" Yankovic* would hit stores just a year after *"Weird Al" Yankovic* and open with a song that would change everything.

12.
MR. FRUMP IN THE IRON LUNG

During the "My Bologna" single and *Another One Rides the Bus* EP stage of his career, Yankovic was the king of the "Funny Five." Though he somehow found the time to graduate from college, *The Dr. Demento Show* was Al's world, the world that helped create and nurture him.

In the 1970s, *The Dr. Demento Show* was a meritocracy, a zany place where an ambitious kid could share airtime with men of distinction like Loudon Wainwright III and Al's idol Frank Zappa if their music was good enough. *The Dr. Demento Show* was a safe, happy place for weird kids with perversely old-timey senses of humor.

"Perversely old-timey" is the perfect description for "Mr. Frump in the Iron Lung," one of four numbers to make the jump from the *Another One Rides the Bus* EP to Al's self-titled full-length debut. The title goes a long way towards establishing the song's retro, Borsht Belt tone. It's one part Shel Silverstein, one part Dr. Seuss and 100 percent vaudeville.

As a young man, Al was already a connoisseur of the ancient, the outdated, the exquisitely anachronistic. Like a true vaudevillian, Al saw the endless comic potential in things that aren't just outdated and creaky, but fascinatingly awful.

"Mr. Frump in the Iron Lung" is an Al specialty: a cheerful tune about something unbelievably depressing. The unbelievably depressing aspect of "Mr. Frump in the Iron Lung" is, of course, the eponymous iron lung. The narrator (again we can safely assume that Al is singing as a character and not as that elusive figure known as his true self) doesn't seem to mind that on a technical level, his pal doesn't actually *do* anything.

Mr. Frump mostly just exists and breathes, although even that's overstating it, since the iron lung handles most of the "breathing" itself. "Mr. Frump in the Iron Lung" is a different kind of duet, one where the singer's "partner" is the dispiriting wheeze of an iron lung in action.

There is a good reason Mr. Frump is "never a chump or a tease" and answers the narrator's questions about world events with the wordless heavy breathing/eerily metallic respirating that is his default answer to everything. Because you see, he's in an iron lung, dying a slow, painful death that finally arrives in the last verse, the song's sick-joke capper.

For a song about friendship (albeit of the one-sided variety), "Mr. Frump in the Iron Lung" is decidedly dark. "Mr. Frump in the Iron Lung" has the curious distinction of being at once too nice and too mean. Or at least, it would seem too mean if Yankovic's preternatural affability didn't rescue it from being hopelessly mean-spirited.

Al would never give up the organ-grinder vaudevillian old-time part of his shtick entirely. The accordion forever tied him to those roots, but that side would never be as pronounced and pure as it is on "Mr. Frump in the Iron Lung."

As with many of Al's later songs, the narrator is gleefully demented and giddily unselfconscious, with a skewed perspective on the world and an utterly inappropriate cheerfulness. It's another chipper song about something bleak that delights in both wordplay and the language and technology of an increasingly distant past.

"WEIRDAL"
YANKOVIC
IN
3-D
(1984)

1.
EAT IT

It's tempting to say that Al peaked early, except that he's still peaking, making music that matters precisely *because* it is so spectacularly silly. That's what we need in our world now. More silliness. More joy. More escape. More that reminds us of what's great and indestructible and happy-making.

Al hit a righteous groove early. The "Beat It" parody "Eat It" kicked off *In 3-D*, and nothing was ever the same. "Eat It" was a game-changer. "Eat It" made Al international. "Eat It" made Al an essential component of MTV's early renaissance, when its name was still associated with borderline avant-garde filmmaking and cutting-edge editing and production design and not the dumbing down of American culture, empty style and mindless T&A.

Early MTV was full of icy Eurotrash weirdoes with strange haircuts and Nordic beauties striking Nagel poses. But Al's heavy presence on the young channel made it seem friendly and approachable to a shy eight-year-old like the painfully self-conscious boy I used to be. So did the even more ubiquitous presence of a fragile creature who had been bullied since childhood into greatness: Michael Jackson.

To my eight-year-old self, who treasured his copies of *Thriller* and "Weird Al" Yankovic's *In 3-D* equally, Al and Michael Jackson were simpatico figures. They were unique. There was no one like them. No one danced like Michael Jackson or sang like Michael Jackson although others have tried, most notably troubled former child star Corey Feldman.

No one wrote songs or made music videos that connected with children and dreamers like "Weird Al" Yankovic. To me at least, they were kings of the 1980s. It would literally be impossible to imagine my childhood without them or the places where they overlapped. Their legacies will forever be intertwined. For all that Al has accomplished, there's still a pretty good chance that his obituary will mention one of his Michael Jackson parodies in its headline.

That connection is darker and more complicated in the aftermath of the harrowing exposé *Leaving Neverland*. But when "Eat It" catapulted Al to superstardom, there was no downside to being associated with the biggest pop star in the world and one of the most indisputably talented.

Al and Michael Jackson helped make MTV a vital cultural force and benefitted from the incredible heat their videos generated. Thanks to MTV, Jackson and Yankovic were nearly as famous for making videos as they were for making music.

Yet Al's songs have always been more than blueprints for music videos. "Eat It" takes what would appear to be a rather threadbare comic conceit – switching the words and letters around so that a tough song about violence and attitude becomes a song about trying to get a picky eater to enjoy a nosh – and builds a vivid cinematic world around it.

It helps that Al and his collaborators were able to piggy-back on the cinematic world of the music video and song they lovingly parodied. The song begins on an eerie, atmospheric note, with a series of icy notes played on a synthesizer called a Synclavier. The Synclavier produced sounds you'd hear in an early John Carpenter movie as darkness descends upon a violent neighborhood.

Al's accordion is nowhere to be heard on "Eat It." Its days as a central instrument on Al's albums on anything other than polka medleys had come to a close, as he wisely sacrificed the useful gimmick of performing rock on an instrument associated with Lawrence Welk's "champagne music" for sounding as much like what he's parodying as possible. On "Eat It," Al and his band don't set out to sound like "Beat It" if "Beat It" was an accordion song. They just set out to sound like "Beat It."

"Beat It" is a tough, macho song from an artist who had to be tough to survive his childhood but otherwise was the furthest thing from macho. Al similarly deviated so far from our culture's conception of traditional masculinity that part of the joke of songs like "Eat It" lies in their feigned toughness and macho posturing.

Even as a kid, I realized that I was far from what our society expects or wants a man to be. So, I gravitated towards figures who did as well, like Al and Michael Jackson. They possessed some strange magic that was particularly potent for children.

If "Eat It" returns to the familiar fodder of food, the perspective has changed. Al previously sang from the unhinged perspective of people with debilitating eating disorders specific to bologna and ice cream. In "Eat It," Yankovic switches things up and sings from the perspective of someone monomaniacally focused on getting a picky young eater to stop being bashful and have something to eat. In our culture, these figures, these food pimps, are known also as "Jewish mothers."

Yet Al is not Jewish despite having, on his breakthrough album, two *separate* songs encouraging people to eat, one explicitly deli-based, and *another* song that finds the humor in the garment trade. I could not imagine more Jewish subject matter, including actual stories from The Talmud or songs about Jewish customs.

In 3-D is more Jewish than "The Dreidel Song." It's more Jewish than "Hava Nagila," despite Al not being Jewish. On "Eat It," Al is every Jewish grandmother trying to convince a fussy grand-child to at least try the brisket, but he's also an alternate-universe version of Michael Jackson and also "Weird Al" Yankovic, pop parodist on the rise.

What really sells "Eat It," along with other standout parodies on *In 3-D*, is its incongruous relentlessness. The lyrics are ridiculous, yet Al brings the same intensity to the parody that Jackson brought to the original.

It's a testament to how intensely Jewish Al's music is that listening to *In 3-D* at a formative age helped me develop a Jewish sense of humor, despite Al inexplicably being a gentile.

Al taught me that food is funny, and mindless consumerism is funny, and people are fools and hypocrites and phonies. But there is laughter and joy to be gleaned from playfully puncturing that pomposity.

2.
MIDNIGHT STAR

Few novels have affected me as profoundly as Don DeLillo's *White Noise*. I was particularly struck by a passage that describes the contemporary American supermarket as an enchanted wonderland where the treasures of the world come together in a paradise of consumer abundance.

Almonds from Spain! Extra virgin olive oil from Greece! Exotic chocolates from Switzerland! Bazooka Joe bubble gum from Israel with comics in Hebrew! All are transported from their homelands to the United States, processed, packaged and distributed in boxes with famous cartoon characters or American flags or Olympic athletes on them.

White Noise made me think of supermarkets as capitalist cathedrals, for-profit museums of the wonders of consumerism that we take for granted because we *can* take them for granted.

I associate supermarkets primarily with Don DeLillo and "Weird Al" Yankovic and, to a much lesser extent, food. The supermarket is the spiritual home of much of Al's work, particularly in his Reagan-era youth.

The grocery store is also where the life of the singer of "Midnight Star" changes instantly and profoundly. For it is within the racks of supermarket tabloids that he encounters a miraculous publication known as the Midnight Star that opens him up to a world beyond his wildest imagination.

He learns that his pet may be an extraterrestrial. He discovers that the ghost of Elvis is living in his den and that "the incredible Frog boy" is on the loose again. His mind is sufficiently blown because, if you do not realize that all the wild yarns in newspaper tabloids are crazy fictional mix-'em-ups, then the stories they contain would seem like dispatches from a crazier, more miraculous and astonishing world.

Like many of Al's guileless obsessives, the tabloid devotee singing "Midnight Star" is so myopically passionate about his greatest love in life that he lacks all perspective on it. He's transformed instantaneously from a total outsider to a neophyte to a true believer.

"Midnight Star" has some of the pop-operatic lushness of Jim Steinman's work with Meat Loaf. Like those songs, it has an outsized sense of melodrama but where Meat Loaf's sweaty, sleazy top 40 symphonies revolved around the two perennials

of young American life – sex and rock – Al saves his outsized passion for a tabloid he sees as a Reagan-era version of *The Matrix*'s Red Pill – the skeleton key that opens the door to hidden realities.

"Midnight Star" is a tribute to the nutty ingenuity of the tabloids as much as it is a parody. You cannot be a grown man who has chosen "Weird" as part of his professional moniker without having an appreciation for the sillier things in life. Few things were sillier in the mid-'80s than supermarket tabloids.

"Midnight Star" lovingly catalogs the time-worn tropes of tabloids, from their peculiar obsession with Hitler's brain being kept alive inside a jar to their equally intense obsession with UFOs and finally to their never-ending jones for all things Elvis-related.

I can't help but look back at 1980s supermarket tabloids with nostalgia. Back then it was easy to delineate between real news found in *The New York Times* and *The Washington Post* and the lurid fantasies of *The National Enquirer* and *Weekly World News*. Now everything is hopelessly mixed up and a president incapable of telling the truth uses the words "fake news" to describe any news he doesn't like, whether it's authentic or not.

We could laugh about someone believing the nonsense in the tabloids back in 1984. The humor of "Midnight Star" is largely predicated on the absurdity of anyone thinking anything chronicled in its pages could be real. These days, people seem not only ready to believe any old implausible, impossible-seeming nonsense, but to also act on those beliefs in scary, alarming ways. We used to be able to laugh about fake news and the tabloidization of our culture. Now it's something we weep about, and laugh about only in the darkest, most bitter possible sense.

3.
THE BRADY BUNCH

The songwriting credits for "The Brady Bunch," Al's parody of Men Without Hat's "Safety Dance," contains the expected names of Yankovic and Men Without Hat's Ivan Doroschuk. But they also contain a name you wouldn't necessarily expect on a pop song: Sherwood Schwartz, the canny hack who created a timeless and tacky empire largely out of *Gilligan's Island* and *The Brady Bunch*, those towering twin testaments to the terrible taste of the TV-watching public.

Schwartz's name is in *In 3-D's* songwriting credits (and publishing) because he didn't just create *The Brady Bunch*, he also wrote (with Frank DeVol, who is also credited as a co-songwriter) a theme song that, in classic sitcom form, doubles as a brisk pitch for the show it's advertising. If you were a television executive and Sherwood Schwartz were to sing you the *Brady Bunch* theme song as a pitch, you'd have him ejected from the building and possibly committed. But you'd probably also buy the show, because Americans famously love things that are terrible.

Sherwood Schwartz is credited as a co-writer of "The Brady Bunch" because the song is simultaneously a parody (of "Safety Dance"), a sneaky semi-cover (of the *Brady Bunch* theme song) and an early mash-up that combines two disparate but insanely catchy pieces of pop culture detritus into something at once radically different and soothingly familiar.

What Al was doing on songs like "The Brady Bunch" is analogous to what early culture-mashing DJ/cut-up artists like Steinski were doing around the time. They were taking sounds and songs and musical ideas apart so that they could put them back together in ways that commented irreverently on the songs themselves as well as the artists, culture and times that created them.

"The Brady Bunch" opens with its singer imploring the listener to avail him or herself of television's infinite wonders. They're encouraged to watch *Fame* and *The Newlywed Game* and *The Addams Family*.

Al's obsessives love the perversely banal objects of their desire with a ferocity that is pathological. The singer of "The Brady Bunch" is equally unhinged in his hatred of the titular trash. Yet in the second half of the song, the singer goes from begging the listener to watch anything but *The Brady Bunch* to faithfully recounting the premise of *The Brady Bunch* via its theme song.

The cloying, weirdly polite lyrics to *The Brady Bunch* feel particularly bizarre in this new context, with Al's uncanny approximation of the Men Without Hats' song's hiccupping, heavily stylized delivery replacing the group sing-along dynamic of the original. The singer despises *The Brady Bunch* but that does not keep him from knowing everything about it.

In its own unpretentious way, "The Brady Bunch" captures how some pop culture can be so ubiquitous and overwhelming that even people who despise it end up knowing a disturbing amount about it. It reminds me of the section in Chuck Klosterman's *Sex, Drugs and Cocoa Puffs* where he writes about how his/my generation ended up mindlessly consuming shows like *Saved by the Bell* regardless of whether they liked them or not.

I didn't watch *The Brady Bunch* and *Saved by the Bell* because they were good. I didn't watch them because I enjoyed them. No, I watched them because they were on TV. When I was a child, that was my sole criteria: if it was on TV, I would watch.

That's true of the singer of "The Brady Bunch" as well. Television and the white noise of clattering consumer culture have colonized his imagination to the extent that he knows the details of what he despises.

Al "honored" Schwartz's other great contribution to the dumbing down of American life with the Tone Loc parody "Isle Thing" later in the decade. I suspect that isn't because Al has any special love for Schwartz's inescapable creations. But these shows cast such a long shadow over pop culture that a man who embodies pop culture and television the way "Weird Al" Yankovic does would almost have to write about them in some context – just as we're all forced to know and watch *The Brady Bunch* and *Gilligan's Island* (and *Saved by the Bell*) no matter how much we hate them.

4.
BUY ME A CONDO

"Buy Me a Condo" is another fascinating first for Al. It's his first (and, to date, only) proper reggae song. The song's narrator leaves behind his island paradise of Jamaica and its spiritual ways to assimilate into a culture that could not be less spiritual.

In "Buy Me a Condo" being an American is largely a matter of buying things. It's less an identity than an assortment of possessions and a "pocket full of credit cards" that will allow this lucky newcomer to our country the opportunity to be in debt for the rest of his life. For him, American life is all about condo ownership, wall-to-wall carpeting, and (in the ultimate piece of mid-1980s preppie conspicuous consumerism) Izod, the "the funny little tee-shirt with the alligator on."

"Buy Me a Condo" is quietly audacious in its depiction of American culture as rooted not in religion, or art, or a shared sense of ideals, but rather a shared mania for consumerism. And a deep-seated belief, found throughout Al's oeuvre, that there is no problem so severe that it cannot be treated through retail therapy.

The song depicts assimilation as a matter of de-evolution. A man who once had fire and passion and idealism trades that all in for a "bowl of plastic fruit" and Amway distributorship. He trades in Bob Marley for Jackson Browne, and the soulful rhythms of island life for empty materialism.

Americans tend to romanticize Rastafarian culture; we see Rastafarians as exotic and pure and more aligned with the natural world than our own degraded society. The singer of "Buy Me a Condo" reverses this dynamic by seeing whiteness and all of the awful, awful, awfully white things that come with it as tantalizingly exotic and foreign. And, consequently, desirable.

Forget "Rhapsody in Blue," *Citizen Kane* or the Constitution: in "Buy Me a Condo," the essence of American life can be found in a "weenie barbecue."

The singer of "Buy Me a Condo" may very well have made a mistake trading in ganja for Izod, weenie barbecues and Tupperware parties. But Al remains an unbeatable advertisement for a sober lifestyle and heroic self-restraint.

5.
POLKAS ON 45

The accordion was central to Al's early career. But by *In 3-D* Al, Al, producer Rick Derringer and Al's band were ready to retire the gimmick of being an accordion-powered rock group.

Al wasn't entirely ready to put his accordion into storage, however. On *In 3-D*, he found a brilliant and surprisingly sustainable way to bring it back to a place of prominence by setting aside one track on every album for a polka.

Al's polka-fied take on the hits of the day afford him a wonderful opportunity to send up the way pop music is packaged and sold.

The title and the format of "Polkas on 45" is a riff on Stars on 45, a novelty group that briefly had enormous international success cranking out medleys of popular hits (sometimes by a specific group like the Beatles) and sometimes grouped by genre. A group of session musicians led by Golden Earring's original drummer would faithfully recreate popular songs and unite them via a common tempo.

The idea was to give consumers maximum bang for their buck. Why buy a Beatles album when you can buy a single combining eight Beatles covers in a ten-minute span? By reducing timeless art like the Beatles into instantly disposable product, Stars on 45 desecrated the music it was ostensibly paying tribute to. Give the Beatles' music all the same backbeat, and the result ceases to be the Beatles in any real way – just a sad simulacrum.

Watching *The Brady Bunch Variety Hour* recently for My World of Flops, my column on notorious show-business disasters, gave me a greater understanding of the primordial ooze from which Al's polka medleys emerged. As brilliant and funny and subversive as Al's polkas are, I'm not sure anything he's done intentionally has been as unintentionally hilarious, perverse and surreal as Mike Brady, television patriarch and former architect, badly singing a medley of the ancient standard "Baby Face" and "Love to Love You Baby", Donna Summer's hyper-orgasmic ode to female sexual pleasure, alongside his entire television family as an introductory number on their ill-fated variety show.

"Polkas on 45" brought Al's accordion back to the forefront for a medley of classic rock hits that brilliantly satirize the cynical calculation of the Stars on 45 series/aesthetic, with its emphasis on hits over coherence and integrity. This landmark first polka similarly comments on the the way medleys were used and abused to condense and destroy songs simultaneously on countless unwatchable 1970s variety shows and specials.

The medley eliminates context and puts everything on bizarrely equal footing. Outside of "Polkas on 45," just about the only thing Berlin's "Sex (I'm A)" and "Hey Jude" have in common is that they're both music.

Within "Polkas on 45," however, these two wildly different songs from different eras and performers bleed right into each other. Al brightly volunteers, "I'm a little girl when we make love together" during the portion of the medley devoted to Berlin's "Sex (I'm A)" just as glibly as he delivers the heart-wrenching chorus of "Hey Jude."

In Al and his band's capable hands, somber masterpieces become spectacularly silly. "Hey Joe" stops being a dour treatise on the emptiness of revenge and becomes a light-hearted goof about a dude getting shot, complete with cartoonish sound effects depicting gunfire as less tragic than "wacky."

"Polkas on 45" casually slaughters musical sacred cows. The Who's "My Generation" may be the ultimate "important" counterculture musical anthem, but in the hands of Al and his merry mirth-makers it becomes pure tomfoolery. "Polkas on 45" is instructive as well for the rare notes of reverence thrown in with all that silliness. Two of Al's favorite groups – Talking Heads and Devo –make the grade, foreshadowing the tributes he'd record to them in the very near future.

Before I began this project, I saw polka medleys as one of the less essential components of Al's career. I look at them much differently now, as one of the cornerstones of Al's satirical aesthetic. The accordion would be employed much more sparingly after *"Weird Al" Yankovic* but on "Polkas on 45" Al made the most out of its fascinating limitations, strengths and peculiarities.

6.
I LOST ON JEOPARDY

How powerful was Al in his mid-'80s prime? He could bring the dead back to life. That's a power that previously only gods and Herbert West, the Re-animator, have possessed. Well, and Dr. Frankenstein from the poorly received 1985 *Bride of Frankenstein* remake *The Bride.*

Whereas Dr. Frankenstein brought the dead back to life in the form of Frankenstein's Monster, Al, in necromancer Herbert West mode, brought back to life a game show called *Jeopardy.*

Today *Jeopardy* is famous for its extraordinary success, longevity, smarts (a rarity in American television) and its host, a quietly, elegantly mustachioed Canadian named Alex Trebek.

The *Jeopardy* that you're almost assuredly familiar with actually represents the third iteration of the show, following the Art Fleming-hosted *Jeopardy*, which ran from 1964 to 1975 and *The All New Jeopardy!* It's the one that would stick and become, like Al, a beloved piece of Americana.

The Alex Trebek-hosted syndicated show debuted on September 10, 1984, the same year *In 3-D* was released and only a few months after the release of "I Lost on Jeopardy" as a single and a music video featuring appearances from Al's parents, Dr. Demento, Don Pardo and Greg Kihn, whose band recorded the smash Al was parodying.

Am I going to claim that "I Lost on Jeopardy" led to *Jeopardy* being revived for an astonishing run that has yielded a Peabody and over thirty daytime Emmy awards? I sure am.

In this book, I'm also going to make the case that Al is responsible for not just the resurrection of *Jeopardy* but for the following as well:

- postmodernism
- mashups
- Girl Talk
- Nerdcore
- Horrorcore
- the fall of Communism
- comedy on MTV
- MTV
- Michael Jackson's success
- James Blunt's failure
- Jimmy Hoffa's disappearance
- the D.B. Cooper heist

Bringing back *Jeopardy* from the dead consequently represents one of Al's lesser accomplishments. When Al recorded

"I Lost on Jeopardy" the show had been off the air for five years, yet made a deep enough impression on the American public that Al could make jokes about features like the Daily Double and "Potpourri" category and trust audiences to get them.

The premise of "I Lost on Jeopardy" is right there in the title. Over a hypnotic disco-funk groove that combines sinister, "Superstition"-style synthesizers and scrappy, ominous guitar to create an air of free-floating paranoia and self-loathing, Al sings darkly of matching intellects on national TV with a "plumber and an architect, both with a PhD."

"I Lost on Jeopardy" locks into the cold-sweat paranoia and shadowy darkness of Greg Kihn's original to tell a much brighter (but still ominous) tale of failure and humiliation on a national scale. Al replaces the romance-noir of the original with an epic exercise in self-deprecation and self-flagellation, as he recounts how he panicked under pressure and disgraced himself publicly.

The song's MVP may be special guest Don Pardo, who engages in wonderfully hammy self-parody during a spoken word bit where he tears into Al for losing.

Pardo didn't spend decades as the voice of *Saturday Night Live* without learning something about comic timing and delivery. Pardo tears into his lines, filling the word "loser" with vast eternities of contempt and taking malicious glee in listing all the wonderful prizes Al won't be taking home.

In a perfect world, *Jeopardy* creator Merv Griffin's estate would send Al a million-dollar check on June 4th, the anniversary of the release date of the "I Lost on Jeopardy" single as a thank you for making him a fortune.

This is not a perfect world, however. I doubt Griffin has sent Al so much as a single million-dollar check, but Al seems to be doing pretty well all the same. If *Jeopardy* benefitted from Al's tribute, he got a lot out of the show as well. It provided the inspiration for one of his funniest and most successful early parodies. In return, he helped bring *Jeopardy* triumphantly back to life, seemingly for good.

7.
MR. POPEIL

Growing up a weird, lonely teenager, I used to amuse myself thinking about Fred Schneider of the B-52s talk-shouting unlikely things in his signature style.

I'd stand there at the Blockbuster Video where I worked as a clerk with a dumb smile on my face as I imagined the tiny little Fred Schneider inside my brain yell-singing things like the following,

> "Mr. Gorbachev, tear down this wall!!!"

> "Abortion stops a beating heart!"

> "I did not have sexual relations with that woman!"

> "I'm here to kick ass and chew bubblegum and I'm all out of bubblegum!"

I was able to distract myself briefly from my adolescent angst by imagining the B-52s leaving their typical subject matter behind to wade into comically incongruous territory. The key was to imagine Schneider singing something howlingly inappropriate.

The essence of comedy often comes down to incongruous juxtapositions. "King of Suede," for example, undercuts the breathless pretension of the Police by applying that somber intensity to the sales pitch of a tailor who works next door to Willy's Fun Arcade.

"Mr. Popeil" takes a different approach. Here, the wackiness of the delivery is matched by its subject matter. Al isn't really spoofing the B-52s so much as he's honoring them, borrowing from the "Rock Lobster" template in using a crazy throwback sound to chronicle kooky subject matter.

"Mr. Popeil" painstakingly recreates the B-52s sound, with its expansive groove, scrappy surf guitar and cascading waterfalls of boy-girl vocals from Al and female back-up singers that include frequent collaborator Lisa Popeil, a member of the prestigious informercial family Al sass-talks/shouts the praises of. I like to think that Al solicited Lisa's services by yelling into her answering machine in his best Fred Schneider shout, "Help me, Ms. Popeil!"

Sam Popeil is a very "Weird Al" Yankovic type of celebrity. He became famous, after a fashion, for yelling on television, and selling on television, and using television for its purest purpose: selling morons crap they don't need.

The song speaks the annoying, exuberant, catchphrase-filled vocabulary of the hard sell, complete with inane infomercial clichés cheerfully repeated like, "Operators are standing by!," "It slices, it dices!," "It's not sold in any store!," "Call our toll-free number!," and of course, Popeil's trademark "But wait, there's more!"

"Mr. Popeil" is about consumer ecstasy, about wonder devices that fill one lunatic's life with meaning. But it's also about how the hard-sell of infomercials becomes, to borrow the title of the book Don DeLillo wrote in 1985 shamelessly ripping off *In 3-D*, part of the white noise of American society - the commercials and jingles and pop songs and TV shows that drive us crazy, but also make us happy. Sometimes these wonder devices even give us something approaching joy, if never quite the sustained ecstasy expressed in "Mr. Popeil."

8.
KING OF SUEDE

Nothing is more deserving of mockery than unearned self-importance. People who take themselves too seriously are irresistible targets for mockery. So it's unsurprising that, on *In*

3-D alone, Al took on the music of the Police and its dour frontman Sting twice, from different angles.

On "Polkas on 45," the Police's "Every Breath You Take" is among the radio staples Al and his band smash together into a giddy medley of seemingly half of the most popular songs of the past twenty years.

Al returns to Sting on "King of Suede," a parody of the Police's "King of Pain." Because it is a Sting composition, "King of Pain" takes itself very seriously.

The singer of "King of Suede" also takes himself very seriously. He's a proud artisan who dropped out of school after second grade so he could channel his energy into providing consumers with the finest quality garments, particularly of the suede variety, for low prices.

How is this man able to provide excellence on such a tight budget? As he concedes with unwise but refreshing candor, "My prices are low, my staff is underpaid." I remember loving that line as a kid because it felt to me like a glitch in the matrix, one of those moments where adult society's mask of phony propriety slips, and we see how the world *really* operates.

But I also love "My prices are low, my staff is underpaid" because it rhymes so beautifully with "You can find me next door to Willy's Fun Arcade." Together and separately, these words conjure up a vivid picture of the Darwinian struggle that was the Reagan-era tailoring world, a harsh realm that Al writes about authoritatively despite (and I cannot make this observation often enough, because it never ceases to amaze me) not being Jewish. Or, presumably, involved in the menswear trade.

If Al had delivered the phrase "Willy's Fun Arcade" in the shriek-shout of Fred Schneider, it would not be funny. What makes the phrase amusing is the seriousness with which Al delivers it, as well as everything else, including a corny but appealing dad joke where the singer admonishes the customer/listener to enjoy his Suede Emporium and its various amenities, but "don't step on my blue suede shoes."

The single-minded focus of the singer of "King of Suede" calls to mind that of "Theme from Rocky XIII (The Rye or the Kaiser)." These songs don't just tell compelling stories; they conjure up worlds. "King of Suede" is somber on the outside and spectacularly silly on the inside, yet nonetheless manages to convey an underlying and oddly moving sense of inner dignity.

9.
THAT BOY COULD DANCE

"That Boy Could Dance" is a movie in song form, a *Footloose* by way of *Airplane!* parody of the crowd-pleasing underdog dance movie. In the annals of musical and dance underdogs, few begin from a sadder place than the hero of "That Boy Could Dance," and even fewer reach as impressive heights.

The gent "That Boy Could Dance" rhapsodizes about is no garden variety klutz. He's closer to feral, more Bat Boy than the cute teen boy in the dance movie who turns into a star when he struts his stuff. Before "That Boy Could Dance" praises its title character, it first buries him with words.

We learn that the titular tragicomic dancing fool is a shambling, embarrassing, only barely human train wreck cruelly nicknamed "Jimmy the Geek" for reasons that soon become apparent. He's described as a "dumb-looking, scrawny little four eyed freak." It only gets less flattering from there.

The dancing maniac "isn't much to look at," and he was "never very bright," but what really makes the song a delight are deliciously mean details like, "He never passed his driver's test, he was always afraid of cars" and "he had a complexion that resembled the surface of Mars."

The singer makes Jimmy the Geek sound like someone who belongs in a circus sideshow rather than a high school. He not only stands out from the rest of the guys, he seems to exist somewhere outside of human civilization as well.

Yet when this foul-smelling, crater-faced, car-fearing, ugly, dumb jerk busts even a single move, he undergoes an amazing transformation. Jimmy the Geek is replaced, *Nutty Professor*-style, by a disco achiever who will someday be known and revered by women and dance-lovers the world over as "Diamond Jim," a titan of dance who "owns half of Montana."

"That Boy Could Dance" is as funny as it is mean. Yet because "That Boy Could Dance" is so upbeat musically, so peppy and propulsive, it ends up feeling oddly good-natured rather than needlessly cruel.

The song is an Al original, yet it's every bit as catchy an earwig as the parodies on the album.

Insane Ian's cover of "That Boy Could Dance" is one of the highlights of *Twenty-Six and a Half,* a nifty and heartfelt Al tribute album from 2011 that focuses on originals, and in

the process highlights Al's extraordinary gifts as an original songwriter, not just a parodist.

Because they're building on hit songs, parodies have an inherent advantage over originals but "That Boy Could Dance" illustrates why originals remain such an essential, if frustratingly overlooked, component of Al's career.

10.
THEME FROM ROCKY XIII
(THE RYE OR THE KAISER)

My nostalgia for "Weird Al" Yankovic is rooted primarily in my love for the man and his work but it's almost as grounded in an overlapping love for everything around it, from the artists and songs he was parodying to the pop culture touchstones he integrated into his art.

In the case of "Theme from Rocky XIII" (The Rye or the Kaiser)", my love of the Survivor parody is inextricably intertwined with my affection for Rocky Balboa.

"Theme from Rocky XIII (The Rye or the Kaiser)" simultaneously sends up "Eye of the Tiger," the Oscar-Nominated theme from *Rocky III*, and the Rocky franchise.

Though he is never identified by name, "Theme from Rocky XIII (The Rye or the Kaiser)" follows the continuing adventures of Rocky Balboa after he gets "fat and weak" and loses confidence in himself, to the point where he sells his gloves, a gesture as dramatic as it is counter-productive.

Rocky famously clobbered massive cuts of beef in *Rocky*. The experience must have left an indelible impression on him, because in "Theme from Rocky XIII (The Rye or the Kaiser)" he decides to forego boxing entirely so that he can make his living from selling meat instead of pummeling it.

"Theme from Rocky XIII (The Rye or the Kaiser)" subscribes to the conventional wisdom that food is funny, Jewish food is even funnier, and food served in a Jewish deli, my God, that is automatic hilarity. "Theme from Rocky XIII (The Rye or the Kaiser)" is one of the most Jewish songs Al has ever recorded, right up there with "Pretty Fly for a Rabbi." Let's face it: singing about salami and rye bread and delis is way more Jewish than singing about Rabbis.

"Theme from Rocky XIII" has a hint of genuine pathos rooted in its defeated hero's sepia-toned memories of his days as a champ. Al and Rocky were made for each other; just two albums later Al would be parodying the theme from *Rocky IV* for one of his least successful and most surgery-specific singles, "Living with a Hernia."

Al the pop culture prognosticator uncannily predicted that the *Rocky* movies would endure the same way his music has. The *Rocky* franchise is currently eight entries deep; there are six films in the *Rocky* series in addition to *Creed* and *Creed II*. If *Creed III* gets made and follows Apollo Creed's son after he gives up boxing to make pastrami sandwiches and homemade chicken soup, I hope they at least give Al a story credit.

11.
NATURE TRAIL TO HELL

In 3-D is Al's sophomore effort but I don't think it takes anything away from *"Weird Al" Yankovic* to argue that in some ways, *In 3-D* is Al's first real album.

For all of *"Weird Al" Yankovic*'s strengths, it still has the feeling of a compilation bringing together songs recorded over a series of years in a series of different contexts for different labels.

The DIY aesthetic of *"Weird Al" Yankovic* provides much of its scrappy charm. But *In 3-D* is the first "Weird Al" Yankovic album that feels like it was conceived and executed as an album.

"Weird Al" Yankovic made Al a recording artist, but *In 3-D* made him an unlikely but inspired pop star.

In 3-D hit the MTV bullseye with "Eat It," but what makes Al's second album so strangely enduring are the components that have nothing to do with hitting the pop charts. Al's legacy is built upon the hits but also the deep album cuts.

"Nature Trail to Hell" is the ultimate deep, crazy album track. It's the perfect way to end the giddy carnival ride that is *In 3-D*. It's a horror-comedy for the ears that doubles as an audio trailer/old school spiel for a 3-D horror movie that does not exist and, for good measure, *should* never exist.

It's a song that's as ambitious sonically as it is lyrically. Al's spooky vocals don't even kick in until after a minute of sinister haunted house organ and creepy-crawly sound effects. "Nature Trail to Hell" is no mere song: it's a bona fide epic.

"Nature Trail to Hell" delights in bloody, bleary, blood-splattered excess, taking great joy in mapping out the myriad horrors of the titular fright flick, a demented slasher film beyond the imagination of even fright master Trent L. Strauss about a "homicidal maniac" who finds "a Cub-Scout troop and he hacks up two or three in every scene."

I'm not sure how many scenes there are in *Nature Trail to Hell,* or how many Cub Scouts are in the pack but a whole lot of people are clearly slaughtered in ways designed primarily to highlight the film's 3-D nature. "Nature Trail to Hell" gives *In 3-D* its title. For it's not just "Nature Trail to Hell" that the singer can't stop kvelling about: it's *Nature Trail to Hell* in *3-D*.

Incidentally, Paul Scheer has a famous anecdote he shared on *WTF* about his mother finding out about "Nature Trail to Hell" and destroying *In 3-D* out of a fierce conviction that it was the devil's handiwork. Decades later, Scheer went from having his mother freak out about a fake 3-D horror film to starring in not just *a* 3-D horror film, but a movie we can all agree is *the* 3-D horror film: *Piranha 3DD*.

Coincidence? I don't think so. Like an accordion-playing Crypt Keeper, Al set out to scare children as well as entertain and amuse them. And with "Nature Trail to Hell," he seems to have succeeded in scaring at least one mother unnecessarily.

"Nature Trail to Hell" is unusually child-centered for an over-the-top bloodbath. The singer even ghoulishly booms, "Bring the kids along, it's good clean family fun" – assuming the family in question is the Mansons.

Scheer's mother may have been onto something in that, like all Satanic records from the 1980s, "Nature Trail to Hell" contains a backwards message, which we all know is the most evil way to convey a message. That backwards message is as sinister as it is enigmatic: Satan loves Cheez Whiz.

"Nature Trail to Hell" joyfully explores what would seem to be a pop culture paradox: a horror buff's intense desire to

experience things that are generally considered to be terrible. Then again, *In 3-D* is rapturously in love with the tacky, the ephemeral, the dated and the televised.

Al isn't content to end the album riffing on the pop culture of the past and the present. No, Al ends his second album and first masterpiece by inventing fictional pop culture too bloody and ridiculous and over-the-top to ever truly exist, yet weirdly plausible, even irresistible all the same.

"Nature Trail to Hell" – the song and the fictional movie – contain horrors beyond our wildest imagination. Yet they pale in comparison to the average atrocity on the 6 o'clock news, which Al suggests is the scariest show on TV because it's all real, or at least as real as anything on television can possibly be.

DARE TO BE STUPID (1985)

1.
LIKE A SURGEON

Weird Al" Yankovic and *In 3-D* **benefitted** from modest expectations, but after "Eat It" Al lost the element of surprise. He'd already gone farther than anyone could have envisioned. By *Dare to Be Stupid* Al had a career to protect and a lot to lose. He nearly cracked the top ten with "Eat It," hitting twelve at its peak, and picked up a Gold and later Platinum plaque for his breakthrough album. *In 3-D* also won Al the first of five Grammys and counting, again for "Eat It."

By the time *Dare to Be Stupid* came out, Al had stumbled upon a winning formula. It was the second album to feature a polka medley, but the first to feature a medley exclusively made up of recent hits.

The half parody/half original songs template was similarly firmly in place by Al's third album, as was his predilection for parodying recent hits rather than golden oldies.

For its lead-off track, first single and music video, "Like a Surgeon" followed the blueprint of *In 3-D*. Al once again locked in on the artist and song of the moment, Madonna. He plugged into the cultural zeitgeist with a canny sensibility that was one part MTV and one part Catskills.

That formula similarly applied to "Eat It." If "Eat It" was about how you should enjoy a nosh, then "Like a Surgeon" was grounded in another staple of Jewish humor: the doctor joke. Only instead of one doctor joke, "Like a Surgeon" was a doctor joke song.

"Like a Surgeon" deliberately eschews Al and his band and producer's generally successful attempts to sound as much like the original as possible with sound effects (in this case hospital noises) that betray almost instantly that this is not Madonna's steamy ode to sexual empowerment but rather a good-natured goof-'em-up.

"Like a Surgeon" operates on the principal of escalation. The song begins with what appears to be the reassuring beeps of the heart monitor of a patient who is still alive. That's no longer true by the end when that reassuring beep-beep-beep is replaced by the ominous hum of a flatline.

Late in the song, the dopey doc concedes, "It's a fact I'm a quack/The disgrace of the A.M.A./'Cause my patients die, yeah my patients die/Before they can pay." That's a line at least as old as vaudeville, a quintessential dad joke, but also a reminder of the homey comfort dad jokes provide.

"Like a Virgin" is such an inherently sexual song that you can't spoof it without addressing that sensuality. Part of the humor in "Like a Surgeon" comes from the surreal incongruity of Al emulating, at times, Madonna's breathy, sex-kitten delivery.

Al has never limited himself to his own gender when choosing artists to parody.

That has resulted in Al spoofing the music, and sometimes the image, of a fair number of female pop stars. When I was working with him on *Weird Al: The Book* around the time *Alpocalypse* came out most of the artists he was parodying were female pop stars in their teens and twenties – Lady Gaga, Taylor Swift, Miley Cyrus and Lorde – so there was an element of cross-generational, cross-gender ventriloquism at play. But when Al recorded "Like a Surgeon" and vamped his way through the video, he and Madonna were generational peers.

This features prominently in *Weird,* the fake trailer Funny or Die put out about a biopic of "Weird Al" Yankovic in the screamingly, sobbingly hyperbolic tradition of *Ray* and *Walk the Line.* What makes the trailer hysterical, beyond its loving recreation of musical biopic conventions, is Al's enduring status as the *least* self-destructive pop star in history.

Musical biopics have a one-size-fits-all structure that transforms wildly different artists into the same drunken, angry, over-sexed monster of id and ego, but this is an area where Al once again breaks the mold. Al is a model of self-discipline and self-restraint, the least traditionally rock star-like rock star in the world.

2.
DARE TO BE STUPID

There's an element of criticism and commentary in nearly everything Al does as a musician. He is both critic and artist, the observer and the observed, the star and the parodist of the star.

Sometimes the commentary is overt and filled with affection, like Al's tribute to Kurt Cobain's adorable idiosyncrasies on "Smells Like Nirvana," or the more ambivalent Lady Gaga parody/homage "Perform This Way."

Al's parodies and pastiches are powered not by derision, but by affection. Al is an evangelist on behalf of the artists he loves. "Happy Birthday" isn't just a brazen homage to Tonio K.: it also functions as borderline subliminal advertising for the artist.

Pastiches are inherently more challenging because Al isn't just swapping out old lyrics for new ones: he's creating music *and* words that are new yet cut from a distinctive, familiar pattern. On "Dare to Be Stupid," Al captures the essence of Devo so uncannily that it feels like an actual Devo song, not just an uncanny recreation of one.

Driven by rampaging synthesizers that give the song a sense of relentless kinetic energy, "Dare to Be Stupid" is largely devoted to dispensing advice, life lessons if you will. It's like Baz Luhrmann's "Everybody's Free (To Wear Sunscreen)" if the person dispensing wisdom was insane rather than casually wise.

Al being Al, the terrible advice the lunatic singing the song dispenses is saturated in pop culture references, particularly television and advertising, and, of course, advertising *on* television.

"Dare to Be Stupid" is a brilliant and weirdly necessary extension of Devo's concept of De-evolution. It's a boldly nihilistic invitation to escape the strictures of sanity and intelligence and embrace every American's God-given, inalienable right to be a boob-tube-worshiping consumerist moron.

Deep into the song, slipped into dangerous, Dadaist and nonsensical advice is the following counsel: "Settle down, raise a family, join the PTA/Buy some sensible shoes and a Chevrolet/ Then party till you're broke and they drive you away." Some of y'all might know that particular hustle as The American Dream, but in "Dare to Be Stupid" it feels just as intentionally nonsensical as everything else.

On *Behind the Music*, Mark Mothersbaugh described how shocked and honored he was by "Dare to Be Stupid,"

describing it, without hyperbole, as "the most beautiful thing I had ever heard."

You know what? He's right. For all its weird angles, there is something beautiful about "Dare to Be Stupid."

"Dare to Be Stupid" isn't technically a collaboration, but it feels like one. Only rather than a traditional collaboration, Al is channeling Devo.

In daring to be stupid, Al further confirmed his own genius, while paying perfect tribute to simpatico geek icons.

3.
I WANT A NEW DUCK

While Al has maintained an extraordinary level of quality control over the course his career, not every song is a classic.

"I Want a New Duck" is far from an embarrassment, but it seems like one of those cases where Al got locked into a comic construct based on a song title and then strained to make that concept work.

The comic conceit of "I Want a New Duck" involves an eccentric man with unrealistic ideas about what ducks are and are not capable of. He wants his duck to show him how to swim as well as dance, wash his car, help him stay in shape and keep his room clean. But he's just as expressive and exhaustive in detailing all the negative characteristics he doesn't want his new pet/soulmate to possess.

As I write this, I am reading a terrific book about pun competitions by Joe Berkowitz called *Away with Words*, so I'm unusually attuned to puns and wordplay and other ways of making your fellow human beings groan and roll their eyes in irritation. So I couldn't help but notice that "I Want a New Duck" is probably the most punny, if not funny, Al song to date. And I've got to admit, not everything about it quacked me up.

The singer threatens to tie up his duck with "duct tape." He expresses a desire for a duck that won't "smell too foul" and longs for one that will show him how to "get down." He wants his pet to know that the "duck stops here." After the "get down" line, Al even shouts, "Get it?"

In addition to a plethora of eye-roll-worthy puns, "I Want a New Duck" features duck-like quacking for background vocals but the kitchen-sink approach to production doesn't really serve the song – which ends on a particularly dark note, with the protagonist threatening to murder and then devour his duck should it ever displease him.

"I Want a New Duck" has a surprisingly involved legacy. Decades after "I Want a New Duck" was released as a single, Al appeared in another Funny or Die video, this one co-starring Huey Lewis. The short film was designed to promote the thirtieth anniversary release of Huey Lewis & the News' *Sports* by spoofing the iconic scene in *American Psycho* where Christian Bale's titular American-born madman discourses pretentiously about the early work of Huey Lewis & the News to a deeply bored colleague shortly before murdering him.

The Funny or Die video casts Huey Lewis and Al, wholesome heroes of countless dorks' childhoods, as, respectively, a deranged mass murderer and a debauched libertine soon to be slaughtered. It's an utterly out of character turn for the sober Yankovic and part of the video's kick comes from seeing familiar faces in such an unfamiliar context.

Al's persona as a good guy is so firmly established that he could only ever play a drunken, dissolute, Bret Easton Ellis-style monster as a joke, one that is darker and funnier than the waterfowl-based humor found in one of the lesser singles from one of Al's best albums.

4.
ONE MORE MINUTE

Al writes funny songs better than anyone else alive. But sometimes Al will write a song so good that it transcends comedy altogether and endures as music – beautiful, beautiful music. That's true of *Dare to Be Stupid*'s title song. It's equally true of "One More Minute."

The song exaggerates, for comic effect, the extent of the singer's heartbreak, but there is a core of genuine hurt underneath the ghoulish comedic excess. "One More Minute" isn't a great parody of a break-up song or a great goof on the tremblingly emotional break-up ballad: it's a great break-up song, period, that just happens to be very funny.

"One More Minute" begins on a deadpan note, with Al channeling the achingly emotional intimacy of "Are You Lonesome Tonight"-era Elvis Presley to address an ex-girlfriend who has dumped him for another man. The singer struggles to at least appear magnanimous, but he does a terrible job. Matters escalate quickly: one minute, he's dutifully ripping his ex's page out of his Rolodex – the next he's burning down one of their old hangouts solely because he associates it with a dead relationship.

The line about burning down the malt shop "where we used to go, just because it reminds me of you!" signals a shift in the song's tone. From that point on, the singer attempts to put a good face on the break-up with hilariously over-the-top descriptions of the torments he'd happily put up with rather than endure another miserable moment with his ex.

Al's affability allows him to get away with murder, literally, but that's a story for another book. "One More Minute" is so overflowing with violent and disturbing imagery that (despite what Tipper Gore might claim) it was actually Al's heartbroken doo-wop tearjerker that inspired the creation of the "Parental Advisory" sticker, rather than Prince's "Darling Nikki."

What year was the Parental Advisory sticker introduced? 1985. What year was *Dare to Be Stupid* released? The same year. Coincidence? No. Tipper Gore and her angry mob pretended to be concerned about metal and funk and rap, but really it was all about Al with her. She helped create the Parental Advisory sticker as a way of taming his tendency towards violent provocation, but Al is such a genius that they could never hang a Parental Advisory sticker on anything he did.

Al has never sounded more masochistic than when he's contemplating just how much he'd rather jump naked on a huge pile of thumbtacks, or dive into a swimming pool filled with double-edged razor blades than endure another moment of romantic misery.

Over velvety waves of doo-wop backup vocals, the singer grows increasingly enraged until he's yelling about his willingness to tear his heart out of his ribcage and stomp on it until death relieves him of the unbearable misery of living rather than experience the less appealing option of one last date with his ex.

"One More Minute" is relatively unique in Al's oeuvre in that it contains a dick joke. Not just a dick joke, mind you, but a masturbation joke, when Al croons forlornly, "I'm stranded all alone in the gas station of love and I have to use the self-service pumps."

Dick jokes are the essence of comedy throughout all cultures and nationalities. From the Lakota Indians to frozen Antarctica, all humor is essentially penis-based, which makes it all the more remarkable that Al has made people laugh for forty years without resorting to dick jokes. Or profanity.

It's a testament to our country's weird puritanism that a mild joke about a heartbroken man masturbating his pain away feels as transgressive as lyrics about ripping out intestines with silverware and having blood sucked out by leeches.

To the rest of the world, it might have seemed like Al was just chasing the zeitgeist with timely parodies of hit songs.

But Al was building a legacy one silly song at a time, and few songs in Al's oeuvre cut deeper than this bleakly hilarious look at romantic despair.

5.
YODA

Al likes to parody new songs, but he made an exception with "Lola," just as he dipped into the big, cornball American songbook to repurpose Don McLean's "American Pie" as the musical backing for "The Saga Begins."

Al wrote "Yoda" around the time *The Empire Strikes Back* was released and a stripped-down version with Al and his accordion is included on *Medium Rarities*. Yet for whatever reason, this sure-fire crowd-pleaser wasn't officially released until *The Empire Strikes Back* was ancient history.

If "Yoda" were about a different film that was popular at the time of its release but had subsequently been forgotten it would never have had much of a life, let alone enjoy one of the most auspicious afterlives in Al's career. But by 1985, it was apparent that even though the original *Star Wars* trilogy had run its course, these movies weren't going anywhere.

The *Star Wars* movies didn't recede with time. If anything, they grew bigger, more important and more central to pop culture.

In "Yoda" Al sings from the perspective of Luke Skywalker as he encounters a fantastical being who upends his sense of reality even more than the title character in "Lola" does its confused protagonist. But where Lola bewilders because the raspy-voiced barroom seductress transgresses the lines separating masculine from feminine and male from female, Yoda blows Luke's mind by doing things like lifting him in the air "just by raising his hand." Yoda is not just magic: he's Muppet magic, the most powerful form of magic.

I interviewed Mark Hamill the day that it was announced that Disney had purchased *Star Wars* and that the enormous machine that is George Lucas' brainchild would soon be roaring back into action. It was a strange, uncertain time for Hamill, who hadn't appeared onscreen as Luke Skywalker since 1983's *Return of the Jedi.*

When I asked Hamill how he felt about the big news, he did not know how to feel. He was overwhelmed. He had no idea whether he'd play a central role in the new movies, or be written out entirely, or just be a framed photograph in the background of a single scene.

Of course, Hamill ended up re-upping in a big way. In "Yoda," Al-as-Luke/Mark Hamill sings, "I'll be playing this part till I'm old and gray." Appropriately enough, the defining characteristic of the Luke found in *The Last Jedi* and *The Force Awakens* is that he is old and gray. *Really* old and gray. To the point where he and Yoda somehow seem like contemporaries.

In "Yoda," the singer frets that the "long-term contract that I had to sign/Says I'll be making these movies till the end

of time." In actuality, *Star Wars'* contractual and professional hold on its performers transcends death. Carrie Fisher is no longer with us, but thanks to CGI and pre-existing footage, she can still appear in *Star Wars* productions.

As a child, the lines in "Yoda" about Luke Skywalker not being able to kill Darth Vader for purely commercial reasons and the protagonist being locked into this ridiculous fictional world for all of eternity were revelatory. It felt like Al was one of those distant mentors you pick up along the way who tell you the way the world really works but manage to be funny and entertaining and relatable while doing so.

Like "Theme from Rocky XIII (The Rye or the Kaiser)," "Yoda" finds impish humor in the mercenary nature of film series that continue for decades, motivated by some powerful combination of nostalgia, greed and commercial calculation.

It took "Yoda" a half-decade to make the leap from *Dr. Demento Show* to *Dare to Be Stupid* album cut, but it was worth the wait. The song's birth is as drawn out and complicated as anything in Al's career, with the possible exception of "Pac-Man", but "Yoda" is immortal. It took a long time to get born, but "Yoda" will never die.

6.
GEORGE OF THE JUNGLE

"George of the Jungle" is a relative anomaly in Al's oeuvre: a faithful cover. That might seem strange, as Al's career is rooted in lampooning the music of others.

So, while "George of the Jungle" may be an anomaly, in other ways it perfectly fits Al's evolving aesthetic. It is, for example, the second consecutive song on *Dare to Be Stupid* about a pop culture figure beloved by children. It's similarly one of many songs in Al's oeuvre about television.

George of the Jungle enjoyed a second life thanks to the 1997 hit live-action adaptation starring Brendan Fraser as a dumb, blankly charming pile of muscles. But when Al tackled "George of the Jungle" back in 1985, it was the kind of oddball cult attraction Al has historically found himself attracted to.

George of the Jungle's initial run lasted a mere three months and 17 episodes, but because it was the brainchild of Jay Ward of *The Adventures of Rocky & Bullwinkle* fame, it has a cult following disproportionate to its modest original 1960s run.

"George of the Jungle" similarly fits into Al's work at the time in the extreme measures Al, producer Rick Derringer and his band took to ensure that these songs were as authentic as possible. For this cover, that meant getting the voice of George of the Jungle, Bill Scott, to reprise his trademark yells – which are as important to the song, if not more important, than Al's unusually orthodox vocals.

Over irritatingly peppy percussion, Al sings gingerly of the titular bungling hero, a Jay Ward take on Tarzan lucky enough to be surrounded by people who are far more capable, or at least less staggeringly incompetent than himself. Scott roars repeatedly over the course of the 64-second novelty ditty with a warble that somehow manages to be defiant, proud, and ultimately overwhelmed and out of control.

12 years after an unexpectedly straight cover of a semi-obscure 1960s cartoon became one of the more bewildering tracks on *Dare to Be Stupid,* Al's version appeared in the Brendan Fraser movie that transformed George of the Jungle from a cult figure to the unlikely star of a hit major motion picture.

Did "Weird Al" Yankovic bring about the resurrection of *George of the Jungle* the same way he did *Jeopardy* simply by reminding a forgetful world about something awesome that had passed too soon? Yes, yes he did. So we can add Fraser and everyone involved with *George of the Jungle* to the list of people who should write Al generous monthly checks in appreciation for all that he's done for the world, and their careers in particular.

7.
SLIME CREATURES
FROM OUTER SPACE

Al paid homage to The B-52s most directly on "Mr. Popeil" from *In 3-D*, but the band's proudly trashy spirit also informs "Nature Trail to Hell" and "Slime Creatures from Outer Space." The songs are so simpatico that "Slime Creatures from Outer Space" feels like a spiritual sequel to "Nature Trail to Hell," or at least a follow-up.

Al's mind was on the pop charts in the mid-'80s, but it was also on movies. Al had perfected the art of making funny little movies for MTV and was dabbling in longer-form narrative filmmaking with the mockumentary *The Compleat Al*, which was released the same year as *Dare to Be Stupid*.

UHF – a movie about TV, appropriately enough – lurked on the horizon. But the movie-mad Al was already making miniature audio motion pictures in the form of "Nature Trail to Hell" and "Slime Creatures from Outer Space."

Over an insistent drum beat and spooky (is there any either kind?) theremin from Al, the song's narrator shares how "things just haven't been the same since the flying saucers came!"

Al has always been good at drawing pictures with words and sounds. The crazily over-the-top science fiction invasion epic he whips up here demands to be projected on a fifty-foot drive-in screen in the 1950s, preferably in 3-D if not full-on Cinerama. But it's also a song that finds campy, delirious joy in the prospect of apocalyptic destruction, a surprisingly consistent theme in Al's work. Al and his collaborators compose a vivid world full of giant-headed monsters with "death-ray eyes" they use to "blow you up real good."

Humanity seems doomed, but the singer manages to maintain a sense of priorities. He's miffed at the evil space aliens because, in his words, "They're not very nice to the human race" and "sure could use some manicures," but also because their penchant for blasting everything could seriously mess up his apartment and he "just shampooed the rug."

"They're an intergalactic disgrace!" Al concludes before more explicitly channeling Fred Schneider's sing-song talk-yell to inquire, "Where did they come from?," "What do they want from us?" and "Why don't they leave me alone?"

The theremin goes a long way towards establishing a campy 1950s science fiction atmosphere. But the production is full of wonderful flourishes, like distorted back-up vocals that sound like space aliens, or at least someone with a strong space alien accent.

"Slime Creatures from Outer Space" is yet another upbeat song about something apocalyptic. It's fascinating for how snugly it fits into Al's emerging sensibility, but it's a lot of fun in its own right, in addition to foreshadowing Al's eventual evolution from making little movies for MTV to making the kind of movies audiences have to pay money to see.

8.
GIRLS JUST WANT TO HAVE LUNCH

The uncharacteristically dire Cyndi Lauper parody "Girls Just Want to Have Lunch" feels sluggish and half-hearted for a very good reason: it was forced on Al by his label, who saw the abundant commercial potential in Al parodying Cyndi Lauper's signature hit the way he did Madonna, Lauper's biggest rival, with "Like a Surgeon."

The record label's request made sense. Lauper was at the height of her popularity; her songs were fun and silly and instantly recognizable the way Al's most popular parodies are.

But the spirit had not moved Al to spoof Lauper. At his label's insistence, he wrote a song that reflected his profound ambivalence at being forced to do something that he did not want to do.

As a parody, "Girls Just Want to Have Lunch" is sorely lacking, but as a passive-aggressive gesture towards "The Man" for trying to dictate the nature of his art, it possesses a certain snotty appeal. "Girls Just Want to Have Lunch" is best understood as a giant "Forget you, pal!" to his record label. It was his way of saying, "Nuts to you, ya big jerks!" to the suits who were trying to tell him what to do. Even at his most enraged, Al keeps it PG.

"Girls Just Want to Have Lunch" feels less like a proper parody of Cyndi Lauper than self-parody. But even as self-parody, "Girls Just Want to Have Lunch" is strangely mean-spirited and off.

The song begins promisingly enough, with familiar, ebullient synths, but things take an unfortunate turn the moment Al's vocals kick in. On "Girls Just Want to Have Lunch," Al sings in a rasp that's creepy for all the wrong reasons. It almost sounds like Al, in protest, decided to sing the first take in an intentionally shrill, abrasive way to mock both the song and his label's insistence on him recording it, and when Derringer asked for a second take, he sneered, "Nah, those are the vocals. Accept it or leave the studio in a body bag."

The song's title similarly reeks of self-parody. It's almost like a "Weird Al" Yankovic Mad Libs equation: take the title of a hit song, alter it slightly to include a reference to food or eating, and voila, the parody writes itself.

Al has slipped inside the sweaty skin of a rogue's gallery of creeps, weirdoes, losers and self-identified groovy guys in his songs. But he can't quite get a handle on the creepiness of the narrator of "Girls Just Want to Have Lunch," who is obsessed with the idea that women are perpetually hungry, but only for lunch.

Yankovic's work benefits from a clear-cut point of view, but it's hard to see what exactly the jerk of "Girls Just Want to Have Lunch" is going on about.

There are certain turns of phrase in Al's work that are so perfect that they never leave your mind. "Girls Just Want to Have Lunch" has the opposite problem: certain lines have lodged themselves in my brain precisely *because* they're so weird and wrong, like when the singer begins by proclaiming, "Some girls like to buy new shoes/And others like drivin' trucks and wearing tattoos."

There's something about the clunkiness of the phrase "wearing tattoos" that's strangely hypnotic. The lyrics don't get any less creepy as the song progresses, thanks to couplets like, "She eats like she got a hole in her neck/And I'm the one that always gets stuck with the check/Can't figure out how come they don't weigh a ton."

"Girls Just Want To Have Fun" reeks of desperation. The crunching-as-percussion feels like pointless busywork, but the song doesn't hit its nadir until the synthesizer solo of the original is joined by the hand-flatulence of "Musical Mike" Kieffer.

Al's record company wanted Al to release a Cyndi Lauper parody in the worst possible way. So, it's sadly appropriate that they got the worst possible version of Al.

9.
THIS IS THE LIFE

The decade? The eighties. Reagan, baby! Morning in America! One man taught a shattered nation to laugh again after the culture-wide funk that followed President Carter's "Malaise" speech. Ah, but this was no mere man. Verily, he was a god among men, a Jersey jester, a muscled-up mirth-maker, a steroid-addled stand-up who worked his magic *live* every Saturday night to the delight of an adoring television audience.

I am talking, of course, about Joe Piscopo. Y'all may not believe this, but at one point, Joe Piscopo was the most popular and successful human being alive. How popular was Piscopo? He was so beloved by Lorne Michaels that he decided to make Piscopo's hilarious catchphrase, "Live, from New York – it's *Saturday Night!*" a fixture of, literally, every opening for decades to come. All in tribute to Piscopo.

Joe Piscopo in his prime was like George Carlin if Carlin was more interested in blasting his quads than incisive social commentary (and also wasn't very good at stand-up comedy). Piscopo's talent, and his roided-out frame, were too big for the small screen. So in 1984 20th Century Fox gave the gift of laughter to an appreciative public in the form of Amy Heckerling's *Johnny Dangerously.* For the all-important theme song, they hired another man of the moment: "Weird Al" Yankovic.

Johnny Dangerously aspired to do for gangster movies from the 1930s and '40s what Al's music did for the hits of the day. But it had to settle for a largely unmerited cult following, a lot of squandered potential, and a great theme song.

That sweet movie money allowed Al and his collaborators to do things musically that they would not be able to do otherwise. "This Is the Life" is no mere song: it's a full-on production, complete with banjo courtesy of Al Viola, whose credits include playing the mandolin on the *Godfather* soundtrack and working extensively with Piscopo's hero Frank Sinatra.

But if "This Is the Life" is a lovingly produced, fleshed-out musical voyage back to the bad old days of the Great Depression, it's also unmistakably a sassy little number about a guy who has it made.

The materialist anthem is sung from the point of view of one of Al's many creeps. We know he's a creep, because in perhaps the song's most memorable lyric, he brags, "You can tell I'm a living legend, not some ordinary creep." Only an ordinary creep would feel the need to tell the world that he's not a creep.

And really, everything that this blessed gent says further confirms his self-absorbed creepiness, but there's nevertheless something incongruously appealing about his narcissism. He's so intent on flaunting his incredible wealth that he wastes ridiculous amounts of money solely for the sake of wasting ridiculous amounts of money.

Al cements his reputation as the Cole Porter of over-consumption with an opening crowing, "I eat filet mignon seven times a day/My bathtub's filled with Perrier/What can I say/This is the life!"

This gentleman is what we Jews call a big *macher*. The music nails the infernal catchiness of Tin Pan Alley songcraft: it's a wonderfully retro little number, at once pleasingly simple and elegantly adorned. It breaks the period mood with a pair of purposefully anachronistic, contemporary touches – a bitching hair-metal guitar solo and the first instance of scratching in Al's work.

Al made the most of an awesome opportunity with "This Is the Life." It's not his fault that the movie the song promoted did not live up to the music he created for it. As for Joe Piscopo? Well, let's just say that things didn't turn out too good for him in the long run. But for a brief idyll, the future radiated nothing

but promise for Piscopo, and Al was blessed to have his own career trajectory overlap with his. They were like the tortoise and the hare, with the once red-hot Piscopo scoring a huge early advantage, but slow and steady Al ultimately winning the race by a decisive margin.

10.
CABLE TV

As a child, television wasn't just a status symbol: it was *the* status symbol. For me, being wealthy meant being able to afford a massive television and the most expensive, deluxe cable package imaginable. What was the point of being rich if you didn't have *all* the cable channels?

In my wasted youth, TV was comfort. It was status. It was pleasure. It was everything. Unfortunately for me, "everything" also meant a ten-inch black and white television that only carried, appropriately enough, UHF channels.

I saw our tiny little television as damning proof that my family was garbage, that we were poor scum who couldn't even afford a decent TV, let alone purchase all the products on it that guaranteed to make our lives perfect forever.

Television was like that in the 1980s. Cable wasn't just part of the white noise of everyday life the way it is now: it was magic, a whole new way of watching the boob tube that radically expanded upon the limited options of network television.

To my nine-year-old brain, there was nothing excessive about the idea of someone's life being completely transformed by the introduction of cable TV, the way the obsessive singing "Cable TV" is.

Of *course* cable TV was going to change an existence so empty our TV fiend was ready to "curl up and die" before he came face to face with the ever-giving glory of television stations beyond the boring networks, uptight PBS and those desperate, disreputable UHF channels.

The glory of cable TV in the 1980s lay in the seemingly unlimited number of options it gave viewers. But as "Cable TV" impishly chronicles, those "83 channels of ecstasy" include such dubious propositions as the "Siamese Faith Healer's Network" and "Celebrity Hockey." The singer's cable package is generous enough to include lots of shows no one could conceivably want to watch.

The comic excess of "Cable TV" has become today's magical, disappointing reality. The HBO-crazed narrator brags about sticking a satellite dish on his car so he can watch MTV while he drives. He could not have foreseen a day when people watching music videos while they drive would constitute both a banal reality and a threat to public safety.

Al spent the 1980s building his career to a place where he could co-write and star in his very own movie, but even when the intensely cinematic Al made the big leap to the big screen, the subject matter was, of course, the small screen.

When he released "Cable TV," Al was only a few years away from making a movie that flopped in theaters but became a huge cult hit on VHS, DVD, Blu-Ray, and of course, cable TV.

11.
HOOKED ON POLKAS

"Hooked on Polkas" is the second of Al's polka medleys to appear on an album but the first to exclusively feature new songs.

On "Hooked on Polkas," Al and his band narrow their focus to contemporary top 40 hits, taking listeners on a speedy, tongue-in-cheek journey through recent pop charts. By the time "Hooked on Polkas" ended Al's third record, Al had firmly established himself as the world's preeminent parodist of pop hits. But he was more than that. He was also a proven hitmaker in his own right with popular favorites like "Eat It," "Like a Surgeon" and "Ricky" to his name. By taking the entirety of top 40 radio and putting it in a blender, Al proved himself uniquely gifted at re-contextualizing hits in ways both goofy and oddly inspired.

Al was taking songs everybody at the time knew due to their ubiquity on radio and on MTV and recreating them in his own goofball image. "Footloose," for example, is radically re-imagined as a jazzy little *a cappella* number instead of a propulsive rocker.

"We're Not Gonna Take It," meanwhile, morphs from a defiant hair metal cry of snotty (if pointless) rebellion into an old-school declaration of defiance. You can easily imagine a barber shop quartet in matching suits performing it while marching in unison down Main Street sometime in the 1930s.

In its original non-polka form, "What's Love Got to Do with It" derives its power from the baggage that Tina Turner brought to it. When Al sings it, however, he's doing it from the perspective of a youthful dullard, a goober devoid of life experience, let alone the kind that allows Turner to sing her signature song with such bittersweet conviction.

The genius of Al and his band is twofold. First and foremost, they can perform any style or genre of music. Secondly, but almost as impressively, they can also transform any genre of music into polka.

Al paved his own lane professionally while still in his twenties, and polka medleys were a big part of that. They allowed Al to disappear inside the words and melodies of screamingly different artists simultaneously, while finding the connective tissue to stitch together songs from across the pop spectrum.

Medleys also allowed Al to be more risqué than he tends to be on his own compositions: Al ends the hit portion of the medley with a riff on the chorus of Frankie Goes to Hollywood's "Relax," an intensely homoerotic song about ejaculation. Al would never record something like this himself, but for a fraction of one medley, he and his band suddenly sound much dirtier.

Dare to Be Stupid's first half ranks alongside Al's best work. The second half is weaker, but ending one of his best and best-loved albums with "Hooked on Polkas" further establishes how important these medleys are to Al. They weren't just filler, or a blast of the familiar in an unfamiliar context, but rather a stealthily satirical ongoing project cheekily subverting rock pretension by crossbreeding it with the goofball world of polka.

POLKA PARTY! (1986)

1.
LIVING WITH A HERNIA

The 1986 flop *Polka Party!* represents Al's bleak mid-1980s nadir, but this is Al we're talking about, so it wasn't particularly bleak, nor was it much of a nadir. Al has had his ups and downs, but as evidenced by 1986's *Polka Party!*, his first real flop, his lows aren't very low while his highs are very high.

It's hard to overstate the importance of the lead-off parody on Al's first four albums. "Ricky" from *"Weird Al" Yankovic*, "Eat It" from *In 3-D* and "Like a Surgeon" from *Dare to Be Stupid* each gave Al a hit single and video riffing on one of the most iconic hits of the era.

"Living with a Hernia" was supposed to do the same. Al filmed a terrific video parodying "Living in America," but the public simply wasn't ready for another surgery-themed spoof so soon after "Like a Surgeon" – nor were they necessarily prepared for *another* parody of a *Rocky* theme song after "Theme from Rocky XIII (The Rye or the Kaiser)." That's too bad, because "Living with a Hernia" is weird and wonderful and punk in its sneering disregard for the demands of the market.

James Brown's music is visceral and physical. The great ones often make it seem effortless, but exuding tremendous effort was central to James Brown's whole deal. He was the hardest-working man in show-business. You *always* saw him sweat. Beyond that, there was something intensely visceral about his delivery that worked in tandem with the sweaty intensity of his dancing.

Part of that physicality lies in Brown's aggressive sexuality. Those grunts and groans and sub-verbal exhortations sure sounded sexual. But they also spoke to how hard he worked, and how hard he pushed himself and the people around him.

So part of the joke in "Living with a Hernia" lies in replacing the grunting delivery of a dancing sex machine who is grunting and groaning and shouting because he feels good with the grunting, groaning and shouting of a man who is in intense physical pain because he's suffering from the titular medical condition. This affords Al an opportunity to return to the doctor jokes that served him well in "Like a Surgeon."

"Living with a Hernia" is one of Al's most underrated singles. That's partially because it manages to once again make surgery funny but also because it is so weird and specific and perversely non-commercial. Al was the 1980s pop star most likely to wear out his library card checking out books relevant to whatever song he's researching. Actually, Al is the *only* pop star of the 1980s likely to wear out his library card researching the subject matter of his latest song.

Some of Al's songs are more educational than others. "Living with a Hernia" is educational and entertaining in equal measure. Al did his homework here and "Living with a Hernia" is consequently the only pop single to feature a fun call-and-response section where the singer helpfully delineates between the various forms of hernias, including Incomplete, Epigastric, Bladder, Strangulated, Lumbar hernia, Richter's hernia, Obstructed, Inguinal and finally Direct.

For a song about a man all too in touch with his body and his body's problems, the singer has a wonderfully wordy way of viewing the world. Who other than Al was going to use words like "ruination" and phrases like "Got a bulge in my intestinal wall!" on a pop single whose audience is partially children?

"Living with a Hernia" has the ultimate adult subject matter. I was ten years old when it came out, and while my father had already had the first of two hernias, even I found the subject matter inaccessible. Then I had a hernia myself as an adult. You can guess what song kept running through my head. I was hurting bad, in a tender location.

"Living with a Hernia" is partially a meditation on James Brown, and since it chronicles a man laid low by an unfortunate bulge in his intestinal wall, it can only end one way, with Al closing out the song with, "I feel bad!"

Polka Party!'s reviews and sales sure didn't make Al or his label feel good. "Living with a Hernia" is indeed a perversely, ingratiatingly non-commercial choice for a big kick-off single (and it's about as commercial as the album gets). But despite its failure to chart, it's nevertheless a funky, kooky delight on an album that's weirder and more fun than it is generally given credit for being.

2.
DOG EAT DOG

Al's pastiches are the ultimate homage. They're even more flattering than parodies, because in parodies Al just provides new lyrics to pre-existing compositions. For his pastiches, Al takes apart the music of his favorite artists and then puts them back together to create something in their image that's still recognizably his own. Al goes all Seth Brundle, mixing his own DNA with the DNA of the artists he's paying tribute to.

In "Dog Eat Dog" that means combining the ineffable essence of Al with Talking Heads and particularly their charismatic head weirdo, David Byrne. The result is one of the purest and most loving homages in Al's discography, as Al pays homage to an act he clearly feels just as connected to emotionally as Devo. How could he not? Who doesn't love Talking Heads?

When musicians make songs about office life, the emphasis is generally on the soul-crushing drudgery of the 9-to-5 grind. "Dog Eat Dog" takes an antithetical tact: the narrator is one of Al's insane over-enthusiasts. But instead of living for cable television or pasteurized lunch meat or potatoes, he's driven to a state of near-ecstasy by the trappings of office life.

"Dog Eat Dog" is rooted in the overall sound and vibe of Talking Heads. But musically it's more specifically based on the nervous, coked-out groove of "Cities" for its verses and the

more triumphant, ascendant chorus of "And She Was" for its chorus. Then there's an entire section rooted in the existential panic of "Once in a Lifetime" when the narrator observes, with acid trip clarity/confusion, "Sometimes I tell myself, this is not my beautiful stapler!/Sometimes I tell myself, this is not my beautiful chair!"

The normally sure-footed Al made some surprising mistakes on *Polka Party!*, more of the commercial than creative variety. But with this tribute to one of the all-time greats, the execution is just as brilliant as the concept and the inspiration.

3.
ADDICTED TO SPUDS

The "Addicted to Love" parody "Addicted to Spuds" follows a blueprint that has served Al well. He took one of those monster radio smashes that everyone knows and everyone recognizes, and then he switched a few letters around.

Voila! A song about drug addiction as a metaphor for overpowering lust delivered with icy sophistication by a debonair English playboy becomes an obsessive but infinitely sillier song about two fiends helpless before their addiction to all things potato-related. "Addicted to Love" is overtly about sex, lust and compulsion. But it also just plain sounds dirty.

Al's mutation is nowhere as lascivious, but at times it captures the intensity of the original when the singer moans of his compatriot's helpless potato addiction: "Your greasy hands, your salty lips/Looks like you've found the chips/Your belly aches, your teeth grind/Some tater tots would blow your mind!"

Never has an overwhelming desire to pop Pringles seemed so compulsive. This is not just someone who enjoys potatoes: he's a man with a problem. A serious problem. A potato problem.

Potato over-consumption is, admittedly, not the most fertile comedic subject matter. On "Addicted to Spuds," Al works up a sweat wringing every last bit of humor out of being unhealthily consumed with consuming every form of a certain starch.

Al's wordplay in the song is dad-joke shameless, but also dad-joke ingratiating and dad-joke mildly-amusing – like when he observes to a fellow French fry fiend of their shared addiction to potatoes, "I understand how you must feel/I can't deny they've got appeal!"

I particularly love the way Al turns "fried" into two syllables when he pronounces it "fuh-ried." And I like the line and sentiment, "Some tater tots would blow your mind!" to the point that I am considering getting it tattooed on my neck.

"Addicted to Spuds" fits the profile of a lead-off parody/ single more than "Living with a Hernia." It's a parody of a massive, unmissable smash that spawned an equally (if not more) massive, unmissable video featuring a sharply dressed Palmer crooning before an all-female band of vacant, dead-eyed sex-doll sentient fashion mannequins barely pretending to play their instruments.

Like the notorious woman-in-a-grinder *Hustler* cover, the "Addicted to Love" video is so grotesquely misogynist that it almost comes all the way around. It becomes a weird, disturbing commentary on the nature of misogyny and the dehumanization of women's bodies in pop culture.

The "Addicted to Love" video would seem to be an obvious satirical target for Al. Indeed, Al parodied it in the "UHF video, but for whatever reason, a full video was never made and the song never became a single.

That's not the greatest loss in the world. But "Addicted to Spuds" is funnier and cleverer than a song with its title and premise has any right to be.

4.
ONE OF THOSE DAYS

Not all "Weird Al" Yankovic songs are created equal. Not every song is a timeless classic. Not every song can be someone's favorite. Not everything can be "Dare to Be Stupid" or "One More Minute." Sometimes Al's songs are disposable goofs meant to be enjoyed in the moment and then forgotten.

That's "One of Those Days." It's an unabashed throwaway as thin (if amusing) musically as it is lyrically. Over bluesy guitar and rollicking piano, the song's hapless singer recounts having possibly the worst day in the history of bad days. It's a day so bad, in fact, that it ensures that no more days will follow for humanity, bad or good.

Things start off on a relatable enough note: the alarm clock is busted, so our luckless protagonist is late to work and gets chewed out by the boss. Then things take a turn, as they do in Al's songs. After losing one of his socks in the drier, the schmuck can't find his wallet. Also, his hair is on fire.

"One of Those Days" is a straightforward exercise in comic escalation. It starts off with the kind of hassles that constitute everyone's idea of a bad day – work troubles, losing things, running late – and quickly ratchets up the danger to apocalyptic levels.

The song alternates between two tracks. On one, the singer grouses about typical, life-sized aggravations. There's nothing good on TV. He's overdrawn on his checking account. He's out of Cheetos. He cuts himself shaving. All that's left to eat are (ostensibly non-mind-blowing) tater tots.

On the other track, the headaches our luckless singer is crooning about are biblical in scope. He's followed by an angry swarm of locusts. The Ku Klux Klan burn a cross on his front lawn. A big steamroller is running over his mother, a misfortune otherwise reserved for cartoon characters.

"One of Those Days" ends with the ultimate headache for an American near the end of the Cold War: nuclear Armageddon. Yet the singer delivers the unfortunate news, "The world blows up and now everybody's dead!" with the same mild annoyance he uses to relate more mundane misfortunes involving lost socks and wallets.

Even with an ending featuring nuclear apocalypse and the death of life on Earth as we know it, "One of Those Days" still feels aggressively inconsequential and inessential.

5.
POLKA PARTY!

Relegating the accordion to the background was a good move for Al both creatively and commercially. *In 3-D* is a big improvement over Al's scruffy, scrappy, hastily recorded self-titled debut.

If Al was intent on downplaying the significance of the accordion in his music, then why is he on the cover of *Polka Party!* grinning big as he plays his trusty squeezebox, surrounded by sneering punks?

Of course, the cover is a very curious, very "Weird Al" Yankovic joke. The humor comes from the incongruous juxtaposition of Alpine and punk rock culture, but it also comes from this mashup – accordion geek and angry punks – being particularly unpalatable and non-commercial.

That goes double for the title. *Polka Party!* is quite possibly the least commercial and also accurate title you could give an album that only features as much, and as little, actual polka content as Al's previous two albums, neither of which had "polka" in the title or Al playing the accordion on the cover.

There's something wonderfully perverse about naming an album after a polka medley that, almost by definition, is doomed to bleed into all the other polka medleys in listeners' imaginations.

Earlier polka medleys got their comic juice from the way Al took serious songs and reimagined them as happy champagne-and-bubbles music. "Polka Party!," in sharp contrast, takes songs that were already ridiculous and makes them even sillier.

It's not like someone must deflate the self-seriousness of Peter Gabriel's "Sledgehammer." On a similar note, the following song "Sussudio" is such disposable fluff that it's practically a novelty song itself. The next nugget in Al and his band's satirical targets isn't just a silly song, it's a song sung by a comedian and comic actor: Eddie Murphy's Rick James-written and produced "Party All the Time."

It's not all goofy larks on the docket, however. "Polka Party!" has fun making solemn songs like Lionel Richie's "Say You, Say Me" and Tears for Fears' "Shout" feel ridiculous. But "Polka Party!" doesn't come into its own in a way that differentiates it from Al's other polka medleys until he closes the hits portion with Madonna's "Papa Don't Preach."

"Papa Don't Preach" is the kind of song Al's polka medleys are made for. It's ubiquitous, so everyone will be able to recognize it even in drastically altered form, but it also takes itself very seriously. It doesn't just want to divert the masses for a few minutes. It wants to say something important about The World That We Live In.

So, it is a subversive delight to hear Al crooning goofily about his determination to hold onto his baby rather than giving it up for adoption or having an abortion.

Titling the album *Polka Party!* after the requisite polka medley was, and remains, an audacious and clever gag, but commercially at least, one that fell extremely flat.

6.
HERE'S JOHNNY

"Here's Johnny," Al's parody of El DeBarge's aggravatingly infectious *Short Circuit* soundtrack smash "Who's Johnny," finds Al once again wading into the warm, comforting waters of television and obsession. It's a tongue-in-cheek tribute to a celebrity who, like Vanna White, became famous for doing not much of anything at all.

Ed McMahon and Vanna White were Warholian celebrities, fascinating in their banality. They're human beings, ostensibly, but also brand names, consumer products, walking punchlines.

McMahon and White were unusually pure creatures of television who lucked into a dream gig. They were paid insane amounts of money for sitting and laughing, and turning letters on a giant board, respectively, opposite someone with the more demanding job. Pat Sajak's gig as the host of *Wheel of Fortune* was so undemanding that he admittedly performed it drunk for decades, which tells you something about his letter-turning sidekick's workload.

"Here's Johnny" is a silly, upbeat bubblegum pop parody about something equally silly, if not sillier: the sedentary yet richly compensated career of America's favorite talk-show sidekick, Ed McMahon.

On "Here's Johnny," Al assumes the perspective of another one of his demented, monomaniacal obsessives. The singer is not just a fan. Unique among television viewers at the time, the singer worships the stocky personification of beefy mediocrity as "such a cool dude" whose mere existence makes his "life worth living."

"Watch him selling beer and dog food" Al sings later in the song, returning yet again to the field of television advertising. There, McMahon was able to leverage a lifetime of sitting on a couch and guffawing excessively at Johnny Carson's jokes into a similarly lucrative, similarly cushy gig reading cue cards in commercials for products than run the gamut from Cash4Gold to Colonial Penn life insurance.

The problem with "Here's Johnny" is that Ed McMahon is just too fat and easy a comic target. There's a strange, pleasing synchronicity in an irritatingly tacky, inescapable pop song that's too sadistically catchy for its own good being used to gently spoof a tacky, inescapable TV treasure who was endearing and unforgettable not despite his cheesiness, but because of it.

7.
DON'T WEAR THOSE SHOES

Polka Party! **remains the kind** of pop culture orphan that attracts defenders more than fans. It's easy to see where the album went wrong commercially. The cover was a mistake, as it failed to increase Al's popularity among punks *or* polka enthusiasts, as was naming the album after the polka medley and a style of music that was only played on ten percent of the album. *"Hillbilly Al" Yankovic's Country Classics* would have been as misleading and uncommercial a title, and more people purchase country albums than polka platters.

Al probably shouldn't have returned so quickly to the comedic well of painful medical procedures with "Living with a Hernia" so soon after "Like a Surgeon," and "Ruthless People" was a poor choice to parody, on account of it being terrible and no one liking it.

Yet I consider Al's first real flop a success all the same thanks to fun outliers like "Don't Wear Those Shoes," a quintessential album cut that joins "Christmas at Ground Zero," "Good Enough for Now" and "Dog Eat Dog" as solid to great originals. They, along with "Living with a Hernia" and "Addicted to Spuds," make *Polka Party!* one of the most underrated albums in Al's career.

With its chiming synthesizer, infectious walking baseline and pop-operatic bigness, "Don't Wear Those Shoes" sounds like nothing else Al had recorded up to that point. Even more impressively, it sounds like nothing Al has done in the decades since. The song is carried by a soaring melody and glossy, dramatic production that seem to mock the non-sequitur absurdity of the lyrics.

"Don't Wear Those Shoes" is sung from the perspective of an obsessive who is willing to tolerate a nearly endless gauntlet of misbehavior, abuse and craziness from the song's subject on the sole condition that that they refrain from wearing specific footwear.

Al has always found the pitch-black comedy in larger-than-life, over-the-top forms of abuse and self-flagellation. The

protagonist of "Don't Wear Those Shoes" invites the subject of his desperate pleas to subject him to the torments of the damned. They're free to wreck his car or shave off all his hair, and run the vacuum during his favorite show, and make phone calls to Europe to people they don't even know.

They're similarly invited to spend his money and waste his time. And, because this is a "Weird Al" Yankovic song, the masochistic offers escalate until the deranged singer is trying to convince himself, the listener, and the song's subject that he could "learn to live" with "a six-inch railroad spike" being shoved through his head – just as long the titular shoes are not worn.

Of course, the singer *could* just be a masochist, and shoes don't really factor into the equation, except to provide an excuse to throw himself into all manner of debasement. We never know *why* these shoes are so dreadfully offensive and unforgivable. We don't need to know. That would just spoil the tantalizing mystery.

8.
TOOTHLESS PEOPLE

Even if you're a casual fan, there's a good chance that when you hear the first thirty seconds of a song that "Weird Al" Yankovic has parodied, you feel an intense surge of recognition.

This might be because you're a big fan of the parody, or at least familiar with it. But it's probably also because, over the course of his 40 years in the recording business, Al has pretty much only parodied monster hits.

Al's golden ear for hits makes "Toothless People" a bizarre anomaly in his oeuvre. For pretty much the only time in his career, Al parodied, in Mick Jagger's "Ruthless People," a pop hit that wasn't actually a pop hit. "Ruthless People" wasn't a song people seemed to like at all, let alone a hit that would be lodged so deeply in the public consciousness that they would recognize a parody.

You know how you know "Ruthless People" was a song no one liked, and no one remembers? Because it's a Mick Jagger solo song. Only Jann Wenner pretends to like those, and that's just to stay in Mick's favor.

"Ruthless People" is an outlier for Al in many ways. It wasn't really a hit, only reaching #52 on the pop charts despite its connection with a sleeper hit movie that would go on to become a cult classic.

People didn't really remember the song "Ruthless People." Even more unfortunately for Al, it wasn't a particularly good or memorable or distinctive song. So instead of a ubiquitous smash for the ages, Al was hanging his spoof on the rickety, shambling frame of a forgettable Mick Jagger solo single.

Judging by the recurring themes of *Polka Party!*, Al's head was in a pretty weird place in 1986. Of *Polka Party*'s ten songs (one polka, four parodies and five originals), two end with a nuclear apocalypse ("One of Those Days" and "Christmas at Ground Zero") and two are about painful, debilitating medical conditions ("Living with a Hernia" and "Toothless People").

While the medical ailment-themed "Living with a Hernia" is a weird and wonderful delight, "Toothless People" is one of the few near complete misses in Al's discography.

Ever the student, Al clearly researched toothlessness, gum disease and tooth decay. The origin story for most pop smashes begins with a songwriter taking out library books about dry sockets and gum disease, but this proved the one instance where that strategy failed. "Toothless People" is plenty educational but even Al can't make this subject matter funny.

Thankfully, "Toothless People" gave Al nowhere to go but up, both in terms of *Polka Party!* and the inherently more successful parodies that would follow.

9.
GOOD ENOUGH FOR NOW

Al and his staggeringly gifted band are proficient in seemingly every form of music. When Al wants to do a reggae song he doesn't make a "Weird Al" Yankovic song with a reggae feel or a reggae vibe. No, when Al wants to do reggae, he writes a reggae song, even if it's a complete anomaly in his oeuvre.

On a similar note, when "Lonesome Al" Yankovic decided to pull a Ray Charles and go country with "Good Enough for Now" he didn't write a song that sounds like a country version of a "Weird Al" Yankovic song. No, he wrote a proper country song that just happened to be funny and satirical.

It helps, of course, that Al and his collaborators sought the assistance of session musicians who'd spent their careers working in the countrified fields into which Al and the gang were gingerly dipping a toe.

No proper country song is complete without pedal steel guitar, so "Good Enough for Now" features straight-faced pedal steel from session musician Jim Cox, and fiddle from Dennis Fetchet.

Lyrically, the song is sung from the perspective of one of Al's signature creepy Casanovas. But where the protagonists in "Weird Al" Yankovic songs tend to see sex and romance through the prism of their own insanity, the country crooner of "Good Enough for Now" is just kind of a jerk.

Country music is full of outsized declarations of love of dubious sincerity but the singer of "Good Enough for Now" takes great pains to establish that his love for what he deems (in a compliment so backhanded it actually qualifies as an insult) an "above average lady" comes with an endless series of caveats.

In his choice of partner, the singer will concede only that he's *relatively* lucky, as he *probably* couldn't ask for too much more. Indeed, she's *"almost just"* what he's been looking for.

When a love comes with back-to-back modifiers like that, it begins to seem not much like love at all.

Love is many things; "acceptable" is not one of them. But the country creep singing "Good Enough for Now" seems willing to settle with the object of his half-hearted semi-desire until a better option presents itself.

The passive aggressive quasi-romantic will offer a country-sized declaration of love like, "Oh, I couldn't live a single day without you." But he immediately undercuts it with, "Actually, on second thought, well, I suppose I could." Our singer is pragmatic, candid and honest to a fault. He's never afraid to establish the limits of his affection or the moderate nature of his romantic feelings.

"Good Enough for Now" is probably more emotionally authentic than straight-faced ballads that pretend that love is eternal, overwhelming and wildly melodramatic. Not, you know, a matter of finding someone somewhat acceptable who will in turn grudgingly tolerate you.

"Good Enough for Now" is like "My Funny Valentine": a love song that could easily pass for a sustained insult. Or, alternately, a sustained insult cannily masquerading as a different kind of love song. And when I mean "different," I mean "condescending and mean." The song's narrator can't praise the object of his lukewarm semi-affection without also insulting her, directly or indirectly.

"Good Enough for Now" is a semi-love song of intense passive-aggression, an exquisitely crafted and performed sleeper that grows on you. It's more than merely good enough; it's legitimately great.

10.
CHRISTMAS AT GROUND ZERO

"Weird Al" Yankovic was never supposed to happen in the first place. The kinky-haired kid with the accordion and the combustible energy was supposed to rule the low-stakes world of *The Dr. Demento Show*'s Funny Five for a few years before growing up and leaving that world behind.

Al wasn't supposed to last four years, let alone four decades and counting. The critical and commercial failure of 1986's *Polka Party!*, following the back-to-back success of *In 3-D* and *Dare to Be Stupid*, could have spelled the end of the line for the young troubadour.

But Al didn't go out like that. *Polka Party!* proved a bump in the road, not an ending.

Polka Party!, which was released during the waning days of the Cold War, didn't just conclude with an ending, it closed with *the* ending: a nuclear apocalypse. That's the second nuclear apocalypse of the album, if you're counting, after the one that concludes "Just One of Those Days."

Al's label wanted a Christmas song from Al, knowing how insanely lucrative a Yuletide perennial can be. So, with the same punky, irreverent spirit that led him to answer their request for a Cyndi Lauper parody with the quietly rage-filled "Girls Just Want to Have Lunch," he answered their Christmas wishes with a blisteringly dark exploration of mankind's horrific capacity for complete self-negation. It just happened to sound like a holly, jolly Christmas perennial from Phil Spector's beloved Christmas album.

They wanted Alvin & the Chipmunks' "Christmas Song." Instead Al gave them *Dr. Strangelove* covered with tinsel and holly.

"Christmas at Ground Zero" was already a bracingly dark title for a holiday jingle, even before the attacks of 9/11 made "Ground Zero" synonymous with a very specific American trauma. It's an audacious sick joke of an album closer that would be almost unbearably grim if it weren't so incongruously, musically chipper.

Al, producer and multi-instrumentalist Rick Derringer and Al's band don't just give the song a big sound: they give it a low-budget Wall of Sound. The ode to Yuletide atomic Armageddon has a lush, super-produced sound topped off with the ghoulish, darkly funny flourish of an air raid siren.

Al's elf of doom delivers news of a nuclear apocalypse with the same saccharine cheer he delivers lines about sleigh bells ringing and carolers singing. Never have phrases like "It's the end of all humanity," "Time to face your final destiny" and "We're gonna get nuked" been sung with such strangely infectious Christmastime cheer.

There's a certain deranged majesty to "Christmas at Ground Zero." Just as "Good Enough for Now" is a credible country song and not just Al and his band's version of one, "Christmas at Ground Zero" is a bona fide Christmas song, with an almost sadistically catchy melody that lodges itself in the brain, in part because it sounds so much like other Christmas staples. It has that instant-vintage kind of feel – like it was always around, but Al just had to capture and record it.

Al made his proper directorial debut with the "Christmas at Ground Zero" video, a stock footage pastiche of old clips involving nuclear apocalypse and Christmas, including a clip of Ronald Reagan in his TV host days, that closes with a shot of Al surrounded by carolers with gas masks.

"Christmas at Ground Zero" isn't entirely bleak, only overwhelmingly so. It at least allows for the possibility that humanity will survive long enough for some "new mutations on New Year's Day." *Polka Party!* ends on a big, bold, confident note, but there's more to recommend than a singularly ballsy, ferociously non-commercial post-apocalyptic Christmas classic.

In the wake of *Polka Party!'s* failure, Al knew that he could do better. He could, and would, do *Even Worse,* the comeback album that would get him back on MTV and the pop charts.

EVEN WORSE (1988)

1.
FAT

The music industry was only going to give an original like Al a limited number of chances. As the late eighties approached, it was imperative that Al score a hit that would help the industry forget *Polka Party!*'s under-performance.

Al once again found inspiration in Michael Jackson and food for the "Bad" parody "Fat."

"Fat" did what it needed to do; while turning "Bad" into "Fat" was not an elegant or unexpected move, Al makes it work through a characteristic combination of craftsmanship, Catskills shamelessness and full-throated conviction.

Yankovic's interpretation of masculinity is unique, if not quite as unique as Jackson's. So the comedy here comes from a white geek getting brash, defiant and proud describing not his toughness, but rather his over-the-top corpulence, i.e. having "more chins than Chinatown."

That "more chins than Chinatown" is what is known as a "street joke." That's a joke that has been told for so long and in so many contexts that no one knows where it originated or who created it. Street jokes belong to everyone and no one. It's a joke book joke, essentially, and it's not the only street joke in the song. It is, after all, about a man who brags, "When I go to get my shoes shined/I gotta take their word!"

Those jokes didn't originate inside Al's brain. But they nevertheless became part of the grand gestalt that makes "Fat," like so many of Al's singles, particularly his parodies, far funnier and more appealing than they have any right to be. What allows "Fat" to transcend the groaningly familiar fat jokes (and it contains its share) is the swagger Yankovic brings to the character.

Yankovic could seemingly inject lard into his bloodstream with an IV drip for months and remain skinny, yet the round mound of sound singing the song is not embarrassed or ashamed to be a larger gentleman. He does not writhe in self-hatred because he does not fit into society's conception of conventional attractiveness.

No, the character Al brought to vivid life in the song's video, and was subsequently cursed to have to bring to life (with the aid of the hardest working fat suit in show business) countless times in concert *owns* being comically obese. He brags defiantly, "The whole world knows I'm fat and I'm proud."

I'm not suggesting that "Fat" is a fat pride anthem. But I am saying that some chubby kid somewhere probably went to a "Weird Al" Yankovic show with their parents and saw their hero scream, "The whole world knows I'm fat and I'm proud," and maybe that meant something to them. Maybe it still does mean something to kids delighted to be given permission to be fat and proud, if only within the context of a pop song parody.

2.
STUCK IN A CLOSET WITH VANNA WHITE

Part of the pleasure of "Weird Al" Yankovic's 2018 Ridiculously Self-Indulgent, Ill-Advised Vanity Tour (where he boldly eschewed the hits and signature theatricality for stripped-down shows of originals and album cuts) lies in hearing beloved pastiches that hadn't been a staple of Al's live show in a while. And part of the pleasure came from hearing ancient obscurities I never imagined I would get to hear live.

"Stuck in a Closet with Vanna White" is a perfect example. It's the ultimate album cut, dates itself instantly with the Vanna White reference in the title, and contains a phrase used to describe little people that was not considered a slur at the time of the song's release but has become offensive in the ensuing decades.

Rather than ignore that inconvenient fact, Al forthrightly acknowledged in concert while performing "Stuck in a Closet with Vanna White" that he had erred out of ignorance rather than malice, and that he would obviously never use a word like that in a new song.

Al had made an honest, understandable error. He learned from it and changed accordingly. That's all you can ask for. We all make mistakes, but if we are good people we learn from them. They help us grow.

Onstage and on record, "Stuck in a Closet with Vanna White" is driven by some of the most audacious fretwork and fancy shredding in all of Al's discography. Jim West's guitar is flashy, hard-driving and aggressive, as is Al's delivery as he tries to make sense of the free-floating insanity of an intense and troubling dream life that always seems to end with the singer in the titular predicament.

Like Ed McMahon, Vanna White became rich and famous for doing not much of anything at all. She elevated the art of smiling, walking, and turning letters into lucrative pop-art, but she also loomed as a preeminent sex symbol of the Reagan decade.

Many people would have loved to be stuck in a closet with Vanna White in 1988. Despite Freudian sexual imagery involving "hot dogs and donuts flying everywhere," however, Al is interested in White as a walking punchline and random pop culture reference rather than as an object of lust.

White was the subject of countless sexual dreams in her prime. But the role she plays in this song more closely resembles a nightmare. The closet that Al and Vanna find themselves in feels more like a coffin or prison than a place to make out.

"Stuck in a Closet with Vanna White" runs an epic five minutes because it has a lot of crazy business to get through, loopy scenarios and vivid imagery tied together with dream logic, silliness - and of course, television, the great common denominator in Al's music.

It's Yankovic-goes-Lewis-Carroll – *Al in Wonderland*, as it were. Al fills the song with a crazy cast of characters that includes a dinosaur, Russian spies and the chest-burster monster from *Alien*.

I'm glad I got to hear "Stuck in a Closet with Vanna White" live. For all its infectious, energetic silliness, it's one of Al's more disposable obscurities. But seeing it performed for an adoring audience in 2018 proved an incongruously unforgettable experience.

3.
(THIS SONG'S JUST) SIX WORDS LONG

Al tends to parody songs from the outside, but at various points in his career Al has attacked the songs he's parodying from the inside out.

In these instances, Al's spoofs double as critical analysis in addition to parody. "Smells Like Nirvana," for example, is about Kurt Cobain's iconic, irresistible incomprehensibility. "(This Song's Just) Six Words Long," meanwhile, uses George Harrison's irritatingly infectious late-period hit "Got My Mind Set on You" to explore a popular theme of Al's: the mind-numbingly repetitive nature of contemporary pop music.

The clattering, mindless repetition of pop hits is a central theme of Al's polka parodies. Al takes songs that are already sadistic in their unrelenting repetitiveness (like Daft Punk's "Get Lucky") and makes them even more psychotically intent on repeating the same earworm of a hook over and over and over and over and over again. Also, Al's polkas mock unnecessary and gratuitous repetition, the kind that just takes up space rather than adding anything new.

"(This Song's Just) Six Words Long" is not, of course, six words long. The chorus alone is six words, but Harrison's late-period smash repeated its six-word chorus so relentlessly that it began to feel like the song consisted of just a few catchy words repeated to the point of madness.

In deconstructing the song, Al assumes the perspective and persona of a pop singer who forgot to write a proper set of lyrics for the song we're listening to, and decides to wing it for three minutes out of a cynical, correct conviction that a catchy melody will distract listeners from the tune's aching emptiness.

So why does the singer of "(This Song's Just) Six Words Long" feel obligated to sing a song he gleefully admits, even brags, has "got nothing to say"?

"Oh, I make a lotta money/They pay me a ton of money/They're payin' me plenty of money/To sing this song, child" the singer concedes with refreshing candor.

As a twelve-year-old, I loved how often Al's characters sang about money as the great motivator, whether they're Luke Skywalker pondering unemployment if he kills Darth Vader or the singer here bragging that, even though he's not willing to put in the work to write an actual song, he will happily accept the financial rewards.

The purpose of most pop songs is to fly by as breezily as possible. "(This Song's Just) Six Words Long" has a different strategy: it wants listeners to feel the singer's desperation as he attempts to fill three and a half minutes' worth of time with absolutely nothing – with throat clearing and repetition and, for the sake of sonic diversity, a guitar solo. Al's parody seems to last twice as long as the original because it's continually calling attention to its own lyrical threadbareness.

It's a silly song that doubles as a sly deconstruction of pop songwriting, particularly the original song's maddening insistence on "rhyming" a word with itself instead of finding actual rhymes. So while the singer insists "I know if I put my mind to it/I know I could find a good rhyme here" the best he can muster is, "Oh, you gotta have-a music/You need really catchy music."

"(This Song's Just) Six Words Long" is about as meta as Al gets, and he's a pretty meta fella. It's a song about a song that's also a song about songwriting, particularly lazy songwriting. It's not the weightiest song in Al's catalog. In fact, it's aggressively featherweight, a meta-trifle. But in its own irreverent way, it has something to say, unlike the hit it's both spoofing and deconstructing.

4.
YOU MAKE ME

Al is a creature of New Wave, to the extent that when he pays tribute to acts like the B-52s, Talking Heads, Tonio K. or Oingo Boingo he isn't lampooning pop stars so much as he's paying homage to his peers.

Like its snottier, more ragged sibling Punk, New Wave attracted larger-than-life characters whose colorful personas informed the art they created. That was the case with Danny Elfman, who, like Al, was creating crazy miniature movies for the ears long before he became involved in the film business.

As with so much of Elfman's work with Oingo Boingo, "You Make Me" sounds like it was created in a stop-motion animation cartoon factory using some manner of crazy, Dr. Seuss-meets-Rube Goldberg contraption involving an assembly line and a cartoon mallet.

The song is one of Al's exercises in randomness and absurdity. It finds humor in comfortingly familiar places, whether in pop culture detritus (*The Gong Show, The Care Bears Movie* and "phone home"), the interplay of the banal and fantastic (the singer expresses a humdrum desire to "eat pork" immediately after announcing a slightly more exciting intention to "break the laws of time and space") or words and ideas which

Al has always, and will always, find funny either separately, or in tandem, like Slurpees, the Limbo, Styrofoam, the Eiffel Tower, trailer parks, shorts, weasels and bagels.

When he made *Even Worse,* movies loomed large in Al's very near future as both a screenwriter and leading man. Films loomed even larger for Elfman, who was well on his way to becoming better known and more successful as a composer (most famously for his collaborations with Tim Burton) than as a rock star and New Wave theatrical weirdo.

Al would break into the motion picture business with 1989's *UHF.* Al's debut was famously a box office flop at the time of its release, but it's become a huge cult classic in the intervening years. In that respect, it's like another cult classic from much earlier in the decade, 1980's *Forbidden Zone,* which found Danny Elfman breaking into the midnight movie realm in a similarly audacious fashion as both a first-time composer and the actor portraying Satan.

5.
I THINK I'M A CLONE NOW

It's poetically apt that "I Think I'm a Clone Now" is on *Even Worse,* because the album features more musical clones than anything Al had done before or since.

There are the musical clones of Al's parodies, of course, which appropriate the melodies and arrangements and instrumentation of the songs they're spoofing while transforming them lyrically.

Beyond that, *Even Worse* finds Al creating weird musical clones of recent hits that are themselves clones of sorts, in that every hit Al parodies on *Even Worse* (with the exception of Michael Jackson's "Bad") is a cover. Even George Harrison's "Got My Mind Set on You" is actually a cover, and Al's cheeky deconstruction of the song's creative and lyrical limitations is obviously referencing Harrison's version and not Rudy Clark's 1962 original.

Al is not just spoofing songs here. He's spoofing specific performances and recordings of songs that are not the originals. For example, the blandly futuristic, plastic version of "I Think We're Alone Now" that "I Think I'm a Clone Now" is based on musically is the work of big-haired teen dream superstar Tiffany and not that of Tommy James and the Shondells.

With "I Think I'm a Clone Now" there is a pleasing harmony of sound and subject matter in that synth pop (a genre more or less created by Al's collaborator Wendy Carlos), like its New Wave cousin, is science fiction music created with eternally futuristic instruments like synthesizers and drum machines.

If a robot were to become a recording artist and release a song, it'd probably sound a lot like "I Think I'm a Clone Now," all futuristic keyboards and technological gloss and zero rock and roll grit.

Where Tommy James and the Shondells' "I Think We're Alone Now" is suffused with the ache of adolescent longing, and Tiffany's with a synthetic recreation thereof, "I Think I'm a Clone Now" instead offers the science-fiction creation story

of a self-professed "Carbon Copy Man," who owes his curious existence to being "part of some geneticist's plan."

If Tiffany's hit was a mall-brat anthem, Al's parody is a puckish pun parade. Lyrics like "Look at the way/We go out walking close together/I guess you could say/I'm really beside myself" are both genuinely clever and eye-roll-inducing, as is the line "Every pair of genes is a hand-me-down."

"I Think I'm a Clone Now" is the punniest (if not quite funniest) Al parody since "Addicted to Spuds." The vibe is half science fiction novel, half wacky, *Small Wonder*-style '80s sitcom, at once smart, silly, sci-fi and unabashedly nerdy.

Like the protagonist of "I Think I'm a Clone Now," Al is on some level a "Carbon Copy Man," a musical superhero who creates sonic duplicates of popular favorites that he corrupts and transforms.

Yet this Carbon Copy Man is also one of our true originals, both in the sense that no one is better or more successful than Al at what he does and that no one else really does what Al does, either. He's dominated the field of parody to the point where it can feel like he's the only person in it.

6.
LASAGNA

Al's music can act as a time machine, hurtling us back into the past and reconnecting us with the children we used to be. Hearing the opening strains of "Lasagna" instantly takes me back to the mid-1980s, when the popularity of *La Bamba*, Taylor Hackford's eminently respectable biopic of Ritchie Valens, briefly ignited interest in the late singer/Hispanic icon, as well as Los Lobos, the beloved veteran band that scored a hit with a faithful cover of the movie's title song.

La Bamba brought the past colorfully (if unimaginatively) to life. It was a rock and roll biopic, but it was also a period film set in the waning days of the Eisenhower era, when the world was in black and white and conformity was king. "Lasagna" seemingly inhabits the same era, if not earlier, since it finds Al resurrecting his "overly aggressive food pusher" persona from "Eat It." But it gives the pasta pimp singing it an Italian accent that runs the gamut from "impossibly cartoony and broad" to "maybe something the Italian-American Defamation League should look into."

"Lasagna" may be blatantly stereotypical, but it's anything but mean-spirited. The protagonist of "Lasagna" may be the most explicitly, overtly, even cartoonishly Italian in Al's work, but his obsession with food connects with Al's other culinary obsessives.

The problem with food songs is that they tend to be thin on jokes, leaning instead on the inherent funniness of food words. Unlike the food it's paying rapturous ode to, there's only one layer to "Lasagna."

There aren't really any jokes in "Lasagna," but there are plenty of exquisitely sonorous, fun-to-rhyme Italian food words like the titular noodle-based delicacy, but also linguini, minestrone, calzone, marinara, zucchini and ravioli. When Al runs out of food words to rhyme, he starts including Italian words that will be familiar to fans of mob movies, like "capisce" and "paisan."

"Lasagna" represents a triumph of perspiration over inspiration. It's the kind of food-based trifle that only Al has ever really been able to pull off.

Revisiting his roots as a food-obsessed accordion jockey with a palpable affection for comedy and pop culture's past on "Lasagna" couldn't help but illustrate how far Al had come in less than a decade as a recording artist. He could still make the old stuff work, but he'd moved onto meatier, more substantive satirical targets. You know, like television.

7.
MELANIE

A good rule of thumb when dealing with Al's softer, slower, gentler songs is that the prettier the melody, the more demented the lyric. "Melanie" has one of the loveliest melodies in Al's oeuvre wedded, inevitably, to one of his most exquisitely warped narratives. With its lush harmonies and gentle acoustic guitar, it'd be perfect for weddings if the man singing it didn't happen to be completely insane, and on the evil and menacing side to boot.

Of all of Al's creepy Casanovas, the lunatic singing "Melanie" may be the most unhinged of the bunch. Like a disturbing number of mainstream romantic comedies, the man's conception of romance looks suspiciously like stalking and criminal harassment from the outside. He furthermore confuses horrifying expressions of psychosis, such as going through the object of his desire's garbage and having her name tattooed on his forehead as extravagant romantic gestures.

The story "Melanie" tells is elegant in its archetypal simplicity. It's the old boy-buys-telescope, boy-spies-beautiful-stranger-in-nearby-building-while-snooping-on-her-with-aforementioned-telescope, boy-begins-"courting"-girl-with-psychotic-acts-of-obsession and then finally boy-deliberately-plummets-out-window-to-his-death-and-is-possibly-singing-the-entire-song-as-a-ghost story you find in pretty much everything Taylor Swift ballad.

The weirdo singing "Melanie" isn't a complicated romantic hero, or even an antihero so much as he is a flat-out villain, a demented misogynist who interrupts his hilariously misguided declarations of love and devotion to ask his would-be partner if she's "too dumb" to realize that their love would last forever and forever if she'd just stop hating and fearing him long enough to fall in love.

Musically, "Melanie" is completely straight-faced, to the point where Al manages to invest a shocking amount of genuine, sincere romantic longing into the character of a creepy, stalker-y Peeping Tom.

"Melanie" is the perfect combination of naughty and nice, sweet and psychotic. It's pretty enough for a summer picnic and insane enough to be committed into Arkham Asylum. It's a gorgeously crafted song of very "Weird Al" Yankovic contradictions.

The lunatic terrorizing the title character labors under the delusion that he just needs to break through his love interest's hatred and fear of him for them to realize their destiny as soulmates. But in actuality, he's a powerful illustration of why restraining orders are not just useful but essential and also maybe should last beyond death. The singer makes it apparent that he's not about to let anything as minor as his own violent demise keep him from continuing his very one-sided courtship of/ psychological warfare with dear, sweet, poor, poor, appropriately terrified Melanie.

In popular music, love is generally more powerful than death. In the warped anti-romantic ballads of "Weird Al" Yankovic, and in this all-time classic, that happens to be true of romantic psychosis as well.

8.
ALIMONY

Tommy James and the Shondells' classic garage rock smash "Mony Mony" doesn't just rock: in a very real way, it *is* rock. It's an inscrutable garage-rock monster so irresistible and undeniable that it's been covered by everyone from Bruce Springsteen to Alvin & the Chipmunks.

Billy Idol loved the song so much that he released it as a single twice, first in 1981 with a studio version, and then later in 1987 with a raucous, sneering live version. On "Alimony" Al is directly spoofing Idol's live take rather than James' incomprehensible, slurry roar of unadulterated, sub-verbal lust.

In its original incarnation, "Mony Mony," like all good rock songs, is about sex and the disorientation of lust and infatuation. It's saturated with sleazy sexuality. If "Mony Mony" is about the exhilarating frenzy of sexual desire then "Alimony" is about the awful price when love goes bad and lust turns to hate.

The give-and-take, call-and-response between Al and his back-up singers give the song a gospel and blues feel. Al isn't just singing, he's testifying, asking listeners to feel his pain.

"Alimony" alchemizes the pain of divorce into high-spirited comedy. Al has fun twisting and contorting words until they're nearly as difficult to make out as James' original, with Al adding a "y" to words willy-nilly until he's crooning about his ex-wife's lawyers calling him on the "telephone-y" and "trying to draw blood from a stone-y stone-y."

The unlucky-in-love fool "working three jobs just to stay in debt" might be in a state of romantic and financial agony, but Al, his band and particularly his back-up singers sound like they're having a blast.

While many if not most rock stars would be able to relate on a deeply painful level to the subject matter of "Alimony," this is another area where Al broke the mold. In managing his heart and his finances, Al has been uncharacteristically sober and restrained for a rock star. He's only been married once, and he hasn't had to declare bankruptcy after buying a series of castles in Europe even a single time.

So for Al, "Alimony" is a glimpse into a road not traveled, and the kinds of expensive, painful mistakes that rock stars seem uniquely prone to making.

9.
VELVET ELVIS

"Velvet Elvis" finds Al once again deriving inspiration from the Police while making yet another serious-sounding song about something spectacularly silly. In this case, that's the titular item of camp Americana, which fills one of Al's signature easily overjoyed seekers with a sense of spiritual completeness disproportionate to its negligible cultural value.

"My life, it used to be incomplete" the song begins over a gloomy approximation of the Police's self-serious reggae-tinged rock. The obsessive art lover could be speaking for any number of warped antiheroes in Al's music whose life similarly lacked all meaning before they were introduced to the stupid, tacky thing that made their souls sing and their lives full.

As with those perversely satisfied protagonists, total fulfillment comes from an unlikely source here. Or at least it would be unlikely if the characters in Al's songs didn't generally find happiness in ridiculous pop culture ephemera rather than love, or spirituality, or religion.

Who needs meaning when you have an archetypal piece of American kitsch that, as the suspiciously overjoyed singer relates here, depicts an idealized Elvis that, unlike the real thing, will never get older, or fat, or lose his androgynous beauty?

"Velvet Elvis" doesn't follow a familiar blueprint but rather a series of familiar blueprints that add up to something uber-Al. Al has always delighted in trash culture, in camp, in the tackier recesses of American entertainment. While "Velvet Elvis" isn't as inspired an homage to the King as "One More Minute" or as brilliant a riff on Sting as "King of Suede," it's a veritable masterclass in the recurring motifs that make Al such an unexpectedly deep and enduring artist.

I gained a new appreciation for "Velvet Elvis" seeing it performed on the Ridiculously Self-Indulgent, Ill-Advised Vanity Tour. Onstage, Al and the band *became* the Police circa 1985. It was uncanny. The song came alive in concert, with Al acting as a funhouse mirror version of Sting and his band raising a righteous ruckus behind him. For one song, they became the world's greatest Police tribute act, only better, because they were playing a "Police" song written not by Sting but by someone more talented, and with a slightly better sense of humor about himself to boot.

10.
TWISTER

Hip Hop has been good to Al, and Al has been good to Hip Hop. Al hasn't recorded many rap songs but some of his biggest, most career-defining hits have been rap parodies. Al has historically treated Hip Hop the way he treats everything else: with caution, care and meticulousness.

Al's parodies share many commonalities with Hip Hop. Like much Hip Hop, Al's parodies begin with another song. Only instead of taking another song and using it as the musical foundation for a new track for a rapper to rhyme over, Al's band faithfully recreates the sonic elements of the song they're parodying, and Al writes parody lyrics he then sings or raps. Al's pastiches are similarly rooted in other songs and other artists, albeit in a more abstract fashion.

Al would go Hip Hop in a big way, but he began small, with "Twister," a Beastie Boys pastiche that's so slight that it barely qualifies as a song. Like Al's *George of the Jungle* theme song cover, "Twister" barely passes the one-minute mark. It feels almost more like a skit than a proper song, and in form and content, it's a fake commercial for a real product.

Commercialism and consumerism are pervasive themes in Al's work, and on this song he goes from singing about commercialism to rapping an actual faux-commercial.

"Twister" painstakingly recreates the minimalist electronic whine and tag-team nasal vocal harmonizing of *License to Ill*-era Beastie Boys, its snotty, irreverent take on macho aggression. Of course, by the time *Even Worse* was released the Beastie Boys had already begun their evolution from ironic party bros to funky bohemians testing the outer limits of sampling with 1989's *Paul's Boutique*.

There's something unmistakably retro about the Beastie Boys. They didn't just constantly reference the pop culture of the distant past: they had a real Bowery Boys vibe as well. Al imagines the Beasties not just as grown men unusually in touch with their inner children but as raucous pitchmen for a child's board game that provides adults an excuse to brush their bodies together in a half-innocent, half-naughty fashion.

Al's attention to detail is extraordinary. The Beastie Boys were brilliant at making three complementary voices sound like one. On "Twister," Al uses the studio to make his one voice sound like three rappers.

A potent recurring theme in Al's work is that, despite all the posturing about art, in our culture music is a business overwhelmingly devoted to making as much money as possible.

"Twister" is perhaps the purest, most succinct representation of this theme. In Al's warped re-telling, Beastie Boys aren't evangelizing on behalf of your right to party or selling attitude and rebellion: nope, they're straight-up salesmen sacrificing their credibility to school all the home boys and home girls on Milton Bradley's game sensation.

"Twister" began Al's fruitful flirtation with Hip Hop on an almost perversely modest, brief note. But even when he was merely cautiously dipping a toe into uncharted waters, Al knew what he was doing. He treated Hip Hop not as a passing fad (like, say, the eponymous board game of the title) but as an art form that he respected enough to take the time to get right.

11.
GOOD OLD DAYS

During Al's Ridiculously Self-Indulgent, Ill-Advised Vanity Tour, I noticed a fascinating phenomenon. During particularly dark songs, concertgoers would audibly gasp with shock. Bear in mind, these were not casual fans, but die-hards who happily paid money for the least commercial tour of Al's career. They still found themselves surprised and pleasantly horrified by some of the bleak turns in songs like "Good Old Days."

Al's album-closing James Taylor pastiche is a brazen exercise in anti-nostalgia with a perversely bifurcated riff on the good old days. On one level, "Good Old Days" lives up to its title with a Norman Rockwell take on a past full of cornball Americana: mom making apple pie, going fishing with dad, the nice older man who runs the corner store dispensing fatherly advice along with gallons of milk and bottles of Coca-Cola.

But behind the *Happy Days* facade lies unfathomable brutality, a horror movie dystopia where evil young men torture rats with chainsaws, repay the kindness of strangers with vicious beatings and leave their date to the homecoming dance in the desert alone to die a hideous, unnatural death.

Al famously likes to pair his gentlest melodies to his most demented lyrics. So when Al turned his attention to the mellow folk stylings of James Taylor, the result was always going to be brutal.

Pastiches like "Dare to Be Stupid," "Dog Eat Dog" and "Happy Birthday" are valentines to the cult artists they're lovingly paying tribute to, but I'm not sure how flattered James Taylor should be by "Good Old Days." The song doesn't just replace Taylor's earnest 1970s Sensitive Man of Emotions with a possible/probable murderer. It also depicts Taylor's music as cloying and overproduced and his crooning as saccharine and bland.

The mellowness of the singing serves the bloody dark comedy of the lyrics. The song's violently insane narrator rhapsodizes about the local corner store owner's gentle ways and smashing his brains out with the same fondness. For him, these are all good memories because he is a sadist with no respect for human life.

"Good Old Days" is a particularly uncompromising exercise in juxtaposing light and dark, the safely nostalgic and the psychotic, but it has a larger satirical point to make about the myopic dishonesty of nostalgia as well. We fetishize the past as a time of dewy innocence, but it is a world of darkness as well as light.

Donald Trump ran for our highest office on nostalgia for America's distant past, but he's a living reminder that the lily-white American past that Trump romanticizes was full of scummy, racist people like Donald Trump's father, Roy Cohn (Donald Trump's mentor) and Trump himself. That dude is old and has been sleazing around and single-handedly making America worse for decades.

Besides, Ed Gein and Norman Bates are as much staples of our collective past as Pat Boone and Lawrence Welk. Or consider Bill Cosby, who took time out of a decades-long serial rape spree to tell young men to pull their pants up and return to the conventional values of tradition-minded, backwards-looking men of honor like himself.

Yes, the past can be a pretty messed up place, full of awful people like Bill Cosby, Donald Trump and the lunatic singing "Good Old Days," who certainly has an insect body count, and probably a human one as well. "Good Old Days" is the rare fond look back at boyhood shenanigans that could be entered into evidence as a confession in a court of law.

Like poor old Mr. Fender, the corner-store owner, in the moments before his brains are bashed in, we encounter a darker side of a familiar face and voice on "Good Old Days." It's yet another Al song that borders on horrorcore in its morbid lyrical content, albeit with a mellow acoustic vibe.

Even Worse begins with a safe choice for a single in "Fat" but closes with the sort of darkly comic oddball album cut that has endeared Al to generations of malcontents. It's the kind of song that reminds them that he's one of them, and that while he may have a singular gift for making popular, accessible and kid-friendly music, Al has also never shied away from releasing songs that might lightly traumatize children, like "One More Minute," "Nature Trail to Hell" or "Good Old Days."

As the father of two boys, I think that's healthy, even essential. Children need to be entertained, after all, but it never hurts to freak them out a little as well.

PETER & THE WOLF

/CARNIVAL OF THE ANIMALS

PART 2 WITH WENDY CARLOS (1988)

1.

PETER AND THE WOLF

Trans pioneer and electronic music legend Wendy Carlos helped develop, refine and popularize the Moog synthesizer through her 1968 album *Switched on Bach*, a smash hit recording of Bach pieces performed on the then-radical new instrument. It won three Grammys, hit the top ten in the United States and topped the Billboard Classical chart for a period of not weeks, not months – *years*.

Switched on Bach helped make synthesizers and classical music fun and accessible, instead of intimidatingly highbrow. It played a big role in popularizing synths and Bach, making them comfortably mainstream, popular and familiar.

Carlos further cemented her place in the annals of pop culture with her scores for Stanley Kubrick's divisive, alienating masterpieces *A Clockwork Orange* and *The Shining* – wildly over-achieving adaptations of pulpy best-sellers elevated to the level of high art by Kubrick's genius.

Yes, Carlos provided the haunting music for some of the most iconic film scenes of all time, from one of cinema's few true uncontested geniuses and visionaries. In the process, she proved herself worthy of collaborating with a true artist like "Weird Al" Yankovic.

I imagine that Carlos thinks of Al and Stan in similar ways – blurring them together into one complicated, demanding genius. I like to think she honestly can't remember which one directed *Paths of Glory* and which one released "Addicted to Spuds."

The project that brought these two very different legends together across generations and genres was "Peter and the Wolf," composer Sergei Prokofiev's oft-told and performed tale about a heroic young exemplar of the pioneering Soviet spirit (a proud member of the Vladimir Lenin All-Union Pioneer Organization if you want to get technical about it) who proves

his courage and the superiority of the Russian people over the decadent American imperialist dogs by outwitting and capturing a fearsome wolf.

Over the years, this family favorite has been performed by just about everybody, including David Bowie, Lorne Greene, Patrick Stewart, Alice Cooper, Sharon Stone, Melissa Joan Hart, Sting, Jonathan Winters, Paul Hogan, William F. Buckley Jr., baseball player Tom Seaver, Mia Farrow, Sean Connery, Leonard Bernstein, Captain Kangaroo, Boris Karloff, Eleanor Roosevelt and Rob Reiner, among others.

In addition to these recordings of varying degree of faithfulness, Al's hero Allan Sherman recorded a parody entitled *Peter and the Commissar*. There, Prokofiev's timeless story about an intrepid boy who disobeys his cautious grandfather and emerges a hero becomes the springboard for a wickedly satirical celebration of individual initiative over the soul-crushing compromises of committee.

In *Peter and the Commissar*, Sherman satirized the genius and innovation-killing groupthink of the Soviet mindset, and by extension the ills of slavish conformity in the United States as well. *Peter and the Commissar* is bold and unapologetically political, something for sophisticates who found Nichols and May embarrassingly gauche.

Al follows in his hero's footsteps in parodying this timeless favorite instead of playing it straight. But his take on the material eschews the sociopolitical satire of Sherman's decidedly continental spoof in favor of wacky audio slapstick that suggests an audio-only version of an old *Looney Tunes* or *Merrie Melodies* cartoon (think *What's Opera, Doc*). It sounds like something directed by Tex Avery (who famously had a thing for wolves).

Peter & the Wolf represents perhaps the biggest of Al's many one-offs. It's his only album of classical music; it's the only album he recorded and released without the backing of his trusty band; it's the only album he narrates, voicing a variety of human and animal characters and reciting humorous verse rather than singing; and it's his only album-length collaboration with another artist. Unfortunately, it's also the only album of Al's career that is nearly impossible to hear legally, unless you splurge for an expensive, extremely out-of-print copy on cassette, LP or CD. It's never made the jump to digital media and isn't available on Amazon or iTunes or Spotify or anywhere else people listen to music online.

But if *Peter & the Wolf* is a decidedly different project for Al, he nevertheless manages to make this all too familiar material his own, just as thoroughly as Sherman did a quarter century earlier.

Al puts his indelible imprint on Prokofiev's timeless classic in part by pulling back the curtain on himself and Carlos until it no longer exists. Listening to *Peter & the Wolf*, we are at once privy to Al and Wendy's furious exertions through words, but also through sound and music. *Peter & the Wolf* is about the telling of the tale nearly as much as the tale itself; this is even more aggressively meta-textual than Al's usual fare.

Peter & the Wolf was designed to educate children about the different instruments in the orchestra and their unique sound, and entertain by having different instruments represent each of the characters.

Al and Wendy's parody follows suit, but not without some bold changes. Al proudly announces that the part of Peter's grandfather will be played by Don Ameche, only to be gruffly informed that he didn't show up. I hope Ameche at least had the decency to call and say he wouldn't make it.

So, in what can only be seen as a major demotion, the grandfather will be played not by the Oscar-winning star of *Cocoon* and *The Story of Alexander Graham Bell* but rather by a bassoon. It's a worthwhile addition to any orchestra, but it hasn't won a single Academy Award.

Al's narrator, who enunciates everything crisply and clearly and classily in his best inside voice, loses the plot pretty much from the outset. He needs to be reminded that the three French horns play the Wolf (after a fashion), and closes the introduction to "Peter and the Wolf" by saying it takes place "a long time ago, in a galaxy far, far away," with Wendy faithfully reproducing John Williams' fanfare for *Star Wars*.

That's true of another story that figures prominently in Al's music and mythology. But certainly not the one Al happens to be telling here, which takes place not long ago in a galaxy far away but rather last Thursday, probably.

"Peter and the Wolf" is a very Russian, very Soviet saga, albeit one that has been successfully adapted all over the world. But Al and Wendy have thoroughly Americanized the proceedings.

In Al and Wendy's newfangled telling, the Wolf talks in the tough guy rasp of Clint Eastwood's Dirty Harry, right down to borrowing his catchphrases. Peter's cranky grandfather, meanwhile, sounds like an old Italian gentleman – think Don Vito Corleone – being softly but continuously strangled.

Peter has a nasal Eddie Deezen inflection to his voice; instead of a strapping illustration of fine Soviet character, he's a typical American creep, easily impressed by something as mundane as a talking bird. Bruce the Duck, meanwhile, is a cross between Daffy at his most frenetic and Al's friend Gilbert Gottfried.

Al and Wendy's "Peter and the Wolf" also educates by teaching kids the sounds of the symphony, or in this case, the synthesized orchestra. This time around the instruments include the accordion – the signature sound of Bob the Janitor. It's a wonderfully pointless addition to the shenanigans that serves little purpose other than to further establish the squeezebox as an intentionally democratic, populist instrument, the natural enemy of pretension and self-seriousness.

Like Prokofiev's original, Al and Wendy's "Peter and the Wolf" follows Peter, a headstrong young boy who disobeys his grumbling grandfather's instruction not to venture out into the dangerous, wolf-infested woods in search of adventure.

In keeping with Al's favored preoccupations of the time, we learn that "boys like Peter are afraid of a lot of things – like nuclear annihilation and flunking algebra – but they're not afraid of wolves."

He should be, though, as there is, in fact, a "big, mean, hairy, ferocious, snarling, carnivorous wolf." This is to be expected, of course, if not angrily demanded, in a story entitled "Peter and the Wolf," Al is quick to assure us.

The beast succeeds in swallowing poor Bruce the Duck in a single chomp, traumatizing our narrator with his horrifically violent demise, causing Wendy to reverently quote Bernard Herrmann's iconic strings from *Psycho*.

In this contemporary take, Peter is videotaping the carnage when he gets an idea prominently involving a dental floss lasso and a nearby tree.

Peter captures Seymour the Wolf in this homemade wolf trap. In the original version, a group of hunters descend upon the Wolf. This takes place in God's own America, however, so the trigger-happy American idiots and proud NRA members who find Seymour and Peter instead emerge out of the woods firing their "Magnums, Uzis and bazookas."

Al pronounces the words as classily as possible, but there's no way to say "bazooka" that doesn't sound ridiculous. This is no mere action story on wax; it's more like a bloody, macho Jerry Bruckheimer action extravaganza full of machine gun fire, rocket launchers and wanton mass destruction.

Peter has the bright idea of taking Seymour the Wolf to the zoo. The NRA gun nuts think that's a swell idea and propose that if he likes it, then they can take him to Disneyland the next week!

Wendy doesn't augment that groaner with a rim shot, synthesized or otherwise, but she very well could have. It certainly wouldn't seem out of place, and heaven knows Al and Wendy aren't above using wacky sound effects, including the dreaded skipped record.

Over the course of a little over twenty-seven minutes, "Peter and the Wolf" cycles through myriad styles of humor – including dark Gothic comedy.

The traditional version of "Peter and the Wolf" ends with a bleak mental image: "If you listen very carefully, you'll hear the Duck quacking inside the Wolf's belly, because the Wolf in his hurry had swallowed her alive."

That's as morbid as something you'd find in a horror movie, or an early "Weird Al" Yankovic album cut. But Al tops it when he lets the kiddies know, "And what about Bruce the Duck? Well, the Wolf had been in such a hurry that he swallowed him... alive, which means the gastric juices slowly dissolved his body and he died a long, painful death."

Al doesn't need to inject morbidity into this story. It's already there. He just needs to gently tease it out in order to close out this nice story for children by asking us to ponder, but not for too long, the unfathomable agony of Bruce the Duck.

"Peter and the Wolf" ends with a glorious non-sequitur: the message that "oral hygiene is very important" and that "you should see your dentist at least twice a year."

Peter was undoubtedly the hero of the original version of "Peter and the Wolf." But in Al's fractured fable, the true hero is dental floss. Peter just happens to be wielding this literal life saver at the right time and place to save the day.

Hooray for dental floss!

With "Peter and the Wolf," Al, with the help of a uniquely gifted new collaborator, turned his satirical gaze from pop to the high-falutin' world of classical music, with delightful results.

In Wendy Carlos, Al had a collaborator uniquely qualified to blur the lines separating high and low culture, art from trash. In their irreverent take on "Peter and the Wolf" these iconoclasts crashed the highbrow halls of classical music in search of laughs, armed with a story sturdy enough to support countless straight versions and parodies of both the politically pointed and proudly silly variety.

2.
CARNIVAL OF THE ANIMALS – PART TWO

In the history of great American wits, few wits were as legendarily witty as the great Ogden Nash, composer of light verse and sayer of famously and fabulously clever, eminently quotable aphorisms.

All the clever things Mark Twain, Dorothy Parker, William Shakespeare and Oscar Wilde did not say were wryly uttered by Nash, or at least the historical record would lead you to believe as much.

So, Al had his work cut out following this giant of American literature in humorously chronicling the peculiarities of the animal kingdom in punchy little poems in a newfangled riff on French composer Camille Saint-Saëns' "The Carnival of the Animals."

"The Carnival of the Animals" was released in 1886, but Nash didn't add words to Saint-Saëns' suite until over a half century later, for a 1950 recording from André Kostelanetz and His Orchestra, featuring narration from no less a legendary *bon vivant* than Noel Coward.

Nash's erudite contributions were so delightful that they were integrated into many subsequent performances of "The Carnival of the Animals." But Al and Wendy weren't intimidated – rather, they were intrigued by the prospect of pitting their romp through the kooky world of critters against the masterwork of Nash and Saint-Saëns.

In the introduction, Al posits "The Carnival of the Animals – Part Two" as an extension, continuation and corrective of Saint-Saëns' most popular work. He quips in rhyming verse: "Camille, in his research, was slightly behind/And I guess some critters just plain slipped his mind/So to fill in the void in the animal kingdom/I'll read some new verses, I'm not gonna sing them."

He ends his introduction on the perfect note of polite belligerence when he implores, "So kindly shut up and I'll narrate for you/Carnival of the Animals – Part Two," a self-described "new composition which features a random assortment of all living creatures."

"The Carnival of the Animals – Part Two" separates music from words; each entry begins with Al drolly delivering humorous verse about animals unaccompanied by music, before Wendy contributes her sonic interpretation of animals that run the gamut from amoebas to vultures to sharks to unicorns. This offers unique challenges. What *does* an amoeba sound like?

As with "Peter and the Wolf," there is wit on the musical and lyrical sides of the equation. "Snail," for example, waggishly references the finale of the "William Tell Overture," albeit at an appropriately glacial speed, executing this rollicking anthem of relentless forward momentum at (literally and figuratively) a snail's pace.

Unsurprisingly, vultures remind Al of the ghoulish avarice of a much uglier and more predatory animal, the lawyer. Al cheekily references the reigning yuppie iconography of Reagan's '80s when he reflects that, despite their predilection for treating human beings as meals instead of friends, at least alligators would never be tacky enough to wear tee shirts with yuppies on the pocket.

Saint-Saëns and Nash left much of the animal kingdom un-goofed upon, so Al is free to pay rhyming tribute to pigeons, the subject and muse of his hero Tom Lehrer's *Dr. Demento Show* favorite "Poisoning Pigeons in the Park." Lehrer's song is a bravely bleak ditty whose eviscerating darkness Al's more kid-friendly version can't hope to approach, let alone match.

"Cockroach" is a ghoulishly dark exercise in animal snuff that anticipates the similarly crunchy and sadistic horrors of "Weasel Stomping Day," while "Amoeba" derives big inspiration from the tiniest of organisms.

"The Carnival of the Animals – Part Two" peaks at the end with a fantastical, aggressively non-factual celebration of the poodle worthy of Shel Silverstein. Al posits this daintiest of pooches as a "slimy, carnivorous beast" whose "fangs measure 23 inches, at least," with "antlers that are simply amazing."

Our deeply misinformed narrator states this miraculous creature is "our main source of pork, ham and bacon" before conceding, correctly as it turns out, "Then again, on the other hand, I could be completely mistaken."

"The Carnival of the Animals – Part Two" features Al puckishly reciting rhyming verse before Wendy's synthesized interpretation of critters big and small, as well as a good bit of rhyming(ish) verse.

Like Nash before him, Al loves to rhyme. But he also likes to twist and contort words so that they *almost* rhyme.

In a meta moment redolent of "Peter and the Wolf," Al acknowledges that his rhymes seem to be getting sloppier and less "rhyme-y" as the piece progresses. He finally begs off, conceding "It's getting late, so I suppose/We should be drawing to a close/Besides, my voice is sounding hoarse/And even my rhymes are getting *woarse*."

"The Carnival of Animals – Part Two" is deliberately modest. Just as Al's spin on "Peter and the Wolf" doesn't aspire to the grown-up sophistication of *Peter and the Commissar*, Al and Wendy don't try to be as riotously clever as Nash's furiously word-happy trip through a literal and linguistic zoo.

Peter & the Wolf/Carnival of the Animals - Part II was nominated for a Grammy for Best Children's recording, a field where Al competed against Meryl Streep *twice*, for two different Beatrix Potter audio adaptations, as well as Glenn Close and the freaking *Bible* (author: God) but lost to Robin Williams and Ry Cooder's *Pecos Bill*. That, friends, is a tough category. If I were Al, I wouldn't take it too hard that I didn't win. Besides, he has his five Grammys to console him.

The legitimate, honest to God unavailability of *Peter & the Wolf/Carnival of the Animals - Part II* in a culture where seemingly everything is readily available lends it a certain mystique. If *Medium Rarities* is something of a rarity, since you can't purchase it separately from the box set, *Peter & the Wolf/Carnival of the Animals - Part II* is an extreme rarity.

That's a shame, because it's a wonderful way to introduce potentially skeptical, if not downright hostile "Weird Al" Yankovic fans to classical music.

Al would follow up this elaborate exercise in musical storytelling with *UHF*, a motion picture prominently involving a considerably more memorable, even iconic janitor.

Al had been building up to *UHF* his entire career. *Peter & the Wolf/Carnival of the Animals - Part II* was an essential step in that journey to cinematic cult immortality, a project cinematic in scope, simultaneously futuristic, retro, digital and symphonic in sound. More than that, it's a fascinating, once-in-a-lifetime collaboration between two geniuses who have left very different, but very important imprints on American pop music and pop culture.

UHF: MOTION PICTURE PICTURE SOUNDTRACK AND OTHER STUFF (1989)

1.
MONEY FOR NOTHING/ BEVERLY HILLBILLIES

In the three decades since its release, Al's 1989 debut vehicle *UHF* has made a remarkable (if unsurprising) transformation from high-profile flop to beloved cult treasure. It's gone from being one of Al's biggest failures to one of his most beloved successes.

But the film's soundtrack has not been quite so lucky. Like *Polka Party!*, Al's biggest failure up to this point, it's an album that attracts defenders more than passionate advocates. It peaked at 146 on the Billboard charts despite being connected to the release of a major motion picture, and remains one of the few Al albums from this era never to go Gold.

Listening to the album today, it's easy to see why. When Al was working on the *UHF* soundtrack he was also working on a movie he not only starred in but co-wrote. And he was still in his twenties. That's an extraordinary amount of work and pressure to throw on anyone that young, even a multi-hyphenate as self-disciplined and scarily efficient as Al.

Something had to give, and the *UHF* soundtrack feels less like an organic companion to Al's big movie break than a collection of tracks Al and his band put together before time ran out.

With "Money for Nothing/Beverly Hillbillies," Al pulled a real switcheroo. He took a song about television and unearned extreme economic upward mobility, took it apart and then put it back together again to create a song about a different kind of television and a markedly different form of unearned extreme economic upward mobility. In this case, Al refers to a country-fried slab of undeservedly beloved hot garbage called *The Beverly Hillbillies*. Of *UHF*'s first four tracks, half are parodies about terrible sitcoms from the '60s.

"Money for Nothing" finds rock stars Mark Knopfler and Sting singing from the perspective of working-class galoots grumbling about how rich rock stars like Mark Knopfler and Sting get their "money for nothing" and their "chicks for free" just for "playing the guitar on the MTV."

It's an enviable racket from the outside, but looks different from the inside, as evidenced by the many songs where rock stars hip an oblivious, jealous public to the surprising truth that, *actually*, rich pop stars have it worse than anyone (on account of the demands of the road and the women, the pills, and the booze) and should be pitied, not envied.

Al's lyrics borrow much of the structure, themes and actual words of the *Beverly Hillbillies* theme song. It's as if Al sat down with the lyrics for both songs and, by cutting and pasting, created something new almost completely out of the raw material that is "Money for Nothing" and the *Beverly Hillbillies* theme song.

The *UHF* soundtrack would close majestically with the all-time classic "The Biggest Ball of Twine in Minnesota." But it seems appropriate, if not inevitable, that Al's big-screen tribute to the small screen would begin with one of Al's patented tongue-in-cheek celebrations of TV dreck, set to a song famous largely for having an innovative video.

Al's career rebounded after *UHF*. Al ended up living the plots of *Beverly Hillbillies* and "Money for Nothing."

This man of modest means, this Lynwood hillbilly, ended up living the good life in the land of movie stars and swimming pools, Beverly Hills, for playing the accordion on the MTV. That's a nice racket, to be sure. But even his harshest critics would have to concede that Al has worked extraordinarily hard to achieve his extraordinary success.

2.
GANDHI II

The first sketch on the *UHF* soundtrack is a television/radio commercial for a *Gandhi* sequel that trades in the original's prestige-film stateliness for a blaxploitation vibe.

Set to wah-wah guitar and disco strings which conjure up a gritty explosion of pimps, players and private eyes, this mock trailer showcases a Gandhi who has traded in passive resistance for punching fools with his furious fists.

The revisionist Gandhi of *Gandhi II* is a sex machine to all the chicks and a man of action. While most of what I know about history and science comes from Al's music, the portrait of Gandhi that emerges here feels historically incorrect. Gandhi was famously a vegetarian, for example, like Al, but the somewhat off-brand Indian icon of peace here orders a "steak, medium rare."

I derive an additional level of amusement from this skit because Gandhi is played by Al's manager, Jay Levey, who I had the honor of working with on *Weird Al: The Book*. Levey's path to managing Al began when he found a Timothy Leary paperback as a young spiritual seeker and sought out a relationship with the man behind the book and its psychedelic, countercultural magic, who somewhat inconveniently happened to be imprisoned at the time.

The two men developed a relationship that led to Levey managing him, and work with that demented doc led to an even more fruitful partnership with the ultimate demented doctor, Dr. Demento. This led to Al, which led to me meeting Jay about seven or eight years ago in New York. We went to the Sony building and raided their archives looking for Al stuff for the book. It was one of many memorable days working on *Weird Al: The Book*, days when I felt like I was communing with the sum of musical history.

I felt humbled and honored to be in a place like that, just as I felt humbled and honored to be in Jon "Bermuda" Schwartz's garage of wonder (where you can feel the history down deep in your bones) while researching *Weird Al: The Book*.

Even today, I have difficulty believing that there's a book credited to Nathan Rabin & Al Yankovic.

"Gandhi II" had effects beyond making me nostalgic for a weird time in my life. Just as Al previously invented horrorcore, postmodernism, MTV, the internet, Nerdcore and mashups, I'm going to lazily assume he also invented the idea of including snippets of dialogue on a soundtrack, and that Quentin Tarantino stole that idea for *Pulp Fiction*.

I'm similarly going to pretend that Al invented the idea of punctuating a skit with the sound of explosive gunfire. Given Al's popularity in gangsta rap circles, it's not surprising that, in the aftermath of the *UHF* soundtrack, suddenly every gangsta rap album featured the roar of fake gunplay and rappers pretending to be tough, violent, over-sexed, gun-toting alpha males like the tough guy protagonist of *Gandhi II*.

Everything comes back to Al. *Everything.*

3.
ATTACK OF THE RADIOACTIVE HAMSTERS FROM A PLANET NEAR MARS

Like "Nature Trail to Hell" and "Slime Creatures from Outer Space," the previous two entries in what I like to call "Creepy Al' Yankovic's Trilogy of Sonic Terror," "Attack of the Radioactive Hamsters from a Planet Near Mars" is enormous fun, a kitschy, goofy, over-the-top romp full of haunted house atmosphere. It's about seemingly adorable but ultimately

malevolent creatures who show up on the narrator's doorstep and, after getting too close to a microwave oven, grew to "forty thousand times their original size."

That proves a game changer not just for the singer, but humanity. The mutated hamsters descend upon the earth in cigar-shaped UFOs and, as he notes unhappily, "Now the whole wide world is their exercise wheel."

As with previous entries in "Creepy Al" Yankovic's Super Creepy Thriller Chiller Horror Theater, this gleans humor from the incongruous juxtaposition of the fantastical and the mundane. While the narrator desperately hopes that the authorities can do something about this rodent menace, he seems as concerned about property values as he does about the looming hamster-driven apocalypse.

If "Slime Creatures from Outer Space" is like *Mars Attack* in song form, then "Attack of the Radioactive Hamsters from a Planet Near Mars" is more like the creature features that flourished in the aftermath of *Gremlins*. As with *Gremlins*, the song begins with something almost oppressively cute and follows them as they go from furry and lovable to a threat to our very survival.

These radioactive hamsters from a planet near Mars aren't just disconcertingly, dangerously large: they're straight-up bastards. According to the appropriately concerned singer, they're "evil and nasty and they glow in the dark," but he grudgingly concedes that they're nevertheless "really kind of cute." The same can be said of "Attack of the Radioactive Hamsters from a Planet Near Mars." If you can ignore a body count probably in the hundreds of millions, it's pretty gosh darn adorable.

4.
ISLE THING

On "Isle Thing," we have another case of Al employing not just a template that had proven successful before (the TV song) but a series of tropes that had proven fruitful. We begin with the Al staple of the song that describes the premise of a beloved pop culture touchstone, while cheekily poking fun of it at the same time. The trash landmark in question is *Gilligan's Island* – a show *Brady Bunch* creator Sherwood Schwartz seemingly created to test the stupidity and gullibility of the American people.

"Isle Thing" also belongs to a subset of Al songs about easily impressed weirdoes whose lives are magically transformed by the ridiculous. In this case the singer, one of Al's creepy Casanovas, tries to get a little something going with a sexy young thing, only to discover that all she's interested in is watching reruns of *Gilligan's Island.*

The singer is skeptical and pokes several holes in the show's premise, but it's not long before this man is as addicted to *Gilligan's Island* and its chintzy collection of broad archetypes as the object of his desire.

"Isle Thing" is the closest Al comes to doing stand-up in a parody. Some of the singer's observations about *Gilligan's Island* wouldn't feel out of place coming from a stand-up comic's set in the 1980s at the Chuckle Monastery.

Comedians have long cracked jokes about the apparent contradiction of the Professor being a scientific genius who somehow can't build a primitive raft that might allow the castaways to finally escape their laugh-track-addled island purgatory. Al might as well begin his verses, "What is the deal with *Gilligan's Island*?" – like the one about the castaways being suspiciously over-prepared for what was supposed to be a three-hour tour.

Al is a comic genius, but his work isn't entirely devoid of open mic night-level riffs. But the grand gestalt of "Isle Thing" – the care Al brings to rapping like a human slab of concrete, the minimalist perfection of The Dust Brothers' production on the original song and the overall air of goofy amiability – helps make up for the dodgy jokes and reheated subject matter.

5.
HOT ROCKS POLKA

"Weird Al" Yankovic nails some of his subjects so right that their respective legacies are forever intertwined. But, as "Toothless People" can attest, Al never quite cracked Mick Jagger or the Rolling Stones.

He's had more success on polka medleys, where the stakes are lower. Al has included the compositions of Jagger and Richards in polka medleys before, but on *UHF*'s "Hot Rocks Polka" he devotes an entire polka medley to a single artist for the first time in his career.

This single-artist twist brings the series back to its initial inspiration, the soul-sucking but lucrative "Stars on 45" series of hit medleys for the undiscriminating. "Stars on 45" frequently devoted discs to a single artist, so if you *really* wanted to hear a bunch of Beatles songs on one 45 and it didn't matter how bland the versions might be, they had you covered, no pun intended.

"Hot Rocks Polka" is named after one of several million Rolling Stones greatest hits compilations, so it's essentially "Rolling Stones on 45" with the sleazy, salacious swagger of snake-hipped Mick Jagger replaced by the mindless cheerfulness of Alpine Al.

Costumes are important to Al's aesthetic: his concerts give his wardrobe as much of a workout as his body and vocal cords, but he frequently tries on musical costumes as well. Al doesn't just study the artists he honors with parodies and pastiches: he gets inside their minds and skins to parody them from the inside out.

The humor in "Hot Rocks Polka" consequently comes from the comic incongruity of the musical costume Al and his band have chosen. Mick Jagger exudes raw, overpowering sexuality. So does Al, in private. But Al's public persona is white and nerdy and aggressively non-sexual. There's a transgressive thrill in hearing "Wholesome Al" Yankovic once again sing lyrics that would be unimaginable in his own work.

This is most glaring during the medley's snippet of "Brown Sugar," a song that is either about heroin addiction, the sexuality of black slave women or the deliciousness of Pepsi.

"Hot Rocks Polka" is a tribute to the impeccable song craft and irresistible melodies of Jagger and Richards. But it also highlights how their big, sing-along choruses are a whole lot more memorable and iconic than the verses.

The novelty of "Hot Rocks Polka" comes from the contrast between the goofy geek and the legendary stud whose words he's giving manic, impish life. But really, "Hot Rocks Polka" is one great pop artist/songwriter's tribute to a legendary duo with a formidable legacy – one that, in some ways, is nearly as impressive as Al's.

6.
UHF

When I think about my childhood, I mostly remember television and trauma. And Al, of course. As a twelve-year-old, my life revolved around a ten-inch black-and-white television set with rabbit ears that didn't get any of the networks, just UHF.

That fit me just fine. The networks were the mainstream. They were the nightly news with Dan Rather. They were *Cheers* and the Academy Awards and the Super Bowl.

UHF represented the fringes. It was overwhelmingly reruns, but it was also a Wild West where you could do whatever you wanted because nobody was paying attention.

"UHF" is simultaneously selling both an actual movie that listeners can pay real money to see, as well as the viewing experience of the nuttiest TV station since those kooks in *Network* got mad as hell and stopped taking it.

On a literal level, "UHF" is a rowdy call to check out the oddballs at an outlaw TV station. But on a more conceptual, Devo level, it's an absurdist spiel to drop contemporary life – jobs, family, leaving your home, school, laundry, dishes – and give yourself over to the all-powerful glowing screen, the glass teat, the televisual Mommy.

"UHF" opens by brashly admonishing listeners/viewers/ television consumers to "put down your remote control" on account of this miracle channel making all other channels unnecessary, and by extension, remote controls pointless.

Al keeps raising the stakes until he's encouraging listeners to not only forsake every other channel, but all other physical activity so that they can focus on the only thing that matters in life: television.

The singer doesn't just want the listener/viewer to abandon shows on other channels: he wants them to abandon their own free will. Why bother thinking for yourself when it's television's job to keep the masses hypnotized into a state of total dependence?

"UHF" is quietly dystopian. When Al howls "we're gonna make a couch potato out of you!" he brings an awful lot of conviction to those words. The song essentially asks (well, demands) that the viewer/listener remove their higher faculties from the rest of their nervous system before they sit down to watch television, so that they can enjoy it better.

"UHF" is hard-driving and full of swagger. Musically and lyrically, it's surprisingly straight-forward for a "Weird Al" Yankovic single, but not for the theme song to what studios and Al hoped would be a hit.

"UHF" had more riding on it than Al's other first singles. It needed to sell *UHF* to audiences that might be skeptical of Al as a movie star. *UHF* was not a box-office success at the time of its release but people keep discovering *UHF* and falling in love with *UHF* and quoting *UHF*, so its theme song succeeded after all. It just took a couple of decades.

7.
LET ME BE YOUR HOG

"Let Me Be Your Hog" runs a mere seventeen seconds and consists of Al howling the title twice and the word "baby" countless times over a greasy, sleazy, lascivious proto-punk blues riff before a skipped-record-needle sound effect ends the track.

The track owes its curious existence to Al being unable to license Carl Douglas' "Kung Fu Fighting" for a scene in *UHF.* So, Al recorded some new music to take its place. It may not be as catchy, but it's certainly less racially problematic.

More than other legendary rock stars, Al's career has been filled with tricky variables, most notably in terms of needing permission to parody songs.

I can only imagine how strange it must be for Al to have to spend so much of his career asking pop stars (who are flaky by nature and probably also on the drugs) for permission to parody their music so that he can go forward with his albums.

How weird must it be to have "Get permission from Iggy Azalea" on your to-do list as a multi-Grammy-winning musical legend?

Having to ask permission for parodies and movie clearance must be a headache. I don't blame Al for creating something nasty and silly and raunchy-sounding like "Let Me Be Your Hog" himself as a low-budget fix.

Seventeen seconds doesn't allow for much in the way of jokes. That's okay; that "Let Me Be Your Hog" not only exists, but is an official cut on a "Weird Al" Yankovic album, and also something Al sometimes even plays in concert, is itself an inspired joke.

8.
SHE DRIVES LIKE CRAZY

There are some things "Weird Al" Yankovic does better than anyone else. No one, for example, is better at making parodies of hit pop songs and pastiches of prominent artists.

There are, alas, some feats not even Al can accomplish. "She Drives Like Crazy" illustrates, unfortunately, that while Al possesses an extraordinary skill set, singing confidently in an otherworldly, Roland Gift-like falsetto is not part of it.

That wouldn't be a problem, except that Al's dedication to recreating the songs he's parodying as exactly as possible means that parodying Fine Young Cannibals requires recreating Gift's falsetto. That's a very tall order, because if you don't have a natural falsetto, singing in that high a register can be incredibly challenging, if not impossible.

UHF may be Al's weakest album to date, but it's also the one that gave Al's vocal cords the biggest workout. He spends many of the parodies here in a gruff, low register as he channels the Dylan-esque rasp of Mark Knopfler on "Money for Nothing/Beverly Hillbillies" and Tone Loc's gravelly delivery on "Isle Thing," but he travels in the opposite direction here.

On "Isle Thing," Al sounds like a sentient cigarette. On "She Drives Like Crazy" he sounds more like a balloon that keeps floating out of view, or a man unsteadily trying to navigate a tricky vocal tightrope.

"She Drives Like Crazy" is a car song about a man in a constant state of fear and panic over a woman's terrible driving. Many of the lyrics are directly addressed to the offending driver, like the opening gambit, "Where'd you learn how to steer?"

The more confident in a song's central conceit Al is, the less he needs to rely upon sound effects. So, it's not encouraging that "She Drives Like Crazy" features extensive automotive sound effects. It's even less encouraging that the screaming and crashing found throughout the track are the most inspired elements of the song.

What's most fascinating to me about "She Drives Like Crazy" is how far outside of Al's comfort zone it finds him. Al took a big chance parodying a song performed in such a tricky falsetto; while it didn't necessarily pay off, the ambition required to even attempt this kind of vocal is admirable, even if he ends up overreaching.

9.
GENERIC BLUES

"Generic Blues" is a transcendent example of the Comically Incongruous White Folks Blues song, a micro-genre he previously explored on "Buckingham Blues."

It begins with its exceedingly white, yet refreshingly reasonable singer moaning only the first in a series of blues clichés he then immediately subverts. The bluesman begins with an opening so familiar that it could be deemed downright generic: "I woke up this morning…"

Al is all about cleverly upending expectations, so he immediately negates what little action has happened in the song by specifying that after waking up in the morning, he went right back to bed.

The singer does eventually emerge from his bed, however, and the lyrics that follow suggest that's a huge mistake.

Other verses begin in a soothingly traditional way – like when the bluesman moans melodramatically, "Well, I ain't got no money, I'm just walking down the road." But the cause for his unfortunate situation is hilariously banal: the poor man done went and forgot the pin-number for his ATM card.

Al exaggerates the blues' emphasis on human misery to delicious comic effect. The bluesman complains, "I was born in a paper sack in the bottom of a sewer/I had to eat dirt clods for breakfast, my family was so poor" before segueing into further absurdist silliness when he continues, "My daddy was a waitress, my mama sold bathroom tile/My brothers and sisters all hated me 'cause I was an only child."

Al throws himself into the soul-consuming self-laceration of "Generic Blues" lines like, "I'm just a no-good, scum-sucking, nose-picking, boot-licking, sniveling, groveling, worthless hunk of slime/Nothing but a low-down, beer-bellied, bone-headed, pigeon-toed, turkey-necked, weasel-faced, worthless hunk of slime." Which makes the incongruously reasonable conclusion he comes to ("Guess I've got a pretty low self-image/Maybe it's a chemical imbalance or something/I should probably go and see a doctor about it when I've got the time") even funnier.

Much of the humor comes from Al's delivery, particularly the whiplash shifts between the despair of the bluesy set-ups and the purposefully deflating common sense of the punchlines.

This is particularly true of the song's central dilemma: the singer is so down on himself that he only sees two paths before him.

He could give into the suicidal despair that is every blues singer's inalienable birthright and end his miserable existence by blowing his brains out. Alternately, he could go bowling instead.

"Generic Blues" follows an intentionally familiar, well-worn template in taking the piss out of blues clichés and the mundane banality of being Caucasian. But it does so with wit, cleverness and full-bodied musical/lyrical conviction. Al doesn't exactly reinvent the Comically Incongruous White Folks Blues here, but he gets the most out of a very limited formula.

Besides, "Generic Blues" is one of B.B. King's top ten favorite blues songs, and that man knows more about the essence of the Blues than even Al's weirdly distinctive generic bluesman.

10.
SPATULA CITY

The curious cult of "Spatula City" embodies Malcolm Gladwell's concept of *stickiness*. *Stickiness* refers to something's seemingly ineffable ability to endure, to last, to stick around in the minds and hearts of the public.

The concept of *stickiness* itself possesses the quality of stickiness.

The idea of Spatula City, a somewhat misguided commercial enterprise that's able to cut out the middleman by dealing only in spatulas, didn't take hold in the psyches of "Weird Al" Yankovic fans despite being such a silly, goofball, ephemeral joke. No, it lodged itself deep in the minds of Al super-fans specifically *because* it's such a silly, goofball, ephemeral joke. Sometimes those are the best ones.

"Spatula City" is only the second skit in Al's oeuvre, but if the form was novel, the content and subject are quintessentially Al. The ineffable Al-ness of the song begins with a title that luxuriates in Al's deep-seated love of words and wordplay. In this case, that word is, of course, "spatula," an intriguingly Italian-sounding name for an appealingly random item.

Spatulas are useful, of course, but in a limited way. They're consummate supporting players of the kitchen universe but in "Spatula City", Al and his collaborators elevate the lowly spatula to a starring role in both a commercial and a very confused business.

"Spatula City" is wonderfully deadpan. It's narrated with a whiz-bam, "Get a load of this miracle product!" over-enthusiasm worthy of Al's previous muse Mr. Popeil. A confidently strolling baseline and jazzy drums (heavy on the hi-hat!) form a groovy musical bed for an absurdist spiel for a uniquely useless business that takes specialization to extremes.

In just over sixty-five seconds, the faux-commercial makes several dubious appeals for the titular business, depicting a "present" no one could possibly want as perfect both for Christmas and as an expression of love.

Late in the skit, "Sy Greenblum" comes on and drones, "Hello, this is Sy Greenblum, President of Spatula City. I liked their spatulas so much… I bought the company." Greenblum is a parody of two famous figures from the world of television advertising: one is Victor Kiam, the Remington spokesman/owner/user who famously bragged that he liked the company's razors so much he "bought the company." But he also spoofs Sy Sperling, who rose to camp fame for wonderfully stilted commercials where he humblebragged that he wasn't just the President of Hair Club for Men, but also a client.

In another context, "Spatula City" would be just another random bit of silliness from a movie and a soundtrack with more than its share. Here, it's a refreshing reminder that Al isn't just funny and smart and semi-secretly satirical: he's also weird in a wonderful way.

11.
FUN ZONE

The full title of the soundtrack to *UHF* slyly subverts the stilted formality of "Original Motion Picture Soundtrack" by following it with the decidedly casual "and Other Stuff." But if the subtitle is a self-deprecating joke from a self-deprecating joker, it's also accurate. More than any of Al's previous studio albums, even his debut, *UHF* feels more like a collection of songs than an organic album.

There's an unmistakably random element to the soundtrack that's particularly pronounced on "Fun Zone." The track was recorded as the theme song for Stanley Spadowsky, the janitor-turned-kiddie-show-host that Michael Richards plays in the film. But the song began life as an unused demo for the theme to *Welcome to the Fun Zone*, an NBC sketch comedy pilot from 1984 that Al's manager Jay Levey co-produced and which featured, as special guests, Al and Dr. Demento, along with a pre-*Saturday Night Live* Victoria Jackson.

Al would seem to be a natural choice to compose and perform the theme song for a comedy show in the mid-1980s. But at the time he recorded the *Welcome to the Fun Zone* theme, he was known primarily for funny parodies of ubiquitous pop songs.

There's something willfully perverse about hiring a man famous for writing and singing funny lyrics to compose a tune with no lyrics and no real singing, just enthusiastic cries of "Hey, hey, hey!" as the song cruises to a close. Al's movie soundtrack is monomaniacally obsessed with television, even in the songs that aren't overtly about the boob tube.

"Fun Zone" is a discarded theme song to a television show that never really happened – one that was cursed to live and die as a one-off. But it's the theme song to a beloved fictional television show as well: Stanley Spadowsky's demented kiddie carnival of fun and trauma.

An upbeat, hard-driving instrumental powered by synthesizers, horns and insistent drums, "Fun Zone" has a kinetic, propulsive quality. It's a musical roller coaster that is continually shifting and contorting, a propulsive music joyride that takes listeners on a journey in just under two minutes.

In an alternate universe, Al's peppy mid-1980s instrumental would have accompanied the opening credits for the show that replaced *Saturday Night Live*. In this world, it was destined for an even more auspicious destiny: it has opened live "Weird Al" Yankovic shows for decades.

I will consequently always associate "Fun Zone" with joy, with laughter, with travel, with the exhilaration and transcendence of live music and the profound spiritual connection between artist and fan. Because of the shows I've been to and the things I've seen, this goofy instrumental will always mean something special to me.

For Al fans at his concerts, there's nothing ironic about the title of "Fun Zone." If anything, it's under-selling the enjoyment of watching Al and his band work their magic in front of ecstatic, invariably satisfied crowds.

12.
SPAM

Al isn't just a diligent student of comedy: he embodies an entire century of comedy, stretching from vaudeville to podcasts, from the cornball Kosher comedy of the Catskills to the anti-comedy of Tim & Eric.

Over the course of his life and career, Al has immersed himself in the comic book anarchy of his beloved *MAD* magazine as well as the cinematic spoofs of the Zucker Brothers and Mel Brooks, the kooky sonic circus of *The Dr. Demento Show* and, of course, television comedy in all its splendor and horror.

To that end, it's unsurprising that Al takes inspiration from the groaningly familiar riffs of stand-up comedy in *UHF*. "Isle Thing" took comic aim at the fattest and laziest of targets, while the R.E.M. parody "Spam" follows closely in its footsteps by asking what the deal is with the canned meat product seemingly nobody likes.

"Open Mic Al" Yankovic returns with a misguided vengeance on "Spam." Now, everyone had their own definition of "hack" in the 1980s, although almost all include doing jokes about *Gilligan's Island* and Spam.

Spam was never for eating. It continues to not be for eating. No, Spam was only ever for making jokes about, and Al isn't averse to making jokes about well-trod comedic territory.

On one level, the singer of "Spam" is one of Al's kooky obsessives, a weirdo whose sad, small life is transformed forever by Spam. The singer posits that Spam is "the best" and makes for a "darn good sandwich," but that doesn't keep him from cracking wise at Spam's expense. The singer wonders aloud if the beef-like substance in Spam is "mystery meat" and proposes using it for home-improvement as well as cuisine.

"Spam" captures the toxic nature of its subject matter so viscerally that I'm starting to get a little queasy just listening to it. Al sings about "ham and pork" in a way that makes listeners never want to consume either, ever again. Maybe that's intentional. Al is, after all, a vegetarian, so maybe the secret purpose of "Spam" has always been to make consuming meat seem so disgusting that it makes vegetarianism look appealing by comparison.

13.
THE BIGGEST BALL OF TWINE IN MINNESOTA

The phrase "formulaic" is seldom used in a positive way except in Al's case, where a steady reliance on formula has helped him stay relevant and popular for four decades.

The seemingly rigid structures of Al's albums allow for an awful lot of playful experimentation and gleeful absurdism, particularly in their final songs. "The Biggest Ball of Twine of Minnesota," which ends *UHF* on a triumphant note, is the ultimate oddball album-closer, a nearly seven-minute long story-song in the vein of singer-songwriter types like Harry Chapin. It packs in so much wonderfully banal detail that it feels like a family road comedy movie on wax, or a short story in song form.

"The Biggest Ball of Twine in Minnesota" embodies Al's genius for treating nonsense as a matter of national, even international importance. In this case, the nonsense is the titular Midwestern home of an exceptionally large assemblage of twine, which the wanderlust-addled narrator and his family seize upon as a sacred Mecca they *must* visit.

The soundtrack-closer doubles as one of the most comprehensive and satisfying character studies Al has ever released. We learn so, so much about the travel enthusiast happily singing the song, from his employer (Big Roy's Heating and Plumbing) to the length of his vacation (two weeks) to his taste in everything from road food (pickled wieners) to country music (Slim Whitman).

We learn far more than we need to know about him, frankly. The sheer accumulation of seemingly pointless and unnecessary details gives the fan favorite an offbeat, shambling rhythm and poetry all its own. But these details also flesh out Al's portrait of the corny dad behind the steering wheel, and the unimportant things he finds important.

We learn that it was exactly 7:37 Wednesday evening when he first encountered the titular twine ball, something he recounts with the kind of awe generally reserved for encounters with the Lord or space aliens. He gushes: "Out on the distance, on the horizon, it appeared to me like a vision before my unbelieving eyes/We parked the car and walked with awe-filled reverence towards that glorious, huge, majestic sphere/I was just so overwhelmed by its sheer immensity."

It's easy to see why "The Biggest Ball of Twine in Minnesota" has attracted an intense, loyal cult following. There's just so much to the song, and so much to love. It's not just a clever tune; it's an entire richly observed universe unto itself. It's an affectionate look at an America that doesn't exist anymore, but lives on in the form of the faded bumper stickers and decals that line the car that transports the song's subjects from one surreally pointless tourist trap to another.

What makes "The Biggest Ball of Twine in Minnesota" such an enduring masterpiece of cornball Americana, in addition to being a sly send-up of cornball Americana, is the enormous affection it has for the campy details of Middle-American life. Sure, the pickled wieners that are constantly mentioned sound as stomach-churning as Spam, but they also sound oddly irresistible.

"The Biggest Ball of Twine in Minnesota" is a gleeful lampoon of tourists, and the human urge to see nonsense that doesn't really need to be seen. But it's a celebration of those same tourists, and the human urge to see nonsense that doesn't really need to be seen, as well. In true "Weird Al" Yankovic form, it's driven by love and affection rather than nastiness or condescension.

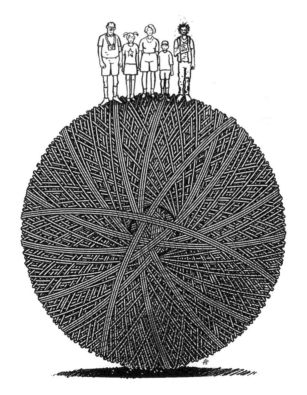

Listening to "The Biggest Ball of Twine in Minnesota" makes you feel like you're there in the car with this archetypal American family in all their All-American weirdness and normality. You can damn near smell the pickled wieners and taste the beer. You want to be one of the brats along for the ride, even if (in one of the song's most darkly winning details) you wouldn't be able to actually see all that glorious scenery on account of the windows being covered up by decals.

If the first song on every Al album is for the radio and the mainstream and people who know Al as the "Eat It" guy, then the final track is generally a gift to his fans that, on classics like this, find him at his biggest, most ambitious, and just plain weirdest. No wonder these oddball final songs tend to be remembered long after the more commercial and less personal singles have been forgotten.

I've always loved "The Biggest Ball of Twine in Minnesota" but I picked up a new appreciation for it while journeying through the highways and byways of our intermittently great nation during my seven stops on the Ridiculously Self-Indulgent, Ill-Advised Vanity Tour.

Though my chariot of choice (or, rather, necessity) was a Greyhound bus, by the end of the tour I felt like I had done more than heard "The Biggest Ball of Twine in Minnesota" performed live multiple times: I'd *lived* it.

OFF THE DEEP END (1992)

1.
SMELLS LIKE NIRVANA

Conventional wisdom holds that pop music had devolved into mindless inanity in the late 1980s and early 1990s until the righteous opening chords of Nirvana's "Smells Like Teen Spirit" kicked off an alternative rock revolution that blasted away the stale machismo of hair metal and emptiness of synth-driven dance pop.

This is a reductive take but there's an element of truth to it borne out by the track listing of Al's second big comeback album (after *Even Worse* washed away *Polka Party*'s relative failure). Remove Nirvana and "Smells Like Teen Spirit" from *Off the Deep End* and you have an album weighed down with parodies from the low-wattage likes of MC Hammer, Gerardo, New Kids on the Block and Milli Vanilli.

It might not have known it at the time, but pop music needed Kurt Cobain. It needed Nirvana. So did Al. "Smells Like Nirvana" sounds like "Smells Like Teen Spirit" might if producer Butch Vig had a Morning Zoo DJ's love of wacky sound effects and animal noises but it also sounds like nothing Al had ever attempted before. It's rawer, louder, angrier and more sonically aggressive.

In that sense, "Smells Like Nirvana" is at once a beginning and a return. Yankovic hadn't yelled his way through a song at such deafening volume since "Another One Rides the Bus." On "Smells Like Nirvana," Al allows himself to be loud, abrasive and obnoxious. The soft/loud dynamic of the original is retained here but feels more like soft/loud/even louder/loudest.

The first single, video and track on *Off the Deep End* finds Al in deconstructionist mode as he picks apart Cobain's original so that he can simultaneously parody Cobain's singing, songwriting and persona in addition to the song itself. It's the best of "Meta Al" Yankovic's songs about songs because it's executed with such affection for its subject matter that it doubles as a tribute to the borderline incomprehensible genius of a fellow original.

After those telltale guitar chords and thunderous drums, "Perplexed Al" Yankovic begins the song on a confused note, mumbling, "What is this song all about?/Can't figure any lyrics out." He's in a very early 1990s fog, which could be the haze of depression, drugs or just the jaded apathy endemic to a generation whose defining album was tellingly titled *Nevermind*.

In one of his most intense and challenging vocal performances, Yankovic seems to be heckling his own song. He's so lost that he's continually beseeching the listener to tell him what he's supposed to be singing. This confusion is existential as well as practical, for what was "Smells Like Teen Spirit" if not a passionate howl of confusion?

As satire goes, "Smells Like Nirvana" is decidedly on the genial side. This is not a blistering takedown of rock star hypocrisy. It's not supposed to be.

When Yankovic screams "We're so loud and incoherent/ Boy, this oughta bug your parents!," it's gently mocking but also celebratory. In rock and roll, being loud, incoherent and bugging parents aren't just positive attributes: they're the whole point. On "Smells Like Nirvana," Al and his band rock as hard, if not harder, than they've ever rocked before.

Cobain was a dark star hurtling towards oblivion but that darkness needed to be balanced out by some sort of light.

That's what "Smells Like Nirvana" provided. Only Al and his collaborators knew that what "Smells Like Teen Spirit," a perfect pop song, was missing all along was kazoos, belching, the "boing!" sound, the mooing of cows and a dude singing/ gargling with water in his mouth.

The silliness in "Smells Like Nirvana" wasn't just the perfect antidote and answer to the grumbling portentousness of Grunge Rock; it was cathartic and liberating. It was a zeitgeist-

capturing smash both for people who loved Nirvana and for people who found Grunge silly.

Cobain famously had an ambivalent-to-traumatic relationship with money and fame. Yet he was, like every pop star, a consumer product whose angst was sold to disaffected young people who saw themselves in his eloquently unintelligible misery.

Yet on "Smells Like Nirvana" he yells at the public to "buy our album!," another reminder that in Al's world, nearly everything comes down to making money.

Given Al's status as the preeminent troubadour of the grocery store as well as our culture's official singer of silly songs about television, commercials and television commercials, there's a neat irony in Al swapping out the name of a tacky consumer product you can buy in grocery stores, Teen Spirit deodorant, for the name of the soon to be legendary band he's spoofing.

By naming his breakthrough single after Teen Spirit, Cobain was re-purposing tacky pop culture detritus to his own ends. Why did Cobain name his generation-defining breakout hit after a deodorant? Because he was a weird dude, and a funny dude, and "Smells Like Teen Spirit" is a very funny song even if it's almost impossible to understand.

There's a whole lot going on in "Smells Like Nirvana." It's overflowing with ideas and jokes and wacky sound effects without feeling cluttered. Like "Smells Like Teen Spirit," it was the perfect song for the moment. It brought Al back in a big way, even if fans knew that he never really went anywhere.

2.
TRIGGER HAPPY

With Al, the more upbeat a song sounds, the more twisted it is likely to be. "Trigger Happy" accordingly marries one of Al's swellest melodies to a darkly comic exploration of American gun lust.

The song cross-breeds the wholesome, Southern California sound of the Beach Boys and Jan and Dean with the "Have you hugged your gun today?" sensibility of the NRA.

"Trigger Happy" lives up to both parts of its title. It's both incongruously happy, even joyous, and most assuredly about a man with a very itchy trigger finger. Al and his band nail the vocal harmonies, California-sized anthemic choruses and air of carefree innocence that characterized the surf sound of the 1960s as well as the misplaced self-righteousness, defensiveness and recklessness of the contemporary American gun enthusiast.

"Trigger Happy" is one of Al's most overtly, savagely satirical songs, but the social commentary emerges organically. I doubt Al would characterize it as an anti-gun song, or political at all, but "Trigger Happy" slyly mounts a credible argument for gun control without seeming didactic or killing the morbid fun.

It's a quietly devastating character study of the Second Amendment radical as an emotionally stunted lunatic who needs to keep an AK-47 by his pillow in order to sleep well at night.

Terrible things happen to the singer throughout "Trigger Happy." Or, more accurately, terrible things happen to the people and animals around him *because* of him.

The only exercise the demented protagonist of "Trigger Happy" gets is in exercising his trigger finger along with his Second Amendment rights. It's sung from the perspective of a man who puts the "nut" in "gun nut" and the "danger" in "danger to himself, his friends and family."

"Trigger Happy" is so much fun, and breezes by so cheerfully, that it can be easy to overlook its underlying bleakness. Never have sentiments like "Better watch out, punk, or I'm gonna have to blow you away!" or "I'll blow their brains out with my Smith & Wesson!" been expressed with such boyish glee.

This pastiche depicts an amoral obsession with deadly weapons combined with total disrespect for the sanctity of human life not as a strange deviation but something endemic to our national character. In "Trigger Happy," gun violence is as all-American as mom, surfboards, the flag, the Beach Boys and apple pie.

"Trigger Happy" gleans pitch-black comedy out of a deadly national addiction to guns that in real life is nothing short of tragic.

3.
I CAN'T WATCH THIS

When Al decided to return to the well of bad television for his "U Can't Touch This" parody "I Can't Watch This," he did not have freshness on his side. But he did have an irritatingly catchy bit of pop-rap built on the hypnotic baseline of Rick

James' "Superfreak" as the musical backbone for his latest attack on the rampaging idiocies of the boob tube.

"I Can't Watch This" is one of Al's first and lesser rap parodies. It's nearly as much a time capsule of the era that created it as a well-worn issue of *TV Guide*.

The TV-hater rapping the song rails good-naturedly against the yuppie whine-fest *Thirtysomething*, Arsenio Hall's mindless enthusiasm and talk shows that are "rude, crude and vile" and make him to want to flip the dial.

The song's freshest, yet most soothingly familiar element is a sonic collage of famous commercials. There's a Negativland-for-Beginners quality to the rapid-fire assemblage of assaultive commercial pleas.

This commercial medley – which mashes together "classic" soundbites like Kelly LeBrock's "Don't hate me because I'm beautiful" and some old geezer's cry of "I've fallen, and I can't get up!" – instantly brought back a flood of memories: It's as if Al is giving a solo not to a musician but to the entire commercial industry.

"I Can't Watch This" is about the innate disposability of television. Yet some of the ephemeral TV fodder referenced in it has endured. A quarter of a century later we're still talking about the donut-eating freaks of *Twin Peaks*, particularly in the aftermath of the glowingly received Showtime reboot. And we're still mourning those Siskel and Ebert bums. Some of us even watch *America's Funniest Home Videos*, apparently, since it's still around.

Most importantly, we're still listening to, and occasionally even reading about, "Weird Al" Yankovic, who seems destined to outlive all of the pop culture detritus he's lovingly spoofed, even when they prove weirdly enduring boomerangs like *Twin Peaks*, which streaked across pop culture like a comet, only to reappear decades later, no worse for wear.

4.
POLKA YOUR EYES OUT

The most wonderfully dated element of any "Weird Al" Yankovic album is generally the polka medley of contemporary hits. Like the unlikely combination of artists parodied on *Off the Deep End* (Nirvana, Milli Vanilli, New Kids on the Block, Gerardo and M.C Hammer) "Polka Your Eyes Out" captures a strange, singular moment in pop music when the grunge and alternative revolution smashed up hard against the dying embers of Hair Metal, pop-rap, boy bands and the traditional metal of Metallica.

"Polka Your Eyes Out" begins differently than any other medley, with a straight-forward recreation of the opening of Billy Idol's "Cradle of Love" bleeding inevitably into a polka goof of the same song. In his medleys, Al and his band polka-fied contemporary hits, but on this medley we hear both a faithful semi-cover of the original version and the polka version immediately afterwards.

One of the transgressive thrills of the medleys involves Al adopting the musical costumes of acts that deal with sex with a bluntness at odds with Al's family-friendly aesthetic. "Naughty Al" Yankovic consequently makes his presence felt on such notoriously dirty songs as Warrant's "Cherry Pie" and the DiVinyls' "I Touch Myself," which is about a woman who finds herself stranded all alone in the gas station of love and has to use the self-service pumps.

Al's polka medleys are a warm, soothing bath of nostalgia, but sometimes the song choices hit particularly close to home and it feels like Al has a unique line into your psyche in addition to possessing a peerless genius for discerning what pop music will endure and what history will quickly forget.

5.
I WAS ONLY KIDDING

Off the Deep End found Al lampooning some of the weakest songs of his career but he nevertheless found ways to express his idiosyncratic sensibility by returning to beloved cult weirdo Tonio K. for inspiration on "I Was Only Kidding," Al's second tribute to the demented New Wave artist after *"Weird Al" Yankovic*'s "Happy Birthday."

This pastiche/homage is unique in a few ways. It's unique because it finds Al returning to a favorite artist a second time and it's unique in the relative obscurity of its inspiration.

Tonio K. falls on the obscure side of just about everything. But Al obviously saw himself in the quintessential cult artist, because "Happy Birthday" and "I Was Only Kidding" aren't just pastiches of K.'s work but rather Al's version of bleakly funny Tonio K. masterpieces "The Funky Western Civilization" and "H-A-T-R-E-D."

"H-A-T-R-E-D" begins with Tonio K. adopting, with ironic detachment, the role of the philosophical troubadour examining the crazy dance of courtship from the wounded perspective of someone nursing a newly-shattered heart.

Initially accompanied only by the gentle strum of a lonesome acoustic guitar, he shifts from folkie to sneering degenerate when the faux-sincerity concludes with him announcing, with just the right hint of impending anarchy, "Let me kind of put this another way, okay?"

"H-A-T-R-E-D" makes a breakneck turn from fake folk to punk aggression as Tonio K. morphs into an angrier, funnier Johnny Rotten as his true feelings come out and he yells his vicious hatred of the song's subject in lines that are as funny as they are mean, like, "You've got me P-I-S-S-E-D off/I'm angry most of the time/Why don't you G-O T-O H-E-double-L/

You tramp, you philandering b****/I'm going to K-I-L-L one of us, baby/When I'm sober I'll decide on which!"

Like "H-A-T-R-E-D," "I Was Only Kidding" begins on an incongruous note of faux-sincerity. Backed by a heavenly choir, the singer sweetly sings, "When I said that I'd be faithful/ When I promised I'd be true/When I swore that I could never/ Be with anyone but you/When I told you that I loved you/ With those tender words I spoke…" before getting to the cruel punchline: "I was only kidding! Now, can't you take a joke?!"

This kicks off a bracing shift from faux-sincerity to genuine aggression. The man cruelly taunting a woman for having the questionable judgement to fall in love with him is another of Al's creepy Casanovas. He may not be as unhinged as the rest of the bunch, but he's a jerk, and unlike the bitter man singing and experiencing "H-A-T-R-E-D," the singer here doesn't even have the excuse of having been cheated on.

"I Was Only Kidding" has the same crazy, heedless momentum as "H-A-T-R-E-D," albeit without the profane rage and with more wacky animal noises. Along with "Smells Like Nirvana," it's one of the punkest (and most animal noise-intensive) songs Al has recorded, and its caustic acidity helps balance out the sugar overload of the album's non-Nirvana parodies.

6.
THE WHITE STUFF

With "The White Stuff," a parody of New Kids on the Block's teenybopper anthem "The Right Stuff," that sugar overload is twofold. Al was spoofing the bubblegum pop of a preeminent boy band, but he was also singing about a sugary treat.

New Kids on the Block were a commercial powerhouse and bona fide pop culture phenomenon, but they did not command respect. They were thought of as a silly cartoon, partially because their merchandising blitz included an actual silly cartoon.

With "The White Stuff," Al once again transformed a song about romance into a song about gluttony, replacing our insatiable hunger for sex with a need for sweets.

"Culinary Al" Yankovic returns to his beloved supermarket aisle for inspiration for a comically over-the-top exploration of a pathological obsession not just with an American snack food but rather for one element of an American snack food.

So, what is the titular white stuff? Is it the booger sugar that fueled the entirety of 1970s and 1980s rock and roll, Al and his band aside? Nope, in "The White Stuff" the titular substance is the white cream found between the cookies in Oreos. If that doesn't sound like a juicy subject for comedy, that's because it's not.

"The White Stuff" is at once a song about nothing and a song about gluttony, consumption and consumerism. Al here returns to a familiar theme: that the result of buying and

consuming all of those amazing wonder products and foods we see advertised on television or on the radio is momentary pleasure followed by obesity and death.

This obsessive gent takes his obsession with cookie filling to extremes, rubbing it on his roast, putting it in his coffee and spreading it on his toast. It's another song of obsession about a man whose life is ineffably enhanced by a consumer product that's also doing a number on his complexion and internal organs. But that's a price Al's fiends are forever willing to pay in exchange for the high of consumer ecstasy.

7.
WHEN I WAS YOUR AGE

Al's originals almost have to be better than his parodies because of the additional pressure on them. *Off the Deep End*, like *Polka Party!* and *UHF* before it, is carried by its originals. On *Off the Deep End*, they're all good to great. "When I Was Your Age" is no different, a rock-solid exploration of the "Get off my lawn after I'm done lecturing you!" mindset of old codgers intent on letting the young people know how rough they had it back in the old days.

Over a working-man groove inspired by the hard-rocking self-pity of Don Henley on songs like "Dirty Laundry" and "If Dirt Were Dollars," Al adopts the persona of a grim old codger addressing a callow ingrate of a young person about how cushy the juvenile delinquents of today have it compared to the Dickensian horrors of their youth.

Al offers a point-by-point comparison between the trials of Job he endured as a young man and the sweet life EVERYONE enjoys now (even those darn Millennials) even though they've done nothing to deserve it.

"When I Was Your Age" is another Al song full of ghoulish imagery, whether the singer is insisting, "Dad would whoop us every night till a quarter after twelve/Then he'd get too tired and he'd make us whoop ourselves" or ending things on a bleak note with the closing image of the singer's abusive father chopping him "into pieces" so he can "play frisbee with my brain," something he insists, not convincingly, he's actually surprisingly cool with.

The belligerent boomer singing the song is apparently cool with everything he suffered through as a young man, from enduring abusive treatment to being murdered and dismembered, except for the ingratitude and entitlement of young people.

"When I Was Your Age" craggily conveys the paradoxical absurdity of grumpy old men insisting that life was a brutal, joyless struggle when they were young, and that, somehow, that suffering made them more real and morally superior to people whose character has not been tested, and strengthened, by a level of adolescent torment that borders on biblical.

8.
TACO GRANDE

Under the "parodies" section of the Wikipedia page for Gerardo's "Rico Suave," Al's spoof is described as being "about a man who visits a Mexican restaurant."

Even for Al, that's a thin conceit to build a song around, but the "Eat It" hitmaker is uniquely skilled at making something out of almost nothing. He's peerless in his ability to take a thin or overused conceit and sell it through energy, affability and goofball charm.

Al accomplishes that alchemy once again in "Taco Grande." The Gerardo parody fits snugly into one of Al's earliest parody templates: taking a hot-blooded radio smash very overtly about romance and sex and making it about food. The song follows very closely in the footsteps of "Lasagna" in focusing not on a single type of food but rather on an entire culture's cuisine.

"Taco Grande" finds Al shopping in the ethnic food aisle of the metaphorical supermarket that is his consumerism-and-consumption-obsessed career. On this guilty pleasure, Al steps inside Gerardo's red blazer (no undershirt, or shirt required!) in order to act as the animated hype man for the cuisine of our neighbors to the South.

"Rico Suave" was already both a complete joke and a *telenovela*-outsized exercise in self-parody when Gerardo, who would go on to become a successful record executive, recorded it and its music video.

With a lascivious wink and a whole lot of bumping and grinding, Gerardo was playing a lusty burlesque of steamy Latino machismo. He was the ultimate Latin lover (even more than the protagonist of 2017's *How to Be a Latin Lover*,

the source of the re-recording of "Happy Birthday" that closes *Medium Rarities,* the box set and this edition of the book), a human cartoon who may have been in on the joke but was a vaguely retro joke all the same.

Al simply changes the joke, from a campy Latin Lover gag to a more family-friendly tribute to the wonderfully sonorous names of Mexican food. Over the space of a little under four minutes, Al name-checks seemingly every Mexican dish in existence, rhyming merrily, "You see, I just gotta have a tostada/ Carne asada/That's right, I want the whole enchilada/My only addiction has to do with a flour tortilla/I need a quesadilla!"

What really makes "Taco Grande" work is the infectious enthusiasm Al brings to it. Al's Mexican food fan sounds way more excited to be munching on a quesadilla than Gerardo is to be making sweet love to the sum of the feminine species on "Rico Suave."

To this day, the phrase "Rico Suave" invariably makes me smile. So does "Taco Grande."

9.
AIRLINE AMY

The creepy Casanovas in Al's oeuvre often mistake mental illness for true love. The myopic romantic of "Airline Amy" is no different but where Al's love-struck oddballs frequently pose a danger to themselves and others, the singer of "Airline Amy" seems fundamentally harmless, even endearing.

"Airline Amy" is sung by a true romantic who mistakes the titular waitress in the sky's devotion to her job for romantic attraction. It's a decidedly one-sided love affair. "Every one of our dates is at thirty thousand feet" the singer boasts without realizing that what he sees as the exquisite dance of *l'amour fou* is actually more a matter of a professional doing her job.

When the titular stewardess points out the exits, refills his coffee, gets him headphones and demonstrates how to use an oxygen mask, our adorably misguided singer is convinced she's flirting up a storm, engaging in high-altitude foreplay.

"Airline Amy" sounds and feels like an infectious, upbeat power-pop love song. You have to really listen to the lyrics to get the song's comic conceit, and even then it's abstract and more than a little conceptual.

"Airline Amy" is strong enough that it doesn't really need to be a comedy song, or even particularly funny. It would be a winner even without the comic hook of a deluded frequent flyer mistaking professionalism for affection and proximity for an actual relationship. If "Airline Amy" was just a catchy power pop love song about a pathologically optimistic young man it would still be a good song, but it would not be a "Weird Al" Yankovic song.

The strange, deluded men of Al's warped love songs comically misunderstand both the emotions of the people they're in love with, and the way love and the world work. Oftentimes that has a sinister quality, but not here. The singer is a fool and a low-key lunatic, but he's also truly lovestruck, albeit misguided.

"Airline Amy" isn't hilarious, but that's by design. Al isn't going for big laughs here, so much as knowing chuckles. "Airline Amy" doesn't reach the comic heights of some of Al's other work but little in his catalog can match it for sunny charm and warped innocence.

10.
THE PLUMBING SONG

Over the course of his extraordinary career, Al has parodied the greats and the not-so-greats alike. Mili Vanilli is an unfortunate, fascinating anomaly among the artists Al has parodied in being less a legitimate act than a low-level criminal enterprise, a strange, cynical case of pop music fraud that briefly catapulted two handsome, talentless morons to international fame for pretending to sing inane pop concoctions that were as infectious as they were banal.

These tacky Eurotrash concoctions didn't call for Freddie Mercury-level pipes, but Rob and Fab, the handsomely vacant singer-model-actor types (minus the whole "singer" part) who fronted the "group" lacked even the modest talent required to sing smashes like "Blame it on the Rain" and "Don't Forget My Number," both of which Al spoofs on "The Plumbing Song."

The premise of "The Plumbing Song" can be divined by its title. Al has never been afraid to nosh hungrily at the trough of Great Joke Subjects, so the only real surprise here is that it took Al this long to finally get around to mining the comic gold of stuffed-up johns and showers gone kaput.

Given the role commercials play in Al's oeuvre, it's fitting that the song begins and ends with snippets of a fake commercial and could itself double as an unusually long, ambitious musical commercial. Mimicking the vocal tics and gimmicky delivery of the original song with annoying meticulousness, Al assumes the perspective of an ordinary man advising a friend with plumbing problems to seek professional help from the kind of guys who make "service calls" in their "overalls" because he himself is helpless in such matters.

The joy in "The Plumbing Song" (and at its best, the silliness here is sublime) comes from how perfectly Al replaces concern over plumbing problems with the original song's romantic lyrics.

But in true "Weird Al" Yankovic tradition, there's also a palpable joy in wordplay and words, particularly the many fun, gross words related to the plumbing industry. Whether he's proclaiming, "If hairballs, grease and goo/Won't let the water through/Blame it on the drain" or "If Drain-O's a joke and your plunger is broke/Baby, call the mensch with the monkey wrench," Al gets the most out of every word.

Al plumbs this material for all its worth. You don't have to be a plumber with a PhD, like one of the contestants on "I Lost on Jeopardy," to appreciate all of the hard work that went into making "The Plumbing Song" so spectacularly over-achieving.

11.
YOU DON'T LOVE ME ANYMORE

By 1992, Al's formula for albums was set in stone. The first song was the big parody for normies who wouldn't know "The Biggest Ball of Twine in Minnesota" from "Slime Creatures from Outer Space." The last track pushes the normies away and rewards fans with some of the darkest, funniest and most audacious songs of Al's career.

The final track of *Off the Deep End* is no different. To its credit, it's one of those songs that worries parents, deservedly so, as it's another masterpiece of the macabre, another portrait of a romantic relationship as a circle of hell. Only instead of one of Al's creepy Casanovas we have a man who is on the receiving end of great cruelty.

He's starting to question his longtime partner's devotion after a series of troubling incidents that makes it apparent to everyone other than the song's singer that the couple's primary problem is one party's intense desire to murder the other party.

But if "You Don't Love Me Anymore" is one of Al's darkest songs lyrically, sonically it's one of his gentlest. Al has seldom sounded more tremblingly sincere than when addressing a lover he fears no longer cares for him the way she once did, as evidenced by her attempts to end his life.

We start off on a gorgeously deadpan note, with crystal-clear acoustic guitar plucking and Al, in sensitive folkie mode, starting things off slowly with "We've been together for so very long/But now things are changing, oh I wonder what's wrong?/ Seems you don't want me around/The passion is gone and the flame's died down."

Things start to take a turn with one of the raunchier lyrics to be found in Al's work: "I guess I lost a little bit of self-esteem/ That time that you made it with the whole hockey team." The following lyrics kicks things into high gear with one of my favorite rhymes not just in Al's work but in all of popular music: "You used to think I was nice/Now you tell all your friends that I'm the Antichrist."

From there, the song becomes a wonderfully dark comedy about a failed romantic relationship as a death pit the unlucky victim is lucky to survive. Al's croon never loses its wounded earnestness no matter how cartoonishly he suffers at his sadistic sweetheart's murderous hands.

The singer is willing to overlook an awful lot for love. At one point he even concedes, "You know, I even think it's kinda cute the way/You poison my coffee just a little each day."

How can you not love a song with lyrics like "You slammed my face down on the barbecue grill/Now my scars are all healing, but my heart never will"? Seldom has Al's juxtaposition of lovely, coffee-house-friendly music and ghoulishly dark lyrics paid such rich comic dividends. Thanks to "You Don't Love Me Anymore," *Off the Deep End* ends as strongly as it begins.

BITE ME
(HIDDEN TRACK)

Though it did not invent the concept, Nirvana's *Nevermind* helped popularize the hidden track with "Endless, Nameless," a song that appeared on some pressings of the CD after ten minutes of silence following "Something in the Way," ostensibly the classic album's final song.

The idea of the hidden track was to make listeners think that that they had lost their mind or that their CD player was possessed by demons when, after an extended silence, the infernal machine roared unexpectedly back to life with a mysterious, possibly Satanic blast of music. In fear, listeners would ritualistically burn their CD players to cleanse it of evil spirits or try to purify it by immersing it in holy water, only to learn that the "secret" unlisted track was intentional. The idea was to reward listeners as a fun little bonus for not turning off a CD immediately after the final note of the final credited song.

As the eight seconds of screaming anarchy of "Bite Me" illustrate, the secret or bonus track was often a "prize" of dubious value, less a reward than a punishment for wasting your time looking for audio treasure that's more likely to turn out to be fool's gold.

The secret track was almost by design something not good enough to make it onto the proper album. The pointlessness of the secret track is the point of "Bite Me," which also gave fans who left the album on for ten minutes after the end of "You Don't Love Me Anymore" a fright and, if they're easily impressed enough, a thrill as well, at least the first time around.

ALAPALOOZA
(1993)

1.
JURASSIC PARK

In the first decade of his recording career, Al released eight albums. In the ensuing twenty-six years, he's released just six. Al has gotten less prolific but more strategic as he's gotten older. Al's '90s oeuvre doubled down on pop culture mashups that combined a zeitgeist-capturing classic song with an equally zeitgeist-friendly hit movie.

Alapalooza piggybacked on the public's affection for such beloved pop culture chestnuts as *Jurassic Park*, *The Flintstones* and *Wayne's World.* Many of Al's biggest singles from the Clinton era aligned so closely with blockbusters that they almost felt like part of their marketing campaigns. "Jurassic Park" sometimes sounds as much like a tongue-in-cheek commercial for *Jurassic Park* as a spoof.

The song Al chose for the musical foundation of "Jurassic Park" was "MacArthur Park," an inscrutable story song written by Jimmy Webb and given screaming, melodramatic life by everyone from Donna Summer to Richard Harris.

The incoherent, self-parodic melodrama of Webb's original song, and particularly Harris' version, perfectly matches the subject matter of "Jurassic Park." If anything, the crooner of "MacArthur Park" seems more distraught over a doomed love affair and a melting cake than the singer of "Jurassic Park" does over their likely impending death-by-dinosaur.

The song is sung from the perspective of a character inside the world of *Jurassic Park* who is understandably alarmed when things at the park devolve from the touristy to the tragic, and they go from being employees to entrees.

"Jurassic Park" traffics extensively in comic understatement; the potential dinosaur lunch undersells the trauma he's going through when he dismisses it as "one lousy day." Later he confides, "I cannot approve of this attraction/'Cause getting disemboweled always makes me kinda mad" – an incongruously chill response.

Yes, "Jurassic Park" has lawyer jokes and Barney the dinosaur jokes, but it also references chaos theory and boasts some of the most realistic dinosaur noises this side of *Jurassic Park.*

"Jurassic Park" has aged better than the movie that inspired it. Joining Michael Crichton and Spielberg's dinosaur-themed cinematic blockbuster to Jimmy Webb's oldies staple might have been a wedding of convenience, but the song and video have endured.

2.
YOUNG, DUMB & UGLY

With "Young, Dumb & Ugly," "Weird Al" Yankovic didn't set out to make a comedy version of a hard rock song. He just made a hard rock song, and a terrific one at that.

This sneakily ingenious sleeper is a riotous riff on the bad-boy posturing and heavy metal swagger of AC/DC. Only instead of luxuriating in the transgression of heavy metal, Al and his band of mild miscreants are more minor annoyances than major threats to the established social order. The rebels without a cause (or a clue) ironically championed here aren't going to steal your girl or your bike but they might cut ahead of you in line, jaywalk or refill their soda without paying.

Over clean, pounding drums and rocking guitars, Al starts off on an appropriately metal note of defiance when he howls, "We're dangerous dudes/We've got bad attitudes/Most of our brain cells are gone!/We were born to be bad/You better not get us mad." The illusion of badassery dissipates instantly once Al specifies the consequences of pissing off him and his crew: "We just might toilet paper your lawn!"

My favorite part of the song is when the moderately-bad boy "boasts" of himself and his fellow rebels that they "wait until the last minute to pay (their) telephone bills." Al and his fellow semi-miscreants aren't even paying their telephone bills late, or not paying them, or throwing their telephones in swimming pools or setting telephones on fire. They're just not being super-prompt about it.

The authenticity of the big, macho, crazily catchy music sells the conceit of an alternate-universe AC/DC, a band boasting about the kind of middle-schooler-level shenanigans that should actually be a source of shame.

3.
BEDROCK ANTHEM

With Al, there are songs of inspiration and songs of opportunity. The songs of inspiration tend to be pastiches, lovingly composed and executed tributes to Al's favorite artists. The songs of opportunity, on the other hand, are almost invariably parodies inspired by the monster anthem of the moment and/or a ubiquitous movie and/or television show.

"Bedrock Anthem" is the quintessential song of opportunity that combines a pair of Red Hot Chili Peppers songs, the libidinal, nonsensical funk workout "Give It Away" and dreamy drug ballad "Under the Bridge" with a mediocre television sitcom that inspired a less-than-mediocre 1994 feature film adaptation – *The Flintstones*.

"Bedrock Anthem" is sung from the point of view of someone who loves *The Flintstones* to the point where they want to escape modern-day reality and live inside its prehistoric, laugh-track-fueled world. He wants to ride a dinosaur to work every day, use sardonic talking animals as kitchen appliances and pal around with Barney Rubble.

Anthony Kiedis' delivery, particularly on "Give It Away," makes everything he sings sound like gibberish. If anything, "Yabba Dabba Doo" would be an unusually coherent lyric from him. Ever the student, Al watched over one hundred episodes of *The Flintstones* as research for "Bedrock Anthem," both for lyrical inspiration and to pull soundbites he could sample for the song.

That might seem like an extraordinary waste of Al's time. But all that research and TV over-consumption helps make "Bedrock Anthem" as knowing and affectionate towards its retro subject matter as "Lucy" was towards *I Love Lucy* – even if *The Flintstones*, unlike *Lucy*, is an affable, deathless mediocrity.

4.
FRANK'S 2000" TV

The transcendent R.E.M. homage "Frank's 2000" TV" opens poetically with a couplet you might find on a college rock song of the era. Al croons, "Rising above the city, blocking out the noonday sun/It dwarfs the mighty redwoods and it towers over everyone."

What is this beast, this monolith, this apex of man's ingenuity and insatiable hunger for bigger, better, higher, *more*? Why, it's the titular wonder of the modern world – an obscenely oversized television set – which inspires such intense reverence.

The 2000-inch TV is a source of endless fascination for our singer. He regards the comically oversized boob tube the way Skull Islanders regard King Kong: something so amazing, so beyond their imagination, that it borders on magic. The reverent TV addict damn near gets down on his knees and worships this false idol. This television is nothing short of a source of civic pride. The overwhelmed singer boasts, "And I'm mighty proud to say/Now I can watch *The Simpsons* from thirty blocks away."

When contemplating the curious sincerity underneath the satire, it's worth noting that, when someone in 1993 referenced *The Simpsons*, they were talking about the greatest television show of all time at its apex. Similarly, when Al references Robert De Niro and his mole, the *Taxi Driver* icon was still a heavyweight thespian whose recent credits included *Goodfellas* and *Cape Fear*, not the prolific schlockmeister of today. Al generally sings about the worst in pop culture, but here he sings about the best.

Despite the timely references, "Frank's 2000" TV" is utterly timeless, a jangly Byrds-ian folk-rock gem that, in a perfect world, would escape the comedy song ghetto and get played on alternative stations alongside R.E.M.

If "Frank's 2000" TV" is not the loveliest song in Al's canon, it's certainly one of them. I never thought the phrase "Robert De Niro's mole" could sound so heavenly.

"Frank's 2000" TV" is strangely subtle, but it's also unusually sophisticated. It's a wry, bittersweet celebration

of a distinctly American form of conspicuous consumerism, Al's ultimate statement on the ridiculous allure of television's American Dream.

Al has written endlessly about pop culture, but he's seldom made it seem more simultaneously absurd and irresistible than he does here.

"Frank's 2000" TV" captures the sound and feel of early to mid-period R.E.M. as well as "Young, Dumb & Ugly" did AC/DC. It's a remarkable feat that the same men could, in the space of a few songs, reproduce the sounds of such dissimilar acts. The soaring, tight harmonies, the chiming guitar, the clean, expansive tunefulness and underlying scope: "Frank's 2000" TV" is perfect.

5.
ACHY BREAKY SONG

There are elements of Al's music that you expect to come back, to be a huge presence in pop culture decades after Al sang about them, like *Star Wars* and *Jurassic Park.*

One subject I never imagined would become timely again is Billy Ray Cyrus having an irritatingly ubiquitous, unmissable hit song on the radio and the annoyance that would result. Yet as I write this in late June of 2019, Lil Nas X and Billy Ray Cyrus' "Old Town Road" has been the number one song for twelve weeks thanks to a chorus so infernally catchy that it's borderline sadistic.

The newly, unexpectedly timely "Achy Breaky Song" resembles deconstructionist parodies like "Smells Like Nirvana" and "(This Song's Just) Six Words Long," where the singer seems to heckle their own song from within.

The singer of "Achy Breaky Song" professes to despise Cyrus' pop-country smash, and rattles off a list of similarly reviled musical acts he'd rather endure than suffer through one more moment of Cyrus' breakout hit.

"Achy Breaky Song" is one of the most mean-spirited songs in Al's catalog. It's the rare instance where Al is unmistakably making fun of the song he's singing, and the singer by extension. Al adroitly captures Billy Ray's "Elvis as 1980s Chippendale's dancer" singing style and persona. But before long he and his collaborators get so understandably bored that they've overloaded the track with random silliness – kazoos, animal noises, the feigned flatulence of "Musical Mike" Kieffer – to compensate for the lack of inspiration at its core.

"Achy Breaky Song" got Al on country radio for the first time, but at a cost. "Achy Breaky Song" is a relative anomaly in Al's work, less because it's a country song and more that it's an uncharacteristically mean track from an artist who has thrived on being nice.

That said, I would love for Billy Ray to prove that it's all good between him and the man behind "Achy Breaky Song" by having Al hop on a remix of "Old Town Road." Forget joining the disparate worlds and sensibilities of Lil Nas X and Billy Ray Cyrus on a genre-mashing, generation-defining smash; putting Al on the remix would *really* bring our fractured nation together and get Lil Nas X and Billy Ray Cyrus back on the only chart that matters: Dr. Demento's Funny Five.

6.
TRAFFIC JAM

Prince had several noteworthy eccentricities. He was a bit of a flamboyant dresser. He spelled things in his own unique, unfortunately imitable way and also he once changed his name to an unpronounceable symbol.

Most inexplicably, Prince refused to let Al parody his songs. Normally that would be strikes one, two and three against an artist in my book. But if I might give the *Purple Rain* icon the highest praise I can give any human being, Prince was a greater creative genius than, yes, even "Weird Al" Yankovic. Prince was a greater artist than just about anyone.

He was an original in every conceivable way. He had his reasons for everything, even if they only seemed to make sense to him, so I respect Prince's decision not to let Al improve on his work, even if I don't agree with it.

Thankfully, Al doesn't need permission to record pastiches, particularly when they're as subtle as the Prince tribute "Traffic Jam."

"Traffic Jam" depicts stopped-up traffic as a circle of hell, an eminently relatable aggravation. Who hasn't known the irritation of being stuck in the kind of traffic jam that renders the road, in Al's words, "one big parking lot"? The irritated driver here could be in Godard's *Week End*, Fellini's *8 1/2* or that one R.E.M. music video ripping off *8 1/2:* like those frustrated souls, he sees the traffic stoppage he's in as not just a temporary headache, but a permanent state of existence.

But if Al's frustrated driver is hopelessly frozen, "Traffic Jam" zips along at a speedy clip, powered by Jim West's righteous shredding and Prince-like soloing and keyboardist Rubén Valtierra's hard-driving contributions.

I gained a new respect for "Traffic Jam" seeing it performed live. It's one of those songs that comes alive onstage and highlights the understated virtuosity of Al's crack band. To be able to play guitar like Prince is no small feat, but West is seemingly also able to play like everyone else as well.

"Traffic Jam" humorously chronicles a situation no one would ever want to find themselves in. But the song's infectious melody and jaunty good spirits make it incongruously pleasant, a fun exploration of an experience the singer wouldn't wish on his worst enemy.

"Traffic Jam" takes inspiration primarily from Prince's "Let's Go Crazy." Only instead of going crazy, Al and his band make going nowhere seem like an absolute blast.

7.
TALK SOUP

Video screens have long been staples of Al's concerts, images from Al's past competing for the audience's attention with the man himself. There's a pleasing synchronicity to this symphony of screens, reflecting each other at odd angles.

It's fitting for Al to be backed by screens in concert, because so much of his music is about screens and the central yet shifting role they play in our lives. In the 1980s, those screens were the television sets that positioned themselves at the epicenter of American life.

Then Al followed larger trends and began to replace TV screens in his songs with computer screens. Computers could perform borderline miraculous feats that have transformed how we live – namely, allowing us to watch television more effectively.

I'm talking about shows like E!'s *Talk Soup*, the Emmy-winning series that made memes out of goofy talk show snippets before memes were even born. E! asked Al to write a theme song for it, then inexplicably chose not to use what he came up with.

The singer of "Talk Soup" is obsessed with being one of the human oddities who populated daytime talk shows like *The Jerry Springer Show*, which helped housewives, heroin addicts, and the unemployed fill the hours with their underclass melodrama and frequent fisticuffs.

Why does this curious man, this self-professed "cross-dressin' alcoholic neo-Nazi porno star" want so badly to expose his eccentricities to the general public? He never quite specifies. He just seems convinced that it's best he publicly expose the kind of secrets most people would want to hide from their closest friends.

"Talk Soup" delights in the randomness and vulgarity of the tabloid realm, in its cynical, mercenary obsession with tawdry transgression.

Like "Midnight Star," "Talk Soup" captures an earlier, more innocent era of outrage, when people were still shocked by things like Bigfoot and Elvis sightings and not beaten down by the inexorable horror of everyday life. In "Talk Soup," tabloids are a fetid sewer that runs underneath pop culture.

In 2019, our whole culture is a fetid sewer lorded over by a reality competition host and close personal friend of *The National Enquirer* named Donald Trump. He's a creature of tabloid sleaze, a monster of id and ego and sex and power and petty feuds and vicious personal attacks and unhinged conspiracy theories.

The craziness satirized on "Talk Soup" is normal now. In 1993, the idea that a man would be so desperate to appear on screens that he'd gleefully debase himself was rooted in reality, but exaggerated to a comic degree. In 2019, it's the underlying basis of the ugly swamp known as "reality TV" – which was just a baby, really, when Al released this song, one which hasn't matured in the ensuing years. If anything, it's devolved.

So there's something incongruously nostalgic about this song's affectionate tribute to something that was already bad, but would only grow bigger and more malignant, as trash TV gave way to trash reality television, and then ultimately trash reality.

8.
LIVIN' IN THE FRIDGE

Not every hit endures, and a lot of classic songs never hit the pop charts. Pat Boone scored hit after hit after hit in the 1950s, while Big Star famously floundered commercially. Big Star failed to become big stars during their brief time as recording artists, but they've proven roughly a million times more important and influential than Boone.

"Livin' on the Edge" was one a series of comeback smashes Aerosmith scored in the late '80s and '90s, after kicking heroin and getting high on life and blockbuster commercial success. It hit the charts alongside other smashes like "Amazing," "Crying," "Janie's Got a Gun" and "Love in an Elevator" but hasn't endured like those songs for a very good reason.

For starters, "Livin' on the Edge" doesn't have an iconic music video over-sexualizing either Alicia Silverstone or (Steven's own daughter) Liv Tyler. But mostly, "Livin' on the Edge" has failed to endure because it's boring. It's one of those "socially conscious" songs veteran bands record when they have nothing to say yet feel compelled to say something all the same.

"Livin' on the Edge" is a well-intentioned, if exceedingly fuzzy, message song about how it's crazy the way the world is today, what with all the problems and social issues and whatnot, and what about the children and the future?

"Livin' in the Fridge" replaces the big social concerns of Aerosmith's original with a more personal sense of horror over the state of a refrigerator – one which long ago ceased to be a conventional repository for foodstuffs. With time and neglect, it became a living, breathing ecosystem, like a marsh or a bog that happens to contain opened, half-eaten, mold-ridden jars of Jiffy peanut butter.

As with "Taco Grande" and Al's other over-achieving food song parodies, there's something weirdly satisfying about how perfectly Al substitutes food obsessions for the original song's much different concerns. The song is filled with loving, perfect details, like the original song's moody background cries of "Ooh, ooh, ooh, ooh" getting replaced by a disgusted "Ew, ew, ew, ew."

By the end, the titular icebox has become a sentient, angry universe all its own, nearly as threatening as Jurassic Park. The song's obsession with mold recalls the stomach-churning culinary comedy of the early B-side "School Cafeteria," but with a slick, full-band sound that perfectly replicates the twisting, Eastern-sounding groove of Aerosmith's pompous original to ends both comic and stomach-churningly disgusting.

9.
SHE NEVER TOLD ME
SHE WAS A MIME

It takes audacity to bring into this sick, sad decaying world a composition called "She Never Told Me She Was a Mime," because the song violates a number of sacrosanct comedy rules simultaneously. First and foremost among these: never lower yourself to dealing with mimes.

Forget *Gilligan's Island* or Spam: jokes about mimes, and people not enjoying the artistry and craft of mime, is the definition of hack. The only thing comic sophisticates abhor as much as jokes about mimes is wordplay. Wordplay *about* mimes that doubles as a particularly corny dad joke? My goodness, "She Never Told Me She Was a Mime" is a veritable perfect storm of comedy-killers. Yet Al has a sneakily consistent way of making you laugh in spite of yourself.

"She Never Told Me She Was a Mime" is another Al tale of a romantic relationship bedeviled by a fatal flaw. In this case, things start off "perfectly normal" before our singer notices some alarming changes in his partner – namely that she's wearing white makeup and a black leotard.

Things escalate quickly. In our disappointed singer's eyes, this is no mere eccentricity or regrettable hobby. No, for him it is a "horrible secret" that has made his life "a living hell." Then comes the exquisitely cornball wordplay of the title. If the song's chorus doesn't make you roll your eyes so hard that they pop out of their sockets and fall to the floor, then you're not human. And if they do, I'm still not sure you're human, 'cause that'd be pretty weird, like the kind of thing you'd only see in a cartoon.

In the end, Al survived "She Never Told Me She Was a Mime" and several songs just as unforgivably/gloriously silly to become an enduring American icon.

"She Never Told Me She Was a Mime" may not be Al's best, or most sophisticated, or most important song. But it could very well be his stupidest. Considering Al also wrote and sang "Gotta Boogie" and "Party in the Leper Colony," that's no small feat.

10.
HARVEY THE WONDER HAMSTER

The highlight of Al's *AL-TV* MTV comedy specials were fake interviews between Al and huge pop stars, where real answers were juxtaposed with Al's "questions" to comic effect through the magic of constructive editing. The specials, which began in 1984 and would continue intermittently over the next two decades, afforded Al a new outlet to lampoon rock pretension.

AL-TV was good, cheap programming for MTV and unbeatable promotion for Al. It also introduced some classic running gags and inside jokes, most notably in Al's beloved pet, Harvey the Wonder Hamster.

Harvey figured prominently in *AL-TV*, including a clip where Al not only talks up his furry little buddy, but sings the official "Harvey the Wonder Hamster" theme song before cavalierly chucking his pal off the roof of a building. It's a jarring gag, both because Al is pretending to casually commit murder and because Al is so famously an animal lover.

Yes, both Harvey the Wonder Hamster and his theme song had been around a while when Al decided to pay tribute to the cute little guy on record. He'd go on to play an even bigger role in another beloved Al cult oddity too good and smart to be successful: *The Weird Al Show*.

"Harvey the Wonder Hamster" is the inverse of "Attack of the Radioactive Hamsters from a Planet Near Mars." Harvey, adorably, doesn't do much at all, while those nasty alien hamsters are doing way, way, way too much in terms of destroying the world and whatnot.

11.
WAFFLE KING

"Waffle King" is a tribute to a very specific era in Peter Gabriel's career, long after he stopped being a poster boy for Prog Rock theatricality and established himself as a solo artist to be reckoned with.

"Waffle King" is a pastiche of Gabriel's mid-1980s music video smashes "Big Time" and "Sledgehammer." It pays homage to a wildly successful period when Gabriel devoted himself to making big, cartoony pop songs for kids with ubiquitous music videos utilizing the same stop-motion animation technique as Al's Grammy-nominated video for "Jurassic Park."

The crazed egotist singing "Waffle King" doesn't just think making excellent waffles makes him special: he thinks it makes him superior to everyone else on earth. He doesn't just want people to eat his tasty treats: he wants to be worshiped as an angry, waffle-making god. The Soup Nazi is a mellow hippie compared to this waffle-selling sociopath.

The Waffle King is a true believer in the "power of the waffle," but mostly he believes in his own innate superiority to the point that he thinks his waffle-addicted fans should grovel at his feet like the worthless peons they are.

Despite being a "Weird Al" Yankovic song, "Waffle King" isn't about food so much as it is about egomania. Waffles are merely the fluffy, syrupy vehicle that transports the Waffle King to a realm of godlike arrogance.

Like "Achy Breaky Song," current events have lent this trifle a new relevance. The "very stable genius" in the White House lends an unmistakable contemporary resonance to the song's satirical depiction of a breakfast mogul with a textbook case of Narcissistic Personality Disorder: both are showmen and entrepreneurs who think success in business renders them superior to the rest of humanity. Both are extremely wrong in that conviction, as well as many others.

12.
BOHEMIAN POLKA

When *Alapalooza* **was released, "Bohemian Rhapsody"** had roared back to life the year prior with the most famous scene in Penelope Spheeris' *Wayne's* World – the feature film adaptation of a TV show sketch about television that bears a distinct resemblance to *UHF.* In that respect, the song was plugged into the cultural zeitgeist on multiple levels, but it also had the benefit of being timeless.

"Bohemian Polka" is an outlier among Al's polkas. It represents the first, and only time that he devoted the polka on his album not to a group of songs but rather to a single song. Then again, "song" doesn't do justice to the majesty of

Queen's creation, which is at once big and ambitious, a typically theatrical musical "statement" and an enormous goof.

But "Bohemian Polka" is less of a departure from Al's other polkas than it might appear, because "Bohemian Rhapsody" is essentially a miniature medley itself, bringing together disparate elements that might as well be from different songs or even different groups. This makes Mercury's timelessly cheeky magnum opus a natural fit for Al to give the polka treatment.

The man emoting wildly through "Bohemian Polka" is overwhelmed with trembling, dark, overwhelming feelings – despair, hopelessness, self-hatred, ennui, anger. But because this is a polka, the overall tone is nevertheless upbeat.

By the time Al recorded "Bohemian Polka" he'd abandoned the gimmick of recording rock songs with an accordion, except for the polka medley. The accordion makes a big comeback here, and its signature wackiness as an instrument serves to push "Bohemian Polka" further from the hyper-produced lushness of its inspiration into something more *MAD* magazine than pop-opera.

"Bohemian Polka" ends *Alapalooza* on an appropriately energetic, madcap note. Al frequently puts his darkest, most ambitious and sometimes brilliant song as the final track on the album; while this doesn't measure up to previous album-closers like "You Don't Love Me Anymore" or "The Biggest Ball of Twine in Minnesota" it's delightful enough to justify its place of distinction all the same.

BAD HAIR DAY (1996)

1.
AMISH PARADISE

The origin of the Coolio-versus-"Weird Al" Yankovic beef began decades before Al parodied "Gangsta Paradise." It started when Stevie Wonder discovered that he could use a sophisticated synthesizer called the Yamaha GX-1 to replicate an entire string section. Wonder used this innovation, along with assists from Hare Krishna musicians and a gospel choir, to give his despairing 1976 song "Pastime Paradise" an almost overwhelming sense of majesty.

With little more than a synthesizer, percussion and voices, Wonder created an overpowering wall of sound that reaches skyward to the heavens while conveying the bottomless pain of the blues. "Pastime Paradise" is not just a song; it's a production. It's an extravaganza. It's a masterpiece.

Just as Al draws on the intensity of the songs he parodies, Coolio, guest vocalist L.V. and producer Doug Rasheed draw upon the solemn gospel glory of "Pastime Paradise" to create something epic and melodramatic, sweepingly orchestral yet as intimate as a dying hustler's prayer for redemption.

Stevie Wonder and Coolio took us to church on "Pastime Paradise" and "Gangsta's Paradise" respectively, but Al took this singularly soaring sonic bed and made it the basis for an extended Amish joke.

"Amish Paradise" is the original White and Nerdy anthem, a tribute to humility delivered through the least humble vessel imaginable: a melodramatic rap song. The comic juxtaposition of Hip Hop arrogance and *really* old time religion fuels the song comedically, but on a larger level it's about the arrogance and hypocrisy of the faithful.

The plainly dressed rapper, truly a creature of the VERY Old School, boasts of his Christ-like ability to literally "turn the other cheek" after a non-Luddite kicked him in the posterior. But his actions are anything but selfless when he brags unbecomingly, "I'll be laughing my head off when he's burning in hell."

The Luddite antagonizing haters is devoid of true humility. His piousness has a specific purpose: to win him a cushy seat in heaven while all the TV-watching, modern-convenience-dependent philistines around him roast in hell.

It can be easy to forget how massive "Gangsta Paradise" was: it was the top-selling single of 1995. Though "Amish Paradise" is huge in the context of Al's career and took up a lot of cultural space, it never rose higher than 53 on the singles chart.

Al's parody was nowhere near as successful as the song that inspired it, but the songs are equally well remembered today. Coolio might have won the sales battle by a decisive margin but Al won the war. Today, Coolio is known primarily for a few unmissable hits and an unusual hairstyle (for him, *every* day is a bad hair day). And last, but not least, being that dude who thought it was a good idea to publicly beef with "Weird Al" Yankovic.

2.
EVERYTHING YOU
KNOW IS WRONG

"Weird Al" Yankovic and They Might Be Giants reign supreme as towering colossuses of the funny music world.

Both acts occupy valuable real estate in the suggestible minds of multiple generations of young geeks, for whom they aren't just favorite musicians but personal heroes.

Like David Bowie and Talking Heads for spooky kids a little later in their development, "Weird Al" Yankovic and They Might Be Giants serve as guides through the uncertain currents of childhood and adolescence. They let misfits know that it is perfectly all right to be, well, weird. In fact, it's far superior to the alternative.

Channeling the spirit of They Might Be Giants on "Everything You Know Is Wrong" liberated Al from the prison of rhyming. Instead of being limited to rhyming couplets, words spill out here in a rapid-fire, stream-of-consciousness torrent in verses that start out gleefully absurd then get more demented, before a mysterious figure up-ends the protagonist's already fractured sense of reality with the titular burst of hard truth.

Al perished in many of his songs in the 1980s. Characters would begin songs alive and well and end them victims of a nuclear holocaust or dead by some other means. That was a big theme in the Reagan decade: we were all adorably afraid of nuclear Armageddon.

"Everything You Know Is Wrong" finds Al returning to this fertile ground in the song's third verse, when he cheerfully observes, "I was just about to mail a letter to my evil twin/When I got a nasty paper cut/And, well, to make a long story short/It got infected and I died."

But in this particularly silly "Weird Al" Yankovic song, death isn't anything near an end. Our luckless hero ends up having a complicated relationship with Saint Peter, who doesn't care for his Nehru jacket. In punishment, our protagonist is doomed to spend eternity next to an ice machine, as every day Saint Peter screams out the titular warning.

Like the Oingo Boingo pastiche "You Make Me," there's something wonderfully Seussian about the way the music moves here. Al captures the Technicolor absurdity and quirkiness of the They Might Be Giants aesthetic perfectly, as well as the runaway sense of momentum that characterizes their most infectious songs.

Like "Dare to Be Stupid," "Everything You Know Is Wrong" is aggressively nonsensical and undeniably anthemic. It's the perfect fusion of Al and the two Johns that underlines how much these two acts have in common, while also establishing what makes them unique.

3.
CAVITY SEARCH

"Hold Me, Thrill Me, Kiss Me, Kill Me" is a relic of the curious phase of U2's career when they decided to eschew the somber earnestness of their early work for trendy irony without understanding irony any more than Alanis Morrissette did.

"Cavity Search" finds Al returning to the shallow well of dental humor that he first mined in "Toothless People," one of the few duds in his discography. "Cavity Search" is a big improvement over "Toothless People" but it suffers from parodying one of U2's most forgettable singles.

Still, even undistinguished U2 is U2, and Al and his band do a masterful job of capturing the pleasantly disorienting mood of the original. "Cavity Search" hijacks Bono's stylized, ironic, half-sarcastic croon and the song's electronic atmospherics, capturing the alternating feelings of horror, disorientation and loopy joy endemic to being pumped full of Novocain and nitrous oxide – essential ingredients for a professional sadist to start sticking sharp objects in your poor bleeding mouth for your own good.

"Cavity Search" is sometimes too evocative. When the unmistakable sound of a dental drill enters the sonic mix, I experienced a weird Pavlovian jab of pain in my mouth. Just hearing that awful instrument of pain brought back agonizing memories of trips to the dentist. "Cavity Search" might not be funny, but it is at the very least painfully amusing (emphasis on the pain).

4.
CALLIN' IN SICK

In the middle of *Bad Hair Day*, Al, whose songs often deal with outlandish phenomena such as Slime Creatures from Outer Space, Yuletide nuclear Armageddons and Spam consumption, gets unexpectedly relatable. "Cavity Search" and "Callin' in Sick" both chronicle universal experiences: respectively, the terror of being in the dentist chair and the half-assed freedom that comes with taking a sick day.

"Callin' in Sick" is Al's post-Nirvana/"Smells Like Teen Spirit" grunge pastiche. Now, we all know that the only "jobs" grunge rockers have involve being depressed and getting addicted to heroin. But "Callin' in Sick" imagines a world in which they work the same kinds of jobs that normal folks do.

The groove here feels effortlessly authentic. It's easy to imagine some long-haired, flannel-clad moaner mumbling something quasi-profound over these crunchy guitars. For grunge rockers were men of intensity, men of drama. They were men who wore too much eye liner and struck tortured poses while bleating, cow-like, in the preferred post-Eddie Vedder style.

The vibe of "Callin' in Sick" is dramatic, but the lyrics are low-key and observational. Al adopts the perspective of an ennui-addled wage slave who decides to engage in everyday rebellion by blowing off work. Al channels the escapist fantasies of clock-watchers everywhere when he insists, "When I'm sick of takin' abuse/I just make up some lame excuse/Freedom's just seven digits away!"

The music and lyrics take on a real bipolar vibe; in the second verse, his list of options for the day include such surreal wastes of time as shining pennies, cleaning his lava lamp, watching *Ernest Goes to Camp*, counting his hair and burping his Tupperware.

By the next verse, however, he's undeservedly full of himself, just like the Waffle King before him – boasting of being truly alive for the first time and blessed with godlike invincibility. He's back to brooding in the next verse, but for a brief, shining moment, escaping the daily grind made him feel better than everyone else.

5.
THE ALTERNATIVE POLKA

The pretension-puncturing, whoopee cushion prankishness of Al's polka medleys was particularly essential during the post-*Nevermind* period, when alternative rock dominated the airwaves with a watered-down version of college rock from previous decades.

In the mid-'90s, Al played with both the songs and the sounds of the alternative rock "revolution." Lollapalooza – the silly name that equally-silly human being Perry Farrell gave his traveling carnival of arts and culture – inspired the title of *Alapalooza*. For *Bad Hair Day*'s polka medley, he chose the title "The Alternative Polka," a medley heavy on what was then known as alternative rock.

We begin with the familiar sound of a slide guitar from Beck's "Loser" that almost instantly shifts from the stoned rhythm of the original to the oompah-band craziness of the polka. The songs (or rather song snippets) that follow alternate between songs that have faded in the public memory (R.E.M.'s "Bang and Blame," Red Hot Chili Peppers' "My Friends") and smashes so ubiquitous that decades later we all know the words to them. Take Sheryl Crow's "All I Wanna Do," or Smashing Pumpkins' "Bullet with Butterfly Wings," whose generation-defining whine of "Despite all my rage I am still just a rat in a cage" cries out angrily for the polka medley tribute the same way the Who's "My Generation" did.

Medleys afford the squeaky-clean Al an opportunity to borrow the scuzzy sensibilities of less family-friendly rockers. That may not be the explicit point of the polka medleys, but that's a consistent pleasure of these manic mix-'em-ups all the same.

On "Alternative Polka," Al lovingly channels Trent Reznor at his most Hot Tropic transgressive when he vows on "Closer" to make love in a purposefully animalistic fashion as a means of ascending to a higher level of spirituality. Al gets nearly as dirty on Alanis Morrissette's "You Oughta Know," but trades sex for drugs by closing the medley with the section of Green Day's "Basket Case" that asks, "Am I just paranoid?/Or am I just stoned?" It's impossible to imagine a non-polka Al song ending this way. That's what makes it the perfect ending for a medley.

6.
SINCE YOU'VE BEEN GONE

Most acts successfully manage to go their entire careers without releasing even a single *a cappella* song, to the delight of their fans and relief of their management. But Al isn't just any musician.

"Since You've Been Gone" fits in perfectly with Al's songs about romantic relationships. Love and romantic entanglements are frequently bittersweet in pop music. In Al's world, however, there's all kinds of bitterness but no sweetness – unless we're talking about the melodies of "You Don't Love Me Anymore" and "One More Minute."

The singer of "Since You've Been Gone" is in a whole world of pain, but it's not the abstract ache of a typical love song. For Al, being apart from his object of desire and derision makes him feel like he's "chewing on tinfoil" and has "got a great big mouthful of cod liver oil."

Al manages to fit a surprising number of graphic, painful and surreal images of visceral physical pain, from a two-ton bowling ball being dropped on his feet to having a red-hot cactus shoved up his nose in just eighty-two seconds, and even manages to close things out with a punchline and a twist.

After letting us know how terrible life has been since the singer's partner left him, he closes by confiding that he feels almost as bad as he did when they were still together.

There's a time and place for *a cappella*. "Since You've Been Gone" establishes that time is somewhere in the eighty-to-eighty-five-second range.

7.
GUMP

The **"Lump"** **parody** **"Gump"** is representative of Al's big singles from this period. It's a movie song directly tied to a cinematic sensation – in this case Robert Zemeckis' controversial smash *Forrest Gump,* which won the hearts of the American people with its smugly satirical, moderately racist, moderately sexist exploration of the saintliness of mindless conformity.

The Presidents of the United States of America's "Lump" is the ultimate earworm: a sadistically infectious pop punk annoyance that takes up space in your psyche the way a sonic leech might. It's evocative and silly and mean in a nonsensical fashion.

With "Gump," Al took a song with silly lyrics that sounds goofy and used it as a sturdy vessel to comedically explore the intellectual shortcomings and life experiences of Forrest Gump. *Forrest Gump* was bursting with incident: Gump's life was just one thing after another, which affords Al ample choices in terms of what to include and what to leave out.

Forrest Gump gives Al much to work with just when it comes to the character's incongruously lowbrow interactions with one-term Democratic Presidents from the 1960s. "Gump" references both the endlessly mourned John F. Kennedy and his less charming successor when Al sings of the title character, "Gump was a big celebrity/He told JFK that he really had to pee" and "He went to the White House, showed LBJ his butt."

For someone who has been making people laugh for forty years, little in Al's oeuvre qualifies as problematic. So it's a little jarring to hear him toss out a line like "His girlfriend Jenny was kind of a slut."

It's out of character for Al to use a word like "slut." He's usually more cautious. But I'm perhaps being unfair in applying a 21st-century conception of cultural sensitivity to a comedy song from 1996.

"Lump" is not a great song, or even a particularly good song. But dear sweet blessed Lord, is it ever catchy. "Gump" is even more of an earworm, with phrases like "His buddy Bubba was a shrimp-lovin' man/His friend with no legs he called Lieutenant Dan" and "Gump sat alone on a bench in the park/My name is Forrest, he'd casually remark" that wedge themselves deep in your subconscious and refuse to leave.

8.
I'M SO SICK OF YOU

Elvis Costello is the master of the witty insult, a sneering poet of prickly tell-offs. With "I'm So Sick of You," Al takes his inspiration's highbrow cleverness in a lowbrow direction. If a song like "Alison" is a musical *New Yorker* short story full of literary details and devastating turns of phrase, then "I'm So Sick of You" is a particularly scatological *MAD* magazine cartoon.

When Al writes about romance, or rather "romance," his creepy Casanovas are usually to blame for screwing everything up. But in this case, it's the girlfriend who's a waking nightmare: she's a toenail-chomping, back hair-sprouting, knuckle-cracking, drooling Neanderthal.

The person being comically excoriated here isn't just hopelessly inadequate as a girlfriend, wife or partner: they're downright sub-human. When the singer frets, "I've never dated anyone this low on the food chain," he doesn't seem to be exaggerating.

"I'm So Sick of You" nails the details of an early to mid-period Elvis Costello rocker: the New Wave roller rink keyboards, the pummeling drums, the sneeringly nasty nasal lead vocals and cheekily chipper Beach Boys-style backup vocals. Al's affection for rock's second most important Elvis comes through in every lovingly gross lyric and stomach-churning image.

"I'm So Sick of You" is as mean spirited as Al gets, but that's only because he's channeling Elvis Costello's misogyny.

Is "I'm So Sick of You" funny enough to justify its uncharacteristic snarkiness? Thanks to wonderfully tart sentiments like "You've got inhuman body odor/You've got the hair of a boxing promoter," the answer is yes.

9.
SYNDICATED INC.

Bad Hair Day closes on a perversely Soul Asylum-centric note. Of the album's final four songs, one is a parody of a lesser Soul Asylum single, the "Misery" parody "Syndicated Inc." and another is the "Black Gold" pastiche "The Night Santa Went Crazy." For a brief stretch, Al derived as much inspiration from these alt-rock also-rans as he did from Michael Jackson.

What's even stranger about Al's mid-career obsession with Dave Pirner is that Al didn't take on "Runaway Train" – a monster single whose groaning earnestness and good intentions would make it ideal for parody. Instead, Al spoofed "Misery" from Soul Asylum's less successful follow up 1995 album *Let Your Dim Light Shine*.

Al made things too easy for himself with "Syndicated Inc." He returned yet again to television for inspiration, one of his most fruitful yet exhausted subjects. The two go hand in hand. It's precisely because Al is so uniquely good at writing funny songs about television that he returns to it so often.

Syndication is such a big subject that anything that's not first-run, sports or news qualifies. Al is able to draw upon decades of easily recognizable, easily rhymable television staples like *Three's Company*, *All in the Family*, *Dynasty* and *Laverne & Shirley*.

About halfway through "Syndicated Inc.," Al throws a musical curveball in the form of an instrument Al tends to reserve for polka medleys: accordion. The squeezebox sounds surprisingly at home here. But it also feels like Al doesn't seem overly enthusiastic about either the half-forgotten song he's spoofing or the overly familiar subject matter.

"Syndicated Inc." is a song about compulsive rerun consumption that feels like a bit of a rerun itself.

10.
I REMEMBER LARRY

"I Remember Larry" is a glorious throwback to the highly synthesized, extravagantly produced New Wave of the late 1970s and 1980s – specifically the solo albums of Hilly Michaels, who rivals Tonio K. and Southern Culture on the Skids for the distinction of most obscure cult artist to inspire a "Weird Al" Yankovic pastiche.

Michaels may be better known as the drummer for Sparks, another titan of quirky musical comedy that inspired one of Al's best originals in "Virus Alert." But Sparks isn't exactly a household name in the United States either.

"I Remember Larry" opens with Al energetically reminiscing about his wacky, traumatic relationship with the titular jokester – a demented, Puck-like imp whose conception of a "prank" generally entails committing an unforgivable crime.

Some of Larry's actions fall loosely under the category of "juvenile mischief": making phony calls, doling out wedgies, pantsing people, the old "Ben Gay in the jock strap" routine. But a good number of Larry's offenses qualify as criminal and psychotic, like dumping toxic waste on lawns and cutting cars in two.

What at first appears to be the song of a good-natured masochist willing to put up with anything in the name of fun turns sadistic when the revenge-crazed singer spends the final verse recounting how he got back at Larry by murdering him. The song sounds as upbeat as ever, only now it's chronicling Larry being abducted and left for dead.

Like the Hilly Michaels music he's saluting, "I Remember Larry" sounds full and ambitious, with trippy, psychedelic backwards background vocals. Actually, that trippy closing part contains one of Al's most audacious gags: if you play part of "I Remember Larry" backwards, you can unmistakably hear Al singing, "Wow, you must have an awful lot of free time on your hands."

Even without that brilliant bit of tomfoolery, "I Remember Larry" would still qualify as a demented gem that's more than just a pretty good gag.

11.
PHONY CALLS

Al is a historian of what I like to call "The Old Jokes." The Old Jokes have always been with us, at least since Vaudeville. They're passed down as folklore, a wacky oral tradition. The wonderful TLC "Waterfalls" parody "Phony Calls" is a loving tribute to the gloriously cheesy subset of the Old Jokes known as the Old Prank Call Gags.

The great thing about the Old Prank Call Gags is that while technology and society are constantly changing and evolving, the Old Prank Call Gags never do. As far as I know, there are no New Prank Call Gags. No one is prank calling strangers these days asking them if their internet is running and, should they answer affirmatively, suggesting that they go out and catch it. No, the Old Prank Call Gags are the same as they were in 1957 or 1967.

So while "Phony Calls" is lush, state of the art R&B rooted in one of the best and most beloved pop songs of the past thirty years, comedically it's frozen in a pre-Jerky Boys conception of prank calling as innocent mischief.

"Phony Calls" is a miniature encyclopedia of "classic" prank calls that were never funny, even once, yet nevertheless endure because of corny dads like myself and songs like "Phony Calls."

"Phony Calls" is spectacularly, transcendently silly, but Al's vocals perfectly capture the moralistic, scolding tone of the original. "Waterfalls" was, and remains, a fundamentally serious song about AIDS, drug addiction and resisting life's temptations.

Where "Waterfalls" was about very Important Social Issues, "Phony Calls" is about schoolyard mischief. Just hearing that warm, unmistakable beat induces a warm, nostalgic flood of emotions, as did hearing Prince Albert in a can being referenced reverently and cameos from Hank Azaria and Nancy Cartwright as Moe and Bart Simpson, respectively.

With "Phony Calls," Al used an intoxicating new groove and a pair of nifty cameos to sell some wonderfully ancient, well-worn gags in a time-warp goof that ranks among Al's very best parodies.

12.
THE NIGHT SANTA WENT CRAZY

"The Night Santa Went Crazy" is an album-closer, which tends to be the darkest, weirdest and most adventurous track on any given album.

Dark, weird and adventurous certainly describes "The Night Santa Went Crazy." In composing a second Christmas classic suitable only for the most morbid of carolers (we're talking people who've seen *The Nightmare Before Christmas* multiple times *and* have merch), Al seems to have challenged himself to write a Yuletide anthem darker, more disturbing and more family-unfriendly than "Christmas at Ground Zero."

Al succeeded by re-imagining Santa Claus not as the kindly, twinkly-eyed living saint of the popular imagination, but as an overworked and under-compensated everyman who finally snaps and takes out his pent-up rage on his poor reindeer, whom he slaughters *en masse* in ways Al describes with ghoulish relish.

"The Night Santa Went Crazy" is Al's version of Kinky Friedman's "The Ballad of Charles Whitman." Only instead of chronicling the dark deeds of a real-life murderer, Al is imagining our culture's ultimate good guy as a man pissed off at having gotten a "raw deal," who decides to transgress societal norms against killing a whole bunch of people and/or flying animals.

The song is a pastiche of "Black Gold," one of those non-"Runaway Train" Soul Asylum hits no one remembers. But in its gutsy roots rock and novelistic working-class detail, it feels a little like Bruce Springsteen as well. "The Night Santa Went Crazy" is unassuming and middle of the road, which helps it get away with being brutal for a song by an artist with a huge family audience.

The "Extra Gory" version of "The Night Santa Went Crazy" is worth checking out for the ways in which it deviates from the original. The plot diverges, and characters meet different, darker fates than they do here. Think of the extra gory version as a sonic alternate ending to a fictional Christmas movie no child should ever be allowed to see, but that every sick little kid who grew up worshiping "Weird Al" Yankovic dearly wished existed.

RUNNING
WITH
SCISSORS
(1999)

1.
THE SAGA BEGINS

It is at this point in the story that Al's career and mine begin to overlap. When *Running with Scissors* was released, I had an opportunity to leverage my nascent power as the 23-year-old head writer of *The A.V Club* into getting to meet "Weird Al" Yankovic – first when he stopped by the *Onion* office to visit a sacred satirical mecca and my then-editor Stephen Thompson, and later that night when we got to meet Al backstage after seeing him in concert.

It was one of the biggest thrills of my career and life up to that point. Who could have imagined how much our paths would cross in the decades ahead?

So if I'm particularly nostalgic for 1999's *Running with Scissors*, it's partially because of my fondness for that period in my life, when all things seemed possible. But I'm also nostalgic for *The Phantom Menace,* the prequel that inspired "The Saga Begins." That's strange, because the first *Star Wars* prequel is famously terrible.

It would be more accurate to say that I'm nostalgic for *The Phantom Menace* as a cultural event. I look back fondly at the incredible anticipation it engendered before the crashing disappointment that followed. Geeks didn't have quite the stranglehold on pop culture back then. These days, everything seems custom-made for geeks; they *are* the mainstream. But in 1999, *The Phantom Menace* still felt like something the geek gods had created specifically for true believers.

At the time of its release, "The Saga Begins" seemed almost suspiciously timely. It came out a little over a month after the film was released, when the cultural consensus hadn't yet devolved from "Well, this is not quite what we expected" to "I demand a personal apology from Mr. Lucas for this abomination."

Al's timing for "The Saga Begins" was perfect. He was latching onto the hottest phenomenon in pop culture, something that he had a long, distinguished, happy history with already. In "The Saga Begins," Al miraculously alchemized the rusted aluminum of *The Phantom Menace*'s plot and characters, two of the film's many fatal flaws, into one of his best-loved songs.

The plot of *The Phantom Menace* is terrible. It's convoluted, bogged down with unnecessary subplots and characters, and so difficult to follow that Lucas had to resort to one of the most rightfully mocked opening scrolls this side of *Alone in the Dark* just so it could make a lick of sense.

On "The Saga Begins," Al transforms Lucas' leaden mythology and hopelessly clumsy plotting into a freewheeling, light on its feet adventure yarn that skips along merrily where its inspiration lumbered.

Listening to "The Saga Begins" in 2019 I found myself grateful that I was merely listening to one of my favorite musicians glide breezily through *The Phantom Menace*'s plot instead of having to watch all the nonsense involving midichlorians and the Trade Federation.

Where George Lucas failed, Al succeeded. Unlike the racist stereotype-based physical comedy of Jar Jar Binks, "The Saga Begins" genuinely made people laugh and continues to do so at Al concerts. There, it's not just a staple, but a sing-along moment of profound spiritual communion, a beloved geek ritual.

Unlike *Episode I,* "The Saga Begins" ended up pleasing *Star Wars* fans in the short and long term. It's the element of *The Phantom Menace* that has aged the best and endured the most.

2.
MY BABY'S IN LOVE
WITH EDDIE VEDDER

In 1992, Al released a song that defined a generation with "Smells Like Nirvana." It was received at the time as the ultimate grunge anthem, easily beating out its inspiration, Nirvana's "Smells Like Teen Spirit." "Smells Like Nirvana" isn't just one of Al's best parodies: it's one of the most important songs ever written.

So it makes sense that Al would revisit the subject of rock star pretension, grunge-style, later in the decade with the Zydeco detour "My Baby's in Love with Eddie Vedder." Alas, Al revisited this subject too late. The song would have had more satirical thrust if it had come out earlier in the decade, when Grunge was more in vogue; but by 1999, Vedder had peaked as a cultural figure. So while Al's tribute/satire of the famously tormented pop star is funny and pointed, it lacked the timeliness of "Smells Like Nirvana."

If Grunge is all about gloom and doom and heavy riffs, heroin addiction and mournful, moaning vocals, then zydeco is all about high spirits, party music and entertainment. Zydeco celebrates the sweetness of life; grunge prays for the sweet release of death.

In "Smells Like Nirvana," Al used Cobain's own music to satirically destroy him by portraying him as a rock star who mumbles a lot. With "My Baby's in Love with Eddie Vedder," the underlying musical satirical conceit is like that of Al's polka medleys: using some of the happiest, goofiest, most upbeat music imaginable to genially mock rock at its most dour. In the 1990s at least, the Pearl Jam frontman epitomized Gen-X angst.

Lyrically, the gag's right there in the title: treating a ponderous "artist" as a dreamboat who has the singer's girlfriend hot and bothered.

It's funny because it is true. Kurt Cobain, Eddie Vedder, Chris Cornell, Scott Weiland and Gavin Rossdale became superstars because of their voices and catchy tunes, but also because they were all extraordinarily handsome. They were grunge heartthrobs whose gloomy good looks got heartbeats racing as much as their songs did.

"Smells Like Nirvana" was half tribute, half loving mockery of Kurt Cobain and the song that began his rocket ride to superstardom. "My Baby's in Love with Eddie Vedder" is less loving and more cutting. In his maiden foray into the world of zydeco, Al paints a withering satirical picture of the "Alive" hit-maker as a caricature of the brooding, pretentious Artiste.

"My Baby's in Love with Eddie Vedder" is a worthy companion piece to "Smells Like Nirvana" and one of Al's strongest, most direct statements about rock star hypocrisy. It's also a straight-up zydeco banger that, unfortunately, seems to have come out at least a half-decade too late.

3.
PRETTY FLY FOR A RABBI

One of the many miracles of Al's career is that he's a white man who has done a fair amount of ethnic material through the years, yet has remained beloved.

Al has slipped inside the personas, costumes and sonic outfits of pop icons of various races, genders, body sizes and ethnicities while always hanging onto his fundamental Al-ness, and with it the public's love (and understanding).

Al's public knows that songs like "Pretty Fly for a Rabbi" (a spoof of the Offspring's "Pretty Fly for a White Guy") are done with love, care and attention to detail. Consequently, they're quick to laugh and slow to take offense.

"Pretty Fly for a Rabbi" doubles as a makeshift encyclopedia of the most commonly employed Yiddish phrases. But it's also a collection of Jewish stereotypes, most notably the one involving Jews being cheap and bargain-hungry. Al doubles down on this line of humor, bragging of his subject, "He does his own accounting," "He shops at discount stores, not just any will suffice/He has to find a bargain, 'cause he won't pay retail price" and "He never acts *meshuggah* and he's hardly a *schlemiel*/ But if you wanna haggle, oy, he'll make you such a deal!"

There are ample jokes about Jews loving to haggle and chase bargains, but they're done with such affection that only a real *schmuck* could find them offensive. This faithful recycling of stereotypes made less of an impression on me than Al's extensive and impressive use of Yiddish slang – as well as his mastery of not just the themes of Jewish comedy, but the specific rhythms and inflections as well.

A lot of people think Al is Jewish. "Pretty Fly for a Rabbi" will do nothing to discourage that belief. Al fluently speaks the language of Jewish humor, with the ease and grace of a native speaker. It's appropriate that Al's big foray into the world of

Judaism is defined by a very Jewish love of the possibilities of language and sounds, Yiddish and English alike.

As a Jew, I'm flattered by "Pretty Fly for a Rabbi" rather than insulted. It's not just *kosher* for Al to put out a song like this despite not technically being a member of the tribe; it's worth *kvelling* about!

4.
THE WEIRD AL SHOW THEME

Succinctness is one of Al's greatest gifts. He's not afraid to stretch things out, "Albuquerque"-style, but he generally doesn't need much time to make an impression.

Al has never crammed more into a tiny space than he did on "The Weird Al Show Theme," one of many unfairly obscure treasures from Al's foray into Saturday morning TV.

"The Weird Al Show Theme" is at once a real TV show theme for a show that actually existed and an absurdist parody of TV show themes.

In classic theme show tradition, "The Weird Al Show Theme" must work musically while explaining the show's conceit. It sets up the basic premise of the show, which is so insane that it plays like a riotous parody of the ultimate convoluted kid's show conceit: for reasons never explained, Al lives in a cave twenty miles under the earth's surface, and is given his own TV show as a reward for saving a hotshot TV bigwig (who was sunbathing in a nearby forest) from a bear trap.

That is the abbreviated, CliffsNotes version. You'd think that's all seventy-four seconds would allow for. You would be wrong.

The humor in "The Weird Al Show Theme" is rooted partially in in-jokes, references to hamsters and spatulas and mind-blowing tater tots and accordions that are like little audio Easter eggs for Al fans. It also traffics in the comedy of randomness, funny words and phrases like "nasal decongestant factory", "lederhosen in a vat of sour cream" and a "mighty fine jellybean and pickle sandwich."

"The Weird Al Show Theme" is overflowing with memorable, zany details that turn out to be exquisitely irrelevant. The genius central gag of "The Weird Al Show Theme" is to set up the appropriately surreal and cartoonish premise of *The Weird Al Show*, but to do so in a way that all but buries that premise in an avalanche of irrelevant details.

Only the second half of "The Weird Al Show Theme" relates to the actual premise of *The Weird Al Show*. The rest is full of hilarious non sequiturs. "The Weird Al Show Theme" unpacks an enormous amount of information in a small amount of time, much of it screamingly, comically irrelevant. Yet it wraps up so quickly that Al spends the last quarter of the song vamping.

On "The Weird Al Show Theme," Al only needs seventy-four seconds to conduct a veritable seminar on silliness.

5.
JERRY SPRINGER

We first encountered the grubby underbelly of the Fourth Estate known as tabloids/trash TV in Al's definitive statement on the subject, the *Weekly World News/National Enquirer* homage "Midnight Star." That song was made with a degree of affection for its subject matter absent from the Barenaked Ladies "One Week" parody "Jerry Springer."

"Jerry Springer" found Al parodying a song that was already a comedy song, a goof from folks who didn't take themselves too seriously. "One Week" doesn't just try to be funny: it tries way too hard to be funny.

The most novel element of "One Week" is its structure, where a sung, college-rock chorus about a complicated romantic relationship alternates with improvised, completely unrelated stream-of-consciousness rap verses.

"Jerry Springer" keeps the sonic structure of its inspiration, with crooned choruses and rapped verses, but this time everything, unfortunately, is rooted in some of the least original subject matter this side of *Gilligan's Island*: the parade of human oddities that constituted the revolving cast of *The Jerry Springer Show* in its heyday.

In "Jerry Springer," "Wholesome Al" Yankovic descends into the gutter of tabloid television and gets a little soiled by its ugliness. Al uses words and phrases you never thought he would, and that he clearly never came close to using again.

Then again, 1999 was a very different era culturally. It was a time when phrases like "s** male," "crack ho" and "slut" were certainly not considered polite, but also weren't considered as offensive as they are today.

The subject matter for "Jerry Springer" is so exhausted that there's a limit to how funny even the most inspired parody can be, and Al and his band brush up hard against it here.

While "One Week" inspired one of Al's weaker parodies, it's opening two words (that forceful "It's been...") was spun into comic gold as a deathless *Comedy Bang! Bang!* running joke by Al's pal Scott Aukerman. So at least someone in the *Comedy Bang! Bang!* family got something special and lasting out of one of the more irritating hits from an unusually annoying period in pop music.

6.
GERMS

The Nine Inch Nails tribute "Germs" is predictably one of the darkest and most sinister pastiches Al has recorded. Al and his collaborators nail (no pun intended) the distinctive sonic elements of the Nine Inch Nails song "Terrible Lie" and to a lesser extent, "Closer": the woozy, ominous broken ventilator groove, the skittering, ominous synths, the wild oscillations between singing in a heightened whisper and an agitated scream.

"Germs" sounds *exactly* like what it's supposed to sound like, to the point where my dumb brain has chosen to categorize it as a Nine Inch Nails song as well as a "Weird Al" Yankovic song.

With Al's originals, the humor sometimes comes from the incongruity of the artist Al is paying tribute to recording a song about a goofily niche subject. The Police, for example, would probably *not* record a song about the life-affirming qualities of owning a velvet painting of Elvis Presley – though it's easy to imagine the B-52s (another group Al has given the parody and pastiche treatment) doing so.

But I don't have a hard time imagining Trent Reznor recording a song about his fear of germs at all. If anything, it's easy to imagine the goth icon as a Howard Hughes-like germaphobe ranting to horrified passersby about the world being hopelessly contaminated with tiny, malevolent organisms, with predators we can't see but are crawling all over our diseased bodies.

As a result, the humor in "Germs" is conceptual and abstract rather than rooted in shtick. It works better as music than as comedy, as an alternate-universe Nine Inch Nails bummer rather than a conventionally funny song.

7.
POLKA POWER!

The late '90s was a halcyon era of Y2K panic, Bill Clinton feeling everyone's pain and a very special compilation series called *NOW That's What I Call Music!* which compiled all the hottest hits on one compact disc.

The series debuted in the United States after much success in the United Kingdom in 1998 (about a year before the release of *Running with Scissors*) and reflected the all-the-hits-all-the-time aesthetic of Al's polka medleys so purely that it inspired the title of the polka medley ("NOW That's What I Call Polka!") on 2014's *Mandatory Fun*.

Medleys like "Polka Power!" offered the hit-laden timeliness of a *NOW That's What I Call Music!* compilation in a fraction of the time, reducing whole CDs of massive radio smashes to four or five minutes of sonic silliness.

Al doesn't just approach music from the perspective of a musician or pop star, but from the perspective of a music historian and critic and filmmaker and music video director and businessman and television sidekick/bandleader and kid's show show-runner and coffee table book editor and copy-editor and about a million other things as well. Al's a renaissance man, and different aspects of his careers reflect his diverse gifts.

The polka medleys, for example, offer Al an opportunity to at once goofily inhabit the role of fun-loving party entertainer *and* satirically comment on the state of pop music using inflection, tone and (of course) zany sound effects rather than parody lyrics. These polka medleys hearken back to the early days of Al's pre-album career as an entertainer. As a young artist, without much in the way of original material, what do you do to entertain a potentially hostile crowd? You play the latest hits.

"Extraordinary how potent cheap music is" goes the Noel Coward epigram. I believe it was in direct reference to the Spice Girls' "Wannabe." Oh, to hear that beloved chestnut of my cherished past performed in any context, but particularly in a "Weird Al" Yankovic polka medley, induces a tidal wave of nostalgia – as does the next song given the business, "Flagpole Sitta" from Harvey Danger. The songs that follow had my nostalgia buttons firing wildly. It's one sing-along guilty pleasure after another.

"Everybody (Backstreet's Back)," "Tubthumping," "Semi-Charmed Life," "MMMBop." It's all the songs I love to hear as a lame Gen-Xer and don't hear often enough despite them being some of the most over-played hits of the past quarter century.

"Polka Power!" hit particularly close to home for me. It inspired a whirlwind of nostalgia. In this medley, Al and the band were giving the business to the music of my generation, the soundtrack to my wasted youth. Listening to "Polka

Power!" made me appreciate anew how infectious, and also how wonderfully stupid and plastic, this music was.

8.
YOUR HOROSCOPE
FOR TODAY

1999's *Running with Scissors* **is a** reminder that the late '90s were a very curious time for pop music, and consequently for Al as well. Pop music has always been a realm of human cartoons and outsized comic book characters; that felt particularly true in those strange days just before the anti-climactic turn of the millennium.

We coped with the possibility of a civilization-ending technological disaster by inexplicably retreating into the coziness of our grandparent's music via the short-lived swing revival. Ska similarly enjoyed a brief surge of popularity in the United States as party music for drunk white college kids.

On "Your Horoscope for Today," Al and his ace collaborators take a trip to the islands. But the superstar parodist and his band weren't merely attempting a new style of music, or offering their comedy take on a genre. No, "Your Horoscope for Today" is ska, all right, albeit of the goofiest variety.

As always, authenticity is key, so Al brought in ringers like Dan Regan and Tavis Werts from Reel Big Fish to fill out the sound on trumpet and trombone, as well as Lee Thornburg from Tower of Power and Tom Evans.

The studio musicians and ska specialists Al recruited give the song the irresistible peppiness and toe-tapping infectiousness endemic to the genre. "Your Horoscope for Today" just plain sounds fun. Al's mirthful music-makers lay down a peppy musical bed for a breezy comic spin through the Zodiac signs.

The horoscope parody is a fascinating subsection of the comedy world. *The Onion*, for example, was a master of the form. My former colleague John Krewson, who wrote a lot of the paper's horoscopes, was a genius at writing funny horoscopes. Al is, too.

There's a distinct structure to mock horoscopes. We generally start with one of a series of stock phrases found in both horoscopes *and* fortune cookie fortunes. These include:

> *There's travel in your future…*
>
> *Try to avoid..*
>
> *The position of Jupiter says that…*
>
> *Now is not a good time to…*
>
> *Get ready for an unexpected trip…*

Only instead of offering some manner of maddeningly vague, "sincere" advice that somehow applies to everyone and no one, Al takes these clichés in dark, violent directions. For example, he specifies that the aforementioned 'unexpected trip' will occur "when you fall screaming from an open window."

Some of Al's advice is so broad that it literally applies to almost everyone, every day, like "The stars predict tomorrow you'll wake up, do a bunch of stuff/And then go back to sleep."

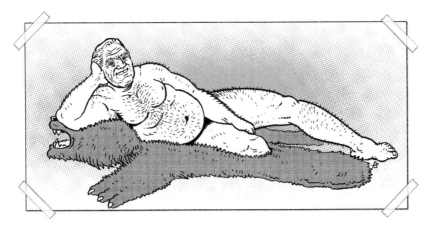

Horoscopes are irresistible to satirists because of the hackneyed tropes they employ, but also because genuinely believing that horoscopes are legitimate represents casual madness.

Deep into "Your Horoscope for Today," Al takes a brief break from rattling off individual horoscopes to eviscerate the concept of Astrology as a whole when he concedes, "Now you may find it inconceivable or at the very least a bit unlikely that the relative position of the planets and the stars could have a special deep significance or meaning that exclusively applies to only you." Then he continues, with exquisite sarcasm, "But let me give you my assurance that these forecasts and predictions are all based on solid, scientific, documented evidence, so you would have to be some kind of moron not to realize that every single one of them is absolutely true."

Horoscopes may be a familiar satirical target, but when approached with this level of zippy brio they can still be a fertile subject for mockery – not unlike a '90s ska revival that resulted in a smattering of guilty pleasures and a whole lot of terrible fashion, rather than lasting works of art.

9.
IT'S ALL ABOUT THE PENTIUMS

Al doesn't always parody the original versions of songs. For example, on his "It's All About the Benjamins" parody "It's All About the Pentiums" Al chose to build his pioneering nerdcore single on the screaming intensity of the song's rock remix, rather than the original album version.

"It's All About the Benjamins (Rock Remix)" is metal. It's punk. It's rap-rock. It's schlock rock. It's pop. It's pop art. It's so '90s it hurts. It's a remix that I enjoy more than the original, because there's just so much going on. It's overflowing with ideas and crazy rock-star energy and Diddy's most inspired screaming.

"It's All About the Pentiums" marks a turning point in Al's discography, one where technology, particularly computers and online culture, became a central focus rather than food or television. Technology would prove a generous muse for Al in the years ahead on standouts like "Virus Alert," "Don't Download This Song," "Stop Forwarding That Crap to Me" and "White & Nerdy."

On "It's All About the Pentiums," Al and his collaborators transform the intensity of Diddy, B.I.G. and company's remix into the belligerent bragging of an arrogant Poindexter who alternates between insulting the listener (a cornerstone of Hip Hop) and boasting of his own technological prowess.

Al's aggro nerd isn't afraid to dip back into our corny collective pop culture history to give his new-school disses unmistakable old-school flavor, like when he taunts, "You think your Commodore 64 is really neato/What kinda chip you got in there, a Dorito?," "I should do the world a favor and cap you like Old Yeller/You're just about as useless as jpegs to Hellen Keller," "Got a flat-screen monitor forty inches wide wide/I believe that your says "Etch A Sketch" on the side," and finally, "Your motherboard melts when you try to send a fax/Where'd you get your CPU, in a box of Cracker Jack?"

If the insults are hopelessly white and nerdy, the aggression that Al brings to his vocals is real. Al is dorkily unrelenting here. Instead of the markedly different flows of the parody's inspiration, Al does everything, double-tracking his vocals so that he can simultaneously be the swaggering central MC and the antic, Diddy-like hype-man cheering him on.

"It's All About the Pentiums" is a time-capsule of a very specific moment in computer culture. Al is the only pop star in existence who can use online slang and make extensive computer references and not come off like a clueless poser trying and failing to keep up with the kids. Al has eternal geek credibility, so when he gets nerdy with his insults, you believe him even if you have no idea what he's talking about.

"It's All About the Pentiums" captured the zeitgeist to such an extent that listening to it now feels like rocketing twenty years back into the past. Music and memory have the power to transcend time and space, even when it's as transcendently silly as this.

10.
TRUCK DRIVIN' SONG

"Truck Drivin' Song" finds "Hillbilly Al" Yankovic venturing south of the Mason-Dixon line for inspiration for his third country song after "Good Enough for Now" and "Achy Breaky Song."

As its title betrays, "Truck Drivin' Song" is not just a country song. No, it is more specifically a truck driving song, a subsection of country devoted to tales of trucks and the hard-living, foul-smelling men who drive them. It's a subculture with its own legacy, traditions and set of heroes, like Dave Dudley and Dale Watson. Country might be the most blue-collar form of music in existence, but the trucking song might be its most working-class sub-genre. Trucking songs aren't just about men whose lives are defined by their thankless jobs: they're about the jobs themselves, and they aren't afraid to scare civilians away with trucker slang.

"Truck Drivin' Song" begins with a flurry of technical truck talk, with the singer singing in a voice deeper than Al has ever attempted before about his "diesel rig" being "northward bound" and it being "time to put that hammer down" on the "twenty tons of steel" in his truck.

But our country crooner isn't just devoted to the grubby romance of the trucker lifestyle. He's equally devoted to cross-dressing. In that respect, "Truck Drivin' Song" is an homage to Monty Python's thematically similar "Lumberjack Song." Both toe-tapping, gender-bending comedy songs glean laughs from the incongruous juxtaposition of an almost cartoonishly manly profession (lumberjack, truck driver) and decidedly unmanly garb.

Al has never sounded more conventionally masculine than when singing about crotchless panties, feather boas, pink angora sweaters, high heels, nipple rings, rhinestones, sequins and chiffon.

"Truck Drivin' Song" may not be the most reverent depiction of gender fluidity, cross-dressing or working-class life, but there's nothing mean-spirited about it. If anything, its singer should be commended for the dedication they bring both to their job as a professional trucker and their passion for women's fashion.

Thanks in no small part to the expert work of pedal steel guitarist Marty Rifkin (whose resume includes credits like Bruce Springsteen, Tom Petty and Dwight Yoakam), "Truck Drivin' Song" is effortlessly authentic, a tongue-in-cheek tribute to the open road and the art of making men look like women.

When I saw Al perform "Truck Drivin' Song" live, he introduced the possibility that this is not a song about a cross-dressing man who loves to drive trucks and wear frilly garb but rather about a truck-driving woman with a very deep, masculine voice who loves to wear frilly, girly lingerie. That would be just as gender-bending as the more traditional interpretation, albeit in a markedly different way.

11.
GRAPEFRUIT DIET

With its energetic horns, frisky rhythms and huge choruses, ska and swing were genres that emphasized fast-paced, short-lived fun. And as the end of one millennium approached and the beginning of another dawned, they roared onto the pop charts as a fad guaranteed to burn itself out quickly.

As such, "Grapefruit Diet" feels at once like a companion piece to Al's third-wave ska tribute "Your Horoscope for Today" and a sequel to "Fat." "Grapefruit Diet" finds Al returning to fat jokes for the first time since his obesity-themed Michael Jackson parody.

The irresistible cheesiness of the tongue-in-cheek, throwback sound is half of what makes "Grapefruit Diet" a guilty pleasure from an artist who usually offers pleasure sans guilt.

The other half is the song's subject matter: "Grapefruit Diet" (a title that screams both "1999" and "guilty pleasure") finds Al dipping deep into the aforementioned "Old Jokes" once again.

The Old Jokes can be found in joke books, but also in the routines of old-school yucksters like Rodney Dangerfield. It's easy to imagine the following lines from "Grapefruit Diet" being delivered in the shtick-slinger's slam-bang cadences:

> *"Every picture of me's gotta be an aerial view!"*
>
> *"Walked down an alley and I got stuck!"*
>
> *"I got more rolls than a pastry truck!"*
>
> *"When I leave a room, first I gotta grease the door!"*

Of course, with Rodney the structure would be different. For the first wisecrack, for example, he'd probably start off by grousing, "My wife is fat, I tell you" to which audiences would respond, "How fat is she?" to which he'd quip, respectively, "Are you kidding? Every picture of her has to be an AERIAL view! She's so fat, she walked down an alley and got STUCK! She's got more rolls than a PASTRY truck!" And finally, "She's so fat, when she leaves a room, first they have to GREASE the door!"

Where "Fat" is defiant, "Grapefruit Diet" is the anguished cry of someone trying to become thinner through the titular fad diet. What could be more quintessentially '90s than a grapefruit diet-themed Cherry Poppin' Daddies parody? Al spoofed the one-hit wonders, and piggy-backed joyously on the infectious idiocy of their tacky little pop radio treasures. He was playing a bigger game all along, one that allowed him to outlast not just the Gerardos and Cherry Poppin' Daddies of the day but beloved icons as well.

Flash in the pans like Cherry Poppin' Daddies come and go. But Al remains. Al persists. Al is eternal.

12.
ALBUQUERQUE

"Albuquerque" is a story song after a fashion, but it's more of an elaborate satirical meditation on the idea of a story song, and stories in general. It's a tongue-in-cheek musical suite that's really three or four or five songs in one, united by a pounding, infectious, hard-driving beat and stream-of-consciousness riffing.

As is sometimes the case with Al's originals, he didn't start entirely from scratch. The sonic and thematic backbone of "Albuquerque" is a song called "Dick's Automotive" by the Rugburns, perhaps the most obscure act Al has ever paid homage to in one of his pastiches.

"Dick's Automotive" runs a comparatively succinct eight minutes and forty-one seconds. Al and his band weren't about to be reined in by such a brief running time, so "Albuquerque" runs eleven minutes and twenty-one seconds, although in concert, Al and the band have been known to stretch the song out even further.

In it its own kooky way, "Albuquerque" captures all the phases in a man's life (not unlike *Citizen Kane*), from childhood and adolescence on through to a surreal and crazed-weasel-packed adulthood.

Like The Rugburns frontman Steve Poltz in "Dick's Automotive," Al talks his way through the verses, taking his time and aggressively emphasizing words. We begin with an appropriately surreal account of the singer's childhood when he enthuses, "Way back when I was just a little bitty boy/Living in a box under the stairs in the corner of the basement of the house half a block down the street from Jerry's Bait shop/You know the place."

Eventually, our hero leaves the basement and a nightmarish gauntlet of unwanted sauerkraut consumption and wins a first-class ticket for a flight to Albuquerque that goes swimmingly, except for *Bio-Dome* as the in-flight movie and the crash that kills everyone onboard (save our hero).

From there, the song goes in about a million directions at once, while simultaneously speeding deliriously and deliberately off a cliff. Our narrator experiences a series of nonsensical adventures involving autographed lucky snorkels, one dozen starving, crazed weasels and our hero cutting off some dude's arms and legs due to an unfortunate misunderstanding.

Wacka wacka doo-doo yeah!

In "Albuquerque," the titular location is less a city than a state of mind, a paradise where the "sun is always shining," "the air smells like root beer" and "the towels are oh so fluffy."

"Albuquerque" is no mere song. Listen closely and you can hear Al's past, present and future all colliding merrily into each other like bumper cars. All in a magical land called Albuquerque.

"The Saga Begins," the song that begins *Running with Scissors*, is the kind of song you can sing along to with your friends. "Albuquerque" has lyrics you get tattooed on your outsized bicep.

How beloved is "Albuquerque"? In a 2012 reader's poll in *Rolling Stone*, it ranked third, just below the slightly more popular and mainstream-friendly hits "White & Nerdy" and "Amish Paradise"

No song in Al's oeuvre is quite as ridiculous, or as self-indulgent, or as ill-advised as "Albuquerque," nor as accidentally majestic.

POODLE HAT (2003)

1.
COUCH POTATO

"Lose Yourself" looms large as one of Eminem's most serious and important songs: It's an adrenaline-pumping, heartstrings-tugging inspirational instant classic from the rapper's brilliant, semi-autobiographical hit movie *8 Mile*, a track characterized by unrelenting intensity.

Al's parody "Couch Potato" still sounds urgent, but lyrically it's about the least urgent subject possible: watching bad television. So instead of the original's iconic spoken-word opening where Eminem asks listeners if they would step up and pursue their dreams when the moment comes, we get Al asking, with the same intensity, "Look, if you had one shot to sit on your lazy butt and watch all the TV you ever wanted until your brain turned to mush, would you go for it? Or just let it slip?"

When Al parodies a pop giant like Eminem, sometimes their musical DNA seeps through, resulting in a mutation that's half Al, half his inspiration. "Couch Potato," for example, uncharacteristically contains not just one gay joke but two. Our singer kvetches, "*King of Queens* jumped the shark the first minute/I can't believe Richard Simmons ain't in it" and later complains, "I only watched *Will and Grace* one time, one day/ Wish I hadn't 'cause TiVo now thinks I'm gay."

Al and company commandeer the solemnly insistent beat of "Lose Yourself" to engage in the kind of gleeful pop culture mockery that defined early smashes like "My Name Is" and "The Real Slim Shady," where Eminem was making fun of the people he saw on TV and who were now, miraculously, also his professional peers.

It's easy to imagine Eminem rhyming "Simon Cowell" and "disembowel" and making fun of Anna Nicole Smith, Ozzy Osborne, the Two Coreys, Rob Schneider and Jennifer Lopez.

"Couch Potato," like Al's "I Can't Watch This," doubles as a time capsule of what was on television when it was recorded, an audio *TV Guide* listing with jokes.

As "Couch Potato" progresses, it moves from real shows to funhouse mirror versions of popular favorites, like *Touched by an Uncle* and *Everybody Tolerates Raymond.* Taking the cruelty and nihilism of reality television to its logical extreme, Al raps about a new FOX sensation involving lions eating Christians.

What sets "Couch Potato" apart from the thematically similar "I Can't Watch This" is escalation. It begins with mild jokes about actual shows and ratchets up the absurdity and the anger until he's threatening to tie executives up and "make them watch all of that junk till their heads explode just like *Scanners.*"

Poodle Hat remains one of Al's least commercially successful albums, due in part to the absence of a music video for its lead single and kick-off track (which Eminem forbade). "Lose Yourself" is about making the most of every opportunity, but Eminem's strange veto of a music video ensured that Al missed his moment. Because "Couch Potato" is very explicitly about television, it sure would have benefited from an attention-grabbing music video. But that was not to be, making "Couch Potato" one of the great what-ifs and disappointments in Al's career.

2.
HARDWARE STORE

In "Hardware Store," the opening of a hardware store is like the premiere of *The Phantom Menace,* minus the crushing disappointment. People (or at least one rather peculiar person) camp out the night before to ensure that they don't miss a moment of the tool-based excitement. Al doesn't just sound excited: he sounds enraptured. The existence of the store and its infinite wonders induces a state of ecstasy in the singer usually attainable only through powerful psychotropic drugs and/or religious epiphanies.

In "Hardware Store," the banal and everyday become transcendent. The song builds in momentum as Al rattles off a hardware store's entire inventory with a speed worthy of rapper Twista or that dude from the Micro-Machines commercials from the '80s.

You can listen to "Hardware Store" a hundred times and still pick up something new with each listen – if only because Al's machine-gun rundown of seemingly every single item you might find in the titular capitalist paradise goes by so quickly that it's impossible to process it all in a single listen. Or a dozen listens.

Al designed it that way. He knows how obsessive his fans are, so he writes songs filled with loving details and in-jokes – like the number 27 reappearing yet again, this time when Al gushes about every 27th customer receiving a ball-peen hammer free.

This certainly isn't the only "Weird Al" Yankovic song about a dude exploding with joy over something silly and banal, but it could be the best. The opening of a hardware store is an awfully silly thing to get psyched about. Then again, so is a song *about* a hardware store, and that doesn't make this any less of a triumph.

3.
TRASH DAY

Music doesn't get better than Nelly's "Hot in Herre," and that includes all of Beethoven's symphonies, which pale in comparison to Nelly's booty-shaking tribute to heat-induced nakedness. "Hot in Herre" is one of those irresistible jams that wow the first time around and never wear out their welcome. "Hot in Herre" may not be high art, but it's pop art at its finest.

To this day, if someone says, "It's hot," "It's hot in here" or "It's getting hot in here," I have to physically fight the urge to answer with an enthusiastic cry of "So take off all your clothes!"

"Hot in Herre" is a perfect pop song, a zeitgeist-capturing collaboration between Nelly and ubiquitous super-producers the Neptunes. They gave the song a sound as carnal as Nelly's lyrics and the flirtatious interplay between the rapper and back-up singer Dani Stevenson.

For his parody, Al took a song that was dirty (in that it was *very* explicitly about sex and nakedness) and made it dirty in the most literal way imaginable. Now, it's about the kind of mess that would require the full resources of the Environmental Protection Agency to properly handle.

In "Trash Day," Al slips inside the undoubtedly foul-smelling skin of a disgusting slob whose unwillingness to take out the trash has caused a rift in his relationship with his significant other. As with "Hot in Herre," a lot of the fun here comes from the battle-of-the-sexes interplay between male and female voices. But where the vibe in Nelly's original is one of playful attraction, "Trash Day" substitutes comic revulsion. Instead of sounding intrigued and turned on, the female back-up singer sounds physically repulsed when she pleads with our Pigpen-like antihero, "Hey, you disgusting slob, you gotta take the trash out!"

In place of the original's grunts of sensual pleasure, "Trash Day" substitutes cries of "Ecch! Ecch!" In place of Nelly's half-sung, half-rapped litany of come-ons, Al offers such surprisingly

sophisticated rhymes as "generatin'/biodegradin'" and "violatin'/resuscitatin'." Or rather, those would be surprisingly sophisticated rhymes from anyone other than Al, who has a proven track record for writing about dumb things in a bracingly smart fashion. For Al, lyrics like, "Look at all this garbage that I keep generatin'/I sit around all day and watch it biodegradin'/Bet there's a hundred health codes that I'm violatin'/Even my dog passed out and needed resuscitatin'" are par for the course.

"Trash Day" is a garbage song in everything other than quality.

4.
PARTY AT THE LEPER COLONY

Like his mentor Dr. Demento, Al takes silly music very seriously. His career has been characterized by caution and care, meticulousness and deliberate planning.

So why did Al find himself breaking into the field of leprosy-based musical comedy decades into his career as a recording artist with "Party at the Leper Colony?" The song would have made more sense on Al's self-titled 1983 debut alongside other exercises in egregious bad taste like "Gotta Boogie" and "Mr. Frump in the Iron Lung," but on 2003's *Poodle Hat* it feels anachronistic.

For the musical foundation of this perverse act of regression, Al chose something similarly retro: the Bo Diddley beat, that rumbling, instantly recognizable groove that reappears over and over in pop music, in songs as dissimilar as Buddy Holly's "Not Fade Away" and Bow Wow Wow's "I Want Candy."

Al opts for an Elvis-style croon as he delves deep into a regrettable well of questionable wordplay involving body parts falling apart as the titular soiree kicks into high gear. The singer is a creepy Casanova whose romantic plans fall apart (along with the limbs of his would-be romantic partner), as evidenced by lyrics like, "I said, 'girl, now don't fall to pieces on me'/But she cried her eyes out, literally."

Normally, when a famous musician says "no" to Al, I'm angry and indignant on Al's behalf. But when the late Clarence Clemons, the legendary saxophonist for Bruce Springsteen's E. Street Band, opted not to play on this track upon hearing its title, his choice made all the sense in the world. I don't blame him. If anything, that was a sound decision, unlike Al making a song with this title and premise this deep into his career.

5.
ANGRY WHITE BOY POLKA

Ideally, we should know every song on a polka medley. These aren't just hits: these are smashes that seemingly everyone knows – that we, as a culture, have collectively learned by heart and can happily sing along to.

That's why, to me, the perfect song for a polka medley is the Who's "My Generation," the Beatles' "Hey Jude" or the Police's "Every Breath You Take."

We need to know the original context of a song in an Al parody for his prankish subversion to register. But listening to "Angry White Boy Polka," I repeatedly found myself thinking, "I don't know this song at all!" and "I have no idea who this is!"

That's partially because Al chose acts for his medley from sections of the pop music landscape I wasn't paying attention to in the early aughts: hip, fashionable hipster rock outfits like the Vines, the Hives, the White Stripes and the Strokes, as well as deeply unhip, unfashionable Nu-Metal artists and rap-rock meatheads like Papa Roach, System of a Down, Disturbed, Limp Bizkit, Staind and P.O.D.

The underlying conceit behind "Angry White Boy Polka" is to subvert the ponderous self-seriousness of white boys in love with their own angst and pain through polka. But since I didn't know many of these songs, Al's cheeky re-interpretation didn't fully register.

That's the tricky thing about the polka medleys: they play very directly to nostalgia both personal and cultural. So my lack of familiarity with the songs being mashed up inhibited my enjoyment of the medley. But I did appreciate the parts that overlapped with my own journey through music, so a brief spin through Kid Rock's "Bawitdaba" and a barbershop quartet-style revisiting of "The Real Slim Shady" were particular highlights.

Nu-Metal is such a tiresome form of music that it taints everything it touches, even something as sturdy and dependable as a "Weird Al" Yankovic polka medley.

6.
WANNA B UR LOVR

The real tragedy of Prince's life and career is that he never gave "Weird Al" Yankovic permission to parody any of his songs. But Al found a way to riff on his work all the same.

Prince's sound pervades *Alapalooza*'s "Traffic Jam" as well as *Poodle Hat*'s "Wanna B Ur Lovr," but this time the inspiration is indirect, as the slinky sex jam (or rather, "slinky" "sex" "jam") is more directly inspired by Beck's *Midnite Vultures*. Beck's tongue-in-cheek foray into lover-man R&B was itself inspired by the baby-making soul of Prince as well as *Young Americans*-era David Bowie.

Midnitet Vultures was Beck riffing on Prince, which makes "Wanna B Ur Lovr" a goof on a goof, something we see a fair amount in Al's career.

What we don't find very often in Al's music are sentiments like, "Do you mind if I chew on your butt?"

"Wanna B Ur Lovr" is a seeming contradiction: a "Weird Al" Yankovic sex song, so the "slinky," "sex" and "jam" elements are even more irreverent than the Beck version. It's a sex song all right, but seemingly sung from the perspective of a space alien who came down to earth, watched *Koyaanisqatsi,* listened to a Barry White album, and then decided that was enough for them to craft baby-making music of their own.

"Wanna B Ur Lovr" is the ultimate creepy Casanova come-on, as the singer glides from one gross line to another, blissfully oblivious as to how he's coming across. Full of unearned cockiness, he begins on a painfully clichéd note, with "I don't have a library card/But do you mind if I check you out?" But it isn't long until he's saying the kinds of things only serial killers would find romantic, like "I'll bet you're magically delicious/Like a bowl of Lucky Charms/You'd look like Venus de Milo/If I just cut off your arms."

Over a slow, carnal groove augmented with horns and DJ Swamp's sexy scratching, Al sounds more confident and turned on than ever before. But his conception of seduction is alternately absurd, insane and insulting to the woman he's attempting to seduce, womankind and humanity.

"Wanna B Ur Lovr" is rather silly, an ironic burlesque of androgynous seduction as filtered through the sizzling myopia of someone who misunderstands both humanity and sex. As second-hand riffs on Prince go, it's decidedly minor but full of goofy charm.

7.
A COMPLICATED SONG

When it comes to the artists he spoofs, Al is like Matthew McConaughey in *Dazed & Confused*: he gets older, and they stay the same age. Because pop music is a young person's grift – a field whose whose most popular participants hover around the legal drinking age.

Al gets older just like the rest of us, but his peculiar life's work calls upon him to regularly take inspiration from pop nymphets still in their teens.

"A Complicated Song," for example, takes its melody from a ubiquitous smash from Avril Lavigne that was released when the pouty chanteuse was only sixteen years old. "Complicated" isn't just an insanely popular song from a strikingly young performer; it's also a very young song, a lyrically mopey yet sonically crisp exploration of game-playing and posturing informed by a decidedly adolescent conception of melodrama.

"A Complicated Song" is a song about words, specifically words that sound like "complicated," of which there are many. We explore three of those words in detail, starting with "constipated" and rising in absurdity and darkness until we get to "decapitated," with a singer whose stubbornness endures even after their head and body are dramatically separated.

In the first verse, the singer is invited to a pizza party and is bummed to discover that he's the only guest. But rather than follow in the footsteps of the original and document adolescent angst, we make an unexpected detour into gastrointestinal distress when our hapless hero takes home the leftover pizza and soon finds himself in the grips of constipation.

Al has fun thinking of words that sound like complicated, but also gets to play with all the vocabulary related to those words – like when he rhymes "constipated" with "bowels evacuated" and then "bowels evacuated" with "colon irrigated."

The second verse explicitly deals with romance, albeit in a decidedly different manner than Avril's original. Our hero is getting ready to propose to his girlfriend when he discovers the horrifying reason they're so wonderfully alike: they're related, as evidenced by the family crest on his object of desire's thigh.

We then segue from the comical complications of incest and inbreeding to even less popular subjects for pop songs: death and dismemberment. In his most foolish decision to date, our misguided anti-hero decides not to let "The Man" tell him that he can't stand up during a roller coaster ride, and ends up literally losing his head.

That would be the end for most people and most songs. Not here. With exquisite understatement, the no-longer-living singer frets, "Why'd I have to go and get myself decapitated?/ This really is a major inconvenience, oh man, I really hate it" before articulating just some of the drawbacks to life without a head: "Can't eat, I can't breathe, I can't snore/I can't belch or yodel anymore/Can't spit or blow my nose or even read *Sports Illustrated*."

It's not all bad, however. Ever the optimist, our singer notes that ever since the unpleasantness involving the roller coaster, his "neck is enjoying a pleasant breeze." That's exactly the kind of deceptively smart line that makes "A Complicated Song" so wickedly wordy and wonderful.

8.
WHY DOES THIS ALWAYS HAPPEN TO ME

Al's friend (and sometimes collaborator) Ben Folds is a sly satirist whose melancholy pop songs take comic aim at the narcissism and toxic self-absorption endemic to the American character. That's also the subject of Al's glorious, bleak Ben Folds pastiche, "Why Does This Always Happen to Me," featuring Folds himself on piano.

The deranged egotist whining his way through "Why Does This Always Happen to Me" begins by watching *The Simpsons*, when the hilarity is interrupted by a news report of an earthquake in Peru so vast that it's difficult to grasp the full scope of the damage.

The sociopath singing the song is disturbed all right, but not by the horrific destruction he's just learned about. No, he's apoplectic that because of the stupid news broadcast his experience watching *The Simpsons* has been hopelessly interrupted, and, in a very real (very minor) way, tarnished.

The most important word in the song's title is "Me." "Why Does This Always Happen to Me" is a song about how our relentless focus on "me" blinds us to the suffering of others. The aggravation of the singer in the first verse is ugly, narcissistic and shameful, but also all too human.

In the second verse, the pain, suffering and cartoonishly over-the-top bloodshed comes closer to our protagonist's life when he's driving to work and encounters a twelve-car pile-up killing everyone involved. Al really lays on the gore and brutality here, singing sensitively, "I saw brains and guts and vital organs splattered everywhere/As well as my friend Robert's disembodied head."

The singer takes exactly one moment to mourn his friend, but that flicker of empathy turns into greed when he thinks about the five dollars his late friend owes him, and how he'll never get that money back.

In the third verse, our increasingly monstrous protagonist moves from watching the aftermath of the violent death of a colleague with a mere iota of compassion followed by a tidal wave of self-interest, to instigating the violence himself. Things start off sleepily enough, but by this point we know what kind of a nasty character we're dealing with. So it's unsurprising that, after being asked to buy toner for the printer repeatedly, the protagonist snaps and stabs his boss in the face.

Thanks in no small part to Folds' piano, "Why Does This Always Happen to Me?" sounds exactly like its inspiration, which adds immeasurably to the comedy. If NPR became sentient it would sound like "Why Does This Always Happen to Me." This pitch-black exercise in scathing social satire is a polished, professional, yuppie-sounding exploration of everyday American self-absorption taken to homicidal extremes.

9.
ODE TO A SUPERHERO

Al's *Spider-Man* themed **"Piano** Man" parody "Ode to a Superhero" is like one of those audio movie storybooks for children you used to be able to buy for your record player. Only instead of merely recounting the plot and action of a movie, Al gives everything his patented satirical spin.

On the subject of Norman Osborne (AKA the Green Goblin) for example, Al sings, "Now Norman's a billionaire scientist/Who never had time for his son/But then something went screwy and before you knew, he/Was trying to kill everyone/And he's ridin' around on that glider thing/And he's throwin' that weird pumpkin bomb/Yes, he's wearin' that dumb Power Rangers mask/But he's scarier without it on!"

As those lines convey, the humor in "Ode to a Superhero" (easily Al's most piano-driven song since "Why Does This Always Happen to Me?" and his most harmonica-heavy until "Bob") is decidedly genial. Al has fun with archetypal superhero mythology and the clichés that come along with it, as well as the movie industry's need to drag everything out as long as possible.

So after recounting how the movie's Peter Parker rejects love interest Mary Jane, Al comforts, "Mary Jane, don't you cry, you can give it a try/Again when the sequel comes 'round."

Back in 2003, even Al couldn't have anticipated that the superhero movie cycle would become so insatiable that sixteen years after Al joked good-naturedly about the latest big tentpole superhero movie, we've not only seen the inevitable hit sequel to *Spider-Man* but also a second sequel *and* a high-profile, big-money, billion-dollar reboot *and* still another reboot, this time starring Tom Holland as the sassy web-slinger. That doesn't even include *Spider-Man: Into the Spider-Verse,* the bonkers, Academy-Award winning animated take on this well-worn mythology. All that in just sixteen years.

Al is as savvy as they come, but sometimes the show business world moves in ways too crazy even for comedy, and too greedy even for Al's cynicism.

10.
BOB

Al is always learning, growing, evolving. He doesn't just possess a formidable creative mind; he possesses the mind of the architectural student he once was. There's an almost mathematical precision to intricate compositions like "Bob," a rollicking tribute to Bob Dylan *and* to palindromes, the geekiest of linguistic conceits.

When I first discovered palindromes as a small child, it blew my young, easily-blown mind that there were words *and* phrases that are spelled the same backwards *and* forwards.

"Bob" is a commentary on Dylan himself and the way he's perceived by both fans and detractors. To people not on Dylan's stoned, exquisitely scrambled wavelength, the Nobel Prize winner's enigmatic wordplay must seem like stream-of-consciousness nonsense.

"Bob" faithfully replicates the sonic trademarks of 1960s era Dylan: the rambunctious, giddy-up rhythm, the insistent, mad-prophet nasal whine as well as the intermittent blasts of wheezing harmonica for emphasis. More than anything, Al and his collaborators reproduce the runaway momentum of Dylan at his most freewheeling.

Al is true to both the spirit and sound of Dylan in that it can be difficult to make out what he's saying at any given moment. "Bob" suggests a spiritual cousin to Al's career-reviving "Smells Like Nirvana," another loving tribute to an artist who came to be known as the voice of their generation despite being incomprehensible to much of the public, particularly those dreary adults/parents/authority figures.

When detractors whine that they can't even understand what people like Bob Dylan and Kurt Cobain are saying, it has several connotations. On the most literal level, they're complaining about a singer's incomprehensibility. But there are larger implications as well: when dreary grown-ups complain that they can't understand an artist, they're also saying that they don't understand the singer's cultural value. It almost invariably speaks to a generational divide, with cryptic geniuses like Cobain and Dylan standing in for youth culture.

On "Bob," Al sings nonsense with the urgency of a protest singer. If you did not know that every single line is a palindrome, it would be easy to mistake the lyrics for Dylan-esque poetry.

Al's Lewis fanciful excursion into word games ends with "Go hang a salami, I'm a lasagna hog," which can only be interpreted as an homage to a certain lasagna-loving, Monday-hating fat cat. Alternately, it might be a reference to Al's own "Lasagna." But I prefer to think it's one American treasure paying tribute to another, and that Al's endlessly versatile brain is more than capable of paying reverent homage to one of our greatest, most important artists, in Jim Davis, and to Bob Dylan as well.

11.
EBAY

In parodying 'N Sync's ubiquitous hit "I Want It That Way" as "eBay," Al transformed a song about romantic yearning into a song about an equally intense yearning to acquire stuff. Al has always been hyper-attuned to the way technology changes the way we live and how we consume.

eBay was an unlikely game-changer. "eBay" captures the weird, ecstatic sense of possibility that came with a suddenly ubiquitous online auction house making everything in the world available for a price. In his best crystalline boy-band voice, Al brags of his eBay prowess, "I'm highest bidder!" with the same zeal other singers reserve for outsized declarations of romantic love.

In the '90s, we thought computers would change everything. In many ways, that happened: iPods, iPhones, Netflix, Amazon and, yes, eBay have all had such a profound impact on the way we live and consume, it can be hard to remember what life was like before them.

In "eBay," the titular website is no mere e-commerce giant: it's closer to a religion, or at least a cult. In Al's parody/tribute, people don't bid on items because they need them, or even particularly want them. No, they bid on items on eBay for the cheap thrill of bidding, and the weird sense of triumph that comes with besting every other anonymous bidder for something of dubious value.

Al captures the old-dressed-up-as-new element of eBay when he sings, "Junk keeps arriving in the mail/From that worldwide garage sale" and later concedes, "Don't know why/The kind of stuff you'd throw away/I'll buy on eBay." It's not the end reward that's intoxicating with eBay, but rather the excitement of the hunt and the thrill of victory. Pointless, pointless victory.

"I Want It That Way" is a masterpiece of pop craftsmanship. It's not just clean and polished: it's pristine. It glistens.

"eBay" benefits from the automatic authority Al brings to singing about computers. Usually when middle-aged musicians reference youth culture or technology, it's embarrassing. When Al does it, we believe him without question. When he sings, "I am the type who is liable to snipe you/With two seconds left

to go," he doesn't sound like a clueless grandpa trying to stay current: he sounds like a tech-savvy dude who knows what he's talking about.

"I Want It That Way" may be a perfect pop song, but "eBay" manages the seemingly impossible feat of improving on perfection.

12.
GENIUS IN FRANCE

For *Poodle Hat's* final track, Al paid tribute to one of his favorite artists and a fellow *Dr. Demento Show* favorite, Frank Zappa, a rock provocateur who thrived on being not just disliked, but outright hated.

The sheer volume of Zappa's work is intimidating. When someone seems to have released four million projects over the course of their career, it's hard to know where to begin. It's easier sometimes to just write the whole thing off. But it's not necessarily right, or fair.

Listening to "Genius in France" made me think, *maybe I should give Zappa a chance.* I was tempted to say "another chance," but the truth is I never gave Zappa a chance to begin with. Instead, I was content to let Zappa's music fall into the outsized category of "Not for me."

Thankfully, Al has a different attitude towards the prickly iconoclast. Al's love of Zappa comes through in every note of this eight-minute, fifty-four-second opus. Frank Zappa was too busy being dead to contribute to "Genius in France," So Al got the next best thing in Frank's son Dweezil, who contributes a guitar solo.

Lyrically, "Genius in France" is a snarky riff on the legend of Jerry Lewis, who is rightly and wrongly considered an obnoxious twit here in his home country, but a towering giant in France. Alas, the singer of "Genius in France" wishes he had the dignity of *Hardly Working/Slapstick*-era Jerry Lewis.

Al's album-closing epic is a spiritual sequel to "That Boy Could Dance," another insult-riddled tribute to an impressively sub-par waste of DNA, who nevertheless possesses something that causes folks to not just excuse their egregious faults, but revere them.

In "That Boy Could Dance," the titular boy's dancing ability renders him a god among men despite being a feeble-minded, drooling halfwit. We never learn exactly what impresses the Frenchies about the subject of "Genius in France," but their affection is as preposterously outsized as it is unmerited.

"Genius in France" combines an entire album's worth of ideas, ambition and genres into a nearly nine-minute epic. It's not written so much as it is composed. Zappa was as fearlessly eclectic as Al, and "Genius in France" is a shape-shifting marvel that's bluegrass one moment and disco-fabulous the next.

"Genius in France" is exhausting in the best way. By the end, you don't just feel like you've come to the close of an unusually long and ambitious song. You feel like Al and his band have taken you on a journey – a ridiculous one, to be sure, but with a certain gonzo wonder all the same.

STRAIGHT OUTTA LYNWOOD (2006)

1.
WHITE & NERDY

With "White & Nerdy," a development that initially seemed like a stroke of bad luck ended up working spectacularly in Al's favor. Even after Al recorded and slated a parody of James Blunt's smash "You're Beautiful" entitled "You're Pitiful" to be the first single on his new album *Straight Outta Lynwood*, Blunt's label Atlantic turned down a request to release it.

Al was in a dilly of a pickle. Thankfully, desperation led to inspiration, and Al recorded a parody of Chamillionaire and Krayzie Bone's "Ridin'" with a skeleton crew of guitarist Jim West (handling synths) and drummer Jon "Bermuda" Schwartz. In doing so, he created a surprise smash that would go on to become the biggest chart hit of Al's career, and his only single to hit the top ten in the U.S.

The last-minute switcheroo paid off not just commercially, but creatively as well. Where "You're Pitiful" is amusing (if mean-spirited and slight) "White & Nerdy" is a brash geek anthem that documents the joys of Nerd Life with palpable affection.

Like "Gangsta's Paradise," "Ridin'" wasn't just a massive crossover hit. It was also a song *about* something – a song that was important, that had substance as well as style. In "Ridin'," the subject is racial profiling and police harassment. It's about a black man targeted by the cops as a probable criminal due to his race and luxurious lifestyle.

"Ridin'" is a song of brash defiance towards corrupt authority, a middle finger to the racist cops that have long been Hip Hop's public enemy number one. Al's song retains that air of raw rebelliousness, but applies it to hilariously incongruous subject matter. Never have the words "Got my name on my underwear" or "I'm nerdy in the extreme and whiter than sour cream" been uttered with such irresistible, misplaced swagger.

"White & Nerdy" presents a sort of de-politicized whiteness, one divorced from the heavy political and ideological baggage it has picked up through the years. It presents whiteness as nerdiness and nerdiness as whiteness, although the beautiful nerd rainbow contains Poindexters of all races and genders.

"White & Nerdy" offers a more benign exploration of race relations than the one found in "Ridin'": the high-status, low-self-awareness geek rapping the song wants to kick it with the gangstas (represented in the video by a pre-superstardom Keegan-Michael Key and Jordan Peele), but he's held back by his inexorable whiteness.

"White & Nerdy" benefits from density as well as specificity. This proud geek doesn't just eschew a 40-ounce of malt liquor (the cartoon gangsta's beverage of choice) for the more prim and proper tea: he specifically favors Earl Grey, the sleepy Caucasian's favorite. Al doesn't just reference MySpace (the Facebook of yesteryear), which lived a tacky life and then

died a tacky, predictable death; he references specific features of the service, rendering the song a fascinating snapshot of a specific time and place in geek culture.

Chamillionaire favors a rapid-fire, singsong, half-sung, half-rapped delivery that Al mimics, but makes several thousand times whiter.

What makes "White & Nerdy" so enduring is the love Al brings to this subject matter. The white and nerdy are Al's people. They comprise much of his fanbase.

When Al raps about computer languages or M.C. Escher or *Star Trek*, it's coming from a place of understanding. "White & Nerdy" is a song that nerds can be proud of, that they can claim as their own. Al speaks their language (or *languages*, since they're fluent in not just Javascript, but also Klingon).

"White & Nerdy" is the only top-ten-charting pop song to reference "vector calculus." I pride myself on knowing all sorts of weird stuff, but vector calculus is one of several phrases I had to Google because, even in context, I only had a vague sense of what "Pascal," "Minesweeper" and "writable media" meant.

Al is like his hero Tom Lehrer: he's not just entertaining, he's educational as well – even when one of your primary fields of knowledge is the life and music of "Weird Al" Yankovic, as happens to be the case with me.

2.
PANCREAS

The exquisitely, perversely detailed Beach Boys pastiche "Pancreas" is indicative of the casual mastery that has defined Al's late-period output.

Al and his collaborators, who include his band and ringers like Tower of Power trumpet player Lee Thornburg, cellist Sarah O'Brien, trombonist Nick Lane, double bassist Miles Jay and French horn player John Dickson, set out to make a song that sounds like it could be an outtake from the *Smile* sessions.

That's a tall order, considering Brian Wilson's work with Van Dyke Parks, the Beach Boys and an overflowing roster of studio musicians during the *Pet Sounds* era is held in high acclaim in no small part because it's so sophisticated and complex.

"Pancreas" expensively, fussily recreates the sound of an era when Brian Wilson, his mind opened to the infinite possibilities of the universe by copious LSD consumption, boldly transgressed the limitations of rock with miniature symphonies that seemingly included every sound in the universe – from the bleat of a baby goat to the death howl of an insane god.

It was as if the only way for Wilson to calm his demons and achieve even a moment of peace was to realize the sounds in his head, no matter the cost or aggravation involved.

Wilson strove for the transcendent, the enduring, the spiritual, sacred and sublime. But he was also a giant weirdo, so that quest for the divine sometimes took the form of writing songs about vegetables – as on the 1967 *Smiley Smile* track of the same name, which contains lyrics like, "If you brought a big brown bag of (vegetables) home, I'd jump up and down and hope you'd toss me a carrot."

How do you top something like that? If you're Al, you imagine Brian Wilson waxing rhapsodic not about his love of celery but rather about the pancreas, his favorite internal organ.

He really, *really* loves his pancreas.

"Pancreas" is the antithesis of minimalism. But while there's an enormous amount going on, the sound is never cluttered. There's a cleanness to it, a hyper-professional polish that speaks to Al's enormous growth not just as a songwriter, but as a producer and a musician as well.

"Pancreas" isn't just a tribute to *Smile*-era Brian Wilson and his glorious eccentricities; in less than four minutes it tracks his fascinating sonic evolution from the relative innocence of his early output to the freaky LSD atmospherics of "Good Vibrations," *Pet Sounds* and *Smile* and the weird sonic experiments that followed.

In an earlier era, "Pancreas" might have ranked as another of Al's songs about weird obsessives and the unlikely things that give them too much joy. But Al had largely outgrown that trope by this point.

With "Pancreas," Al and his collaborators created a song of great, unlikely beauty about unlikely subject matter that Al manages to make seem oddly beautiful.

Incidentally, Al played accordion on "Let's Stick Together" from *Sweet Insanity,* an album Wilson recorded while he was under the care of controversial psychiatrist Dr. Eugene Landy that was never released.

It would have been a coup if Al had been able to get Wilson to contribute to "Pancreas." But he did magnificently, even without the assistance of the eccentric genius behind the Beach Boys.

3.
CANADIAN IDIOT

Despite its title, the real target of "Canadian Idiot," Al's parody of Green Day's "American Idiot," is American boorishness, just like the snotty Dubya-era political provocation it's spoofing. The nationality of the Canada-disparaging dude singing the song is as important (if not more so) than the country that he's singing about.

"Canadian Idiot" is about the way we demonize people who are different, even when those differences make them better than us. The singer here notes that Canadians possess national health care, that their medication is cheaper and their air isn't quite as poisoned. But what does that matter when the populace is so poorly armed?

The Canada-basher doesn't hate Canadians because they're culturally inferior, but because they're superior. "Canadian Idiot" is really a song about American idiots so suspicious of Canadian's politeness, harmless eccentricities and lack of personal firepower that they're ready to launch a preemptive strike against Canada rather than learn from them.

When Americans profess to be filled with rage towards our neighbors to the North, it's almost always seen as fantasy, comedy and satire. Who could actually hate or fear Canadians? They're white! And polite! When Americans profess to be filled with rage towards our neighbors to the South, on the other hand, it's rightly seen as racism, and/or the basis for Trump's foreign policy.

That's because our Canuck neighbors are widely seen as white & nerdy instead of dark & threatening. So the very idea that they might be up to something is seen as inherently comic, instead of indicative of our deep-seated, poisonous xenophobia.

"Canadian Idiot" may be a song of opportunity rather than inspiration, but there's a lot going on all the same. Al's brand of satire and social commentary is less ham-fisted than the tune it's spoofing. He's always been something of a sly, sneaky secret satirist, whereas Billie Joe's *American Idiot* project shouted its satirical ambitions from the rooftops, starting with its title.

4.
I'LL SUE YA

Rage Against the Machine's signature, both on record and onstage, is righteous rage, ferocious sonic fury. However, the angry screamer of Al's Rage Against the Machine pastiche "I'll Sue Ya" is anything but righteous. He's another of Al's demented narcissists, an entitled loser who thinks that the world owes him everything in exchange for doing nothing, and is unforgivably late in delivering.

So he takes to the nation's courts in search of redress and justice – but mainly in pursuit of a wholly unearned payday, the legal windfall that is every opportunistic American sleazebag's birthright.

"I'll Sue Ya" explores another unfortunate element of the American psyche: our inveterate litigiousness. It's rooted in bits of contemporary pop folklore like the famous 1994 "hot coffee" case of Liebeck vs McDonald's, where a 79-year-old woman named Stella Liebeck was awarded 2.86 million dollars after she received third degree burns after spilling McDonald's coffee on her lap.

Liebeck case was seen (wrongly, it turns out) as what is pejoratively known as a "nuisance lawsuit." What's a nuisance lawsuit? Well, it's something the dude shouting "I'll Sue Ya" files

in abundance. He sues for nonsensical reasons, like his belief that Colorado looks "a little bit too much like Wyoming." He sues for petty reasons, like Earthlink putting him on hold and his Starbucks Frappucino being too cold. But mostly he sues companies and people and places for his own stupid, eminently avoidable mistakes, from wearing Fruit of the Loom underwear on his head to visiting New Jersey.

The eternal litigant yelling his way through "I'll Sue Ya!" makes his shabby case in the court of public opinion not through facts or evidence (which most assuredly are not on his side) but through deafening volume and overwhelming, if ultimately pointless, intensity.

5.
POLKARAMA

Al's polka medleys are invariably informed by a combination of guilty delight and genuine appreciation. Al takes the piss out of the top hits of the day, using the inveterately unserious vehicle of the polka medley to render somber hits silly, silly hits preposterous and sexy songs cartoonish and buffoonish.

"Polkarama" kicks off with the Black Eyed Peas' "Let's Get it Started," which made it onto the multi-platinum album *Elephunk* as "Let's Get R*tarded" before someone realized that that was wildly offensive. Why didn't anyone figure that out before the album was released with that song title? The whole thing seems pretty elephunked up, if you ask me.

Al uses the non-offensive version of the chorus as the gleeful kick-off to his tour through the highs and lows of the pop charts, from the cheeseball douchebag pop of Weezer's "Beverly Hills" to the arena-rock pomposity of Coldplay's "Speed of Sound" to the gender-bending, neurotic neo-new wave of the Killers' "Somebody Told Me."

"Polkarama" is a real blast from the past, a musical magic carpet ride to a time when I knew and cared about pop music (within reason). At the time, I considered it, if not a sacred obligation, then at least an important part of my job to keep up with what the kids were listening to. Here, that includes Kanye & Jamie Foxx ("Golddigger"), Snoop Dogg and Pharrell ("Drop It Like It's Hot"), Gorrilaz and De La Soul ("Feel Good Inc.") and many more.

On a purely personal and selfish level, I dug this medley because it reconnected me to a time when I went to shows and eagerly debated the merits of new albums. In those days, I felt a responsibility to my readers and to pop culture to keep current.

"Polkarama" reminded me why I love pop music, even when I'm not professionally obligated to do so.

6.
VIRUS ALERT

By 2006, the internet had supplanted television as our primary source of pleasure, while simultaneously warping our minds, destroying our attention spans and methodically ruining civilization. We no longer tuned in, we logged on.

In a related development, computers supplanted television as Al's subject matter of choice. Al had previously explored this fruitful field of geek comedy with "It's All About the Pentiums," but *Straight Outta Lynwood* was the album where Al's Computer Age really began.

One quarter of the album's twelve songs are computer-themed: "White & Nerdy," "Virus Alert" and "Don't Download This Song." Those are not only three of the best songs of the album, but three of the best songs from this period in Al's career.

"Virus Alert" is a particularly overlooked gem, a hilarious and bracingly smart homage to rock band (and cult weirdoes)

Sparks that perfectly lampoons our fear of terrifying, exhilarating new technology.

They say that when technology surpasses a certain point it becomes a form of magic. In "Virus Alert," technology has advanced to the point where it's not just a form of magic, but dark magic capable of destroying not just the person using it, but all of civilization.

We start off innocently enough with the alarming news that "a dangerous, insidious computer virus" is making its way through cyberspace and causing wreckage in its wake.

According to the song, this menace will do the following and more:

- Translate your documents into Swahili
- Make your TV record *Gigli*
- Neuter your pets and give you laundry static cling

Our paranoia about technology is often inextricably rooted in sexual shame. We're terrified our sexual kinks will become public knowledge. So it's another perfect detail that the horrors promised by the spread of this virus include your grandmother being sent your entire porn collection.

The sick joke underlining the song, and virus alerts in general, is that this hysterical, hyperbolic attempt to keep paranoid computer users safe from malevolent malware is itself almost assuredly a computer virus itself.

If computers and technology can be miraculous in positive ways, then by extension they must also be all-powerful in terrifying ways as well. The online malady of "Virus Alert" is downright Shiva-like in its destructiveness.

Like the best pastiches, this doubles as a covert plug for the music of its inspiration, one destined to send curious souls like myself racing to Spotify and Amazon to rectify our lack of knowledge about this nifty-seeming cult act.

7.
CONFESSIONS PART III

"Confessions Part III," Al's parody of Usher's Jermaine Dupri-produced smash "Confessions Part II," represents the first entry in a late-period R&B trilogy. The series continues with "Trapped in the Drive-In," his brainy deconstruction of the gimmicky songcraft of R. Kelly's endless "Trapped in the Closet", and closes with "Whatever You Like."

"Confessions Part III" is an unusually direct parody of both "Confessions Part I" and "Confessions Part II," to the extent that it opens with Al directly referencing them not just as prequels to his parody, but also as things that happened to the man singing the song.

Al crudely summarizes the earlier songs as first being about the singer cheating on a lover with someone whom Al uncharacteristically refers to as a "skank," and then about the confessor getting a woman of easy virtue pregnant.

The first two confessions are about secrets. Sexy, sexy secrets about sex stuff. That's not how Al rolls, however, so "Confessions Part III" is about confessions that aren't just non-sexy, but *anti*-sexy.

On a larger conceptual level, "Confessions Part III" takes satirical aim at the oily opportunism of a musician recording a sordid laundry list of his misdeeds to appeal to sensationalism-craving fans by following it up with a mercenary sequel recounting even more ethical transgressions when the first song proved a monster hit.

Al had attained a state of creative mastery by this point in his career, but "Confessions Part III" illustrates that not everything he did was a masterpiece.

8.
WEASEL STOMPING DAY

It's on the originals that Lynwood's own Alfred Matthew Yankovic truly gets "weird." "Weasel Stomping Day" is a beautiful example of just how strange and ghoulish Al can get when he's not worrying about appealing to the narrow sensibilities of the pop market.

Al's sadistic streak finds perhaps its purest reflection in this chipper ditty about a fictional holiday where (for reasons lost to time) children and adults alike put on Viking helmets, slather mayonnaise on the lawn and brutally torture weasels.

Why? No one knows. As the morbidly syrupy voices crooning the tune in horrific harmony assert, "Why do we do it, who can say/But it's such a festive holiday/So let the stomping fun begin/Bash their weasely skulls right in/It's tradition, that makes it okay!"

"Weasel Stomping Day" sounds like the kind of annoyingly catchy kid's song you might hear outside a ride at Disneyland. "It's a Small World" is the undisputed king of those clamorous contraptions. Like "Weasel Stomping Day," its catchiness is sadistic. You simply can't get these songs out of your head. This means that a disturbingly large number of people had lyrics like "You'll know what this day's about/When you stomp a weasel's guts right out" and "All the little girls and boys/Love that wonderful crunching noise" going through their minds at inopportune moments, like making love or the birth of their first child.

"Weasel Stomping Day" is as sonically cloying as it is thematically deranged, a wholesome 1960s family-friendly song about the mindless slaughter of blameless animals by Americans driven into a violent frenzy by a barbaric holiday.

Holidays, real and imagined, are invariably dark days in Al's world, as evidenced by his pair of apocalyptic Christmas songs and his equally apocalyptic birthday song. "Weasel Stomping Day" starts dark and gets increasingly brutal until words cheering the ritualistic killing of small animals are augmented by the *crunch* of weasel bones as they're beaten senseless en masse.

Deep into his career, Al retained the power to shock and delight even his most devoted and obsessive fans with bracingly brutal yet perversely upbeat numbers like this.

9.
CLOSE BUT NO CIGAR

On the 2018 Self-Indulgent Vanity Tour, when a curious instrument known as the vibraslap was in Al's hands and a look of excitement swept across his wildly expressive face, it could mean only one thing: "Close But No Cigar" was next.

The vibraslap is one of the signature instruments of Cake, whom Al lovingly pays tribute to on "Close But No Cigar." Al's

Cake pastiche is about a man who can't deal with even the most minuscule imperfections in otherwise preposterously perfect partners, but from a musical perspective, "Close But No Cigar" is close to perfection.

"Close But No Cigar" is yet another song about romance that posits our need for love and sex as a form of madness. But where the creepy Casanovas of Al's other songs about the dark side of romance and human nature scream their violent insanity from the mountaintop, the impossible-to-please singer here suffers from standards so high that even microscopic flaws are deal-breakers.

In each of the verses, Al sings the praises of his imperfect and consequently inadequate objects of desire in hilariously hyperbolic ways. We begin with case study 1: Gillian is her name, and "she was sweeter than aspartame" to the point where her smooches reconfigured the singer's DNA, after which he never was the same.

Our lovesick lunatic didn't just love Gillian: he "loved her even more than Marlon Brando loved soufflé," until he was finally unable to look beyond her use of the word "infer" when she clearly meant "imply." The two words are close to synonymous, but "Close But No Cigar" is ferociously devoted to splitting hairs.

"Close But No Cigar" is the ideal combination of smart and silly, romantic and misanthropic. It's full of bracingly smart, eminently quotable lyrics. The first verse has that wonderful line about Gillian's kisses reconfiguring DNA. The second verse is about young Janet, the "prettiest thing on the planet," who has "a body hotter than a habañero" and "lips like a ripe pomegranate" as well as "a smile so incredibly radiant you had to watch it through a piece of smoked glass."

"Close But No Cigar" is a delight in every conceivable way. The lyrics are hilarious and unforgettable, the groove slinky and the shout-along chorus insanely catchy.

Nothing is ever good enough for the simultaneously lucky and unlucky-in-love creep singing the song, but "Close But Cigar" beautifully hits its own mark.

10.
DO I CREEP YOU OUT

Silver-haired cheeseball and Soul Patrol leader Taylor Hicks didn't write "Do I Make You Proud," but its achingly sincere lyrics reflect his journey from scruffy anonymity to unlikely television star after he won *American Idol*, instead of an undoubtedly more talented and deserving woman or minority.

"Do I Make You Proud" is sung from the perspective of a man oozing gratitude for a partner who has spurred him on to great heights, convincing him he could achieve far more than he ever imagined possible (like winning *American Idol* and having a song parodied by "Weird Al" Yankovic).

It's a song of unashamed, unabashed excess that begins on a note of trembling sincerity and builds to a string-laden chorus.

Al transforms this slice of American cheese into a showcase for one of his creepy Casanovas. Instead of filling his partner with pride, the lunatic crooning this warped anti-love song is more likely to engender fear, physical and psychological revulsion and a need for a restraining order, or possibly round-the-clock security.

Like "Do I Make You Proud," "Do I Creep You Out" starts off soft and intimate before getting bigger and bigger until it couldn't get any more melodramatic. And then it closes with the rapturous applause of a phantom *American Idol* audience, one roped into aggressively cheering the yucky self-disclosure of one seriously unpleasant human being.

"Do I Creep You Out" works because Al throws himself into the clammy creepiness of the song with the same outsized melodrama Hicks brings to the original.

Like Hicks, Al doesn't merely sing. He *performs* the song.

So while "Do I Creep You Out" might feel a little over-familiar lyrically, on a conceptual level it soars as a sly commentary on the glossy over-production and cornball over-emoting of *American Idol*-derived pop product.

11.
TRAPPED IN THE DRIVE-THRU

For parodists, R. Kelly's multi-media extravaganza "Trapped in the Closet" proved an irresistible yet daunting target. The R&B superstar and sex cult leader's epic story suite is a delirious, hyper-sexualized musical melodrama whose total lack of self-awareness renders it perfect for satirical puncturing.

Yet "Trapped in the Closet" is so surreally unselfconscious that it renders outside parody redundant. How can a parody make R. Kelly and his horny storyteller aesthetic seem more ridiculous than the sex criminal's own music already does? How can you exaggerate something that already exists in a state of crazed excess?

Al's answer? Go in the opposite direction. While R. Kelly wrote a song about everything, Al transformed it into a song about nothing – or rather the most banal possible subject: an ordinary guy on an ordinary day who goes out for fast food and ends up getting his order slightly wrong.

Conceptually, "Trapped in the Drive-Thru" is tremendously sophisticated. The underlying joke of the parody is that there are no jokes. "Trapped in the Drive-Thru" is not quite anti-humor, but it finds Al at his most sneakily deconstructionist.

We begin with that distinctive, oddly hypnotic dripping-faucet groove and our hilariously mundane storyteller sharing the mundane details of another boring night at home. It's early evening, he's zoned out on the couch watching television when his wife poses a question of very little importance: is he hungry?

The carnivore crooning the song isn't terribly famished, but he eventually vows to take his spouse out to eat, setting in motion a series of banal events of almost no significance even to the people experiencing them.

Like "Trapped in the Closet," "Trapped in the Drive-Thru" is full of conflict and disagreements. And repetition! Like the original, "Trapped in the Drive-Thru" goes so overboard with repetition that repeating the same words over and over again becomes as hypnotic as it as annoying.

Instead of being rooted in the sordid, steamy foundation of sex, lies and deceit like "Trapped in the Closet," Al's parody is rooted in the minor aggravations of everyday life.

"Trapped in the Drive-Thru" starts off quiet and builds in musical and vocal intensity until it reaches a furious climax wildly disproportionate to the everyday nonsense being discussed. Then the process starts all over again with the next movement.

Vocally, Al could not sound more enraged and engaged about the gauntlet of minor irritations he encounters – from pimply, distracted fast food employees to annoying relatives calling him to his wife thinking he's proposing that they eat liver for dinner when he's just asking about delivery.

In terms of length, ambition and conceptual weirdness, "Trapped in the Drive-Thru" feels more like an album closer than the terrific but comparatively modest "Don't Download This Song." But Al's successful formula dictates that albums end on originals, not parodies.

Like the song it's so parodying, "Trapped in the Drive-Thru" is an elaborate production that lasts over ten minutes, includes an interpolation of Led Zeppelin's "Black Dog" and is the only song of Al's to be listed on Wikipedia as belonging to the sub-genre of "Hip-Hopera."

"Trapped in the Drive-Thru" helps close out one of Al's best albums in a very big yet banal way; it's a standout parody with the oddball soul and epic audacity of an album-closing original.

12.
DON'T DOWNLOAD THIS SONG

The first single from *Straight Outta Lynwood* (and a song Al impishly made available to fans online for free), "Don't Download This Song" brilliantly juxtaposes a screamingly 2006 topic —the music industry hypocritically shaming the public out of downloading music – with a sound rooted inextricably in the saccharine message songs of the '80s: "Hands Across America," "Do They Know It's Christmas?" and especially "We Are the World."

"We Are the World" succeeded in opening the wallets of the first world with a heavy-handed, saccharine appeal to compassion. It was a song about something almost too important to be the subject of a mere pop song – an epidemic of suffering and starvation in Africa, particularly in Ethiopia.

"Don't Download This Song" is appropriately plastic and overwrought, over-produced and shameless. But instead of tackling a matter of genuine significance, Al satirizes the transparent hypocrisy of the money-crazed, parasitic ghouls in the music industry wagging a finger in sour judgment at listeners for downloading a song for free online, instead of ponying up seventeen dollars for a Limp Bizkit album to listen to the one song on it they kind of like.

"Don't Download This Song" exaggerates the recording industry establishment's ridiculous arguments to sublime effect.

Its singer presents the ethical misdemeanor of media piracy as a gateway crime that will inevitably lead to "robbing liquor stores" and "selling crack," and ultimately "running over school kids with your car."

If downloading music illegally is a crime, then that makes people who've downloaded the new Dave Matthews Band album before its release date criminals. As Al pleads here, "It doesn't matter if you're a grandma/Or a seven-year-old girl/They'll treat you like the evil hard-bitten criminal scum you are."

In the song, and the music industry's warped logic, tech-savvy seven-year-olds and grandmas are criminals who must be punished. Conversely, multi-millionaire rock stars with comically decadent lifestyles to support are the real victims.

Channeling the epic self-pity of the "Napster must be stopped" set, Al implores, "Don't take away money from artists just like me/How else can I afford another solid gold Humvee?/And diamond studded swimming pools, these things don't grow on trees!"

The faux-message song gets angrier and more apoplectic until the self-pitying singer can't contain his rage any longer and condemns downloaders to the bowels of hell.

Al is just one man, but on "Don't Download This Song" he and his back-up singers sound like a full chorus of pompous pop stars singing on behalf of their corporate masters' interests.

At the very end of "Don't Download This Song," buried deep in the sound mix, is an almost imperceptible shout of "You cheap bastard!" In this moment, the singer's preposterous mask of decency falls off and we see him for who he, and the recording industry establishment he represents, really is. They don't care about compensating artists or making sure that everyone gets their fair share. No, they're pissed that file sharers are ripping off artists, when that has historically been the music industry's job.

Juxtaposing the smarmy sanctimoniousness of the Reagan-era all-star message song with the recording industry's high-minded campaign against downloading made "Don't Download

This Song" timely as well as resonant and hilarious. But it's the song's scathing satire of corporate greed masquerading unconvincingly as basic human decency that makes it timeless.

ALPOCALYPSE
(2011)

1.
PERFORM THIS WAY

"Perform This Way" is a big song for Al, but it's a particularly important song for me.

I was working with Al on *Weird Al: The Book* when the "Perform This Way" kerfuffle happened. I had a front row seat to pop culture history when, in a frenzy of inspiration, Al parodied Lady Gaga's ubiquitous LGTBQ anthem "Born This Way" as "Perform This Way." It's a send-up of the *A Star is Born* diva, at once loving and more biting than his usual fare in that it takes aim at the singer as well as the song.

Yankovic sent the song to Gaga for approval (per his custom) and word got back to Al that Gaga's camp had rejected Al's request. This left Al in the lurch, unclear on how to proceed with either the single, or the music video, or the album it was supposed to launch.

How could Lady Gaga not recognize Al as a kindred spirit? Surely it all had to be some manner of misunderstanding, right?

Eventually it came out that it was all a big mix-up. Lady Gaga's manager, thinking he was doing her a solid, rejected the parody on her behalf. Once she found out what happened, she had him publicly executed (tough, but fair).

"Perform This Way" is an unusual parody for Al in that it's satirical towards the subject of its parody in a way Al's spoofs generally aren't. "Smells Like Nirvana" is the closest song Al had come to "Perform This Way" at that point, and that earlier hit pointedly lacks a line as scathing as, "I'm sure my critics will say it's a grotesque display." That line lands a little hard, because otherwise "Perform This Way" is a loving valentine to the boundary-pushing pop icon's Dadaist fashion choices.

Crazy or art? That's the question at the heart of "Perform This Way," which offers a third option: commerce. "Ooh, my little monsters pay/Lots 'cause I perform this way," Al-as-Gaga sings here, continuing a theme that pops up throughout Al's albums.

"Perform This Way" spoofs a version of Lady Gaga that largely doesn't exist anymore. It took some doing, but Lady Gaga is better known these days for her talent and her music than her clothes. That wasn't true in 2011, when Gaga made headlines more for her outlandish style sense than her catchy tunes and knockout voice.

The exhibitionist singing "Perform This Way" dresses in a manner equally likely to attract the attention of the fashion press, tabloids, mental health professionals and the police. They might even turn heads at the FDA, since some of the outfits described here violate not just the rules of propriety and good taste, but probably a health code or two as well.

When I look at Gaga in her gaudiest get-ups, I see someone hiding behind an outrageous image and revealing something important about themselves at the same time. I see the same thing in Al's most out-there ensembles. With Lady Gaga, there's bold pop artistry and heady, trippy ideas behind these outrageous looks, but also a lot of pretension and being weird for the sake of being weird. That's what Al's parody is all about.

I wrote about Al and Lady Gaga as simpatico figures back in 2012's *Weird Al: The Book* because they were famously theatrical and outrageous. They both made their names performing dazzling multi-media extravaganzas in wild costumes and stages filled with screens and props.

They remained oddly parallel figures in 2018 as well: that's the year Al and Lady Gaga took bold steps to prove to the world that there's so much more to them than outrageous get-ups, wild sets and brazenly theatrical performances. In Al's case, it was in touring without all of the spectacle; in Gaga's, it was playing someone heartbreakingly real in *A Star is Born*, a serious prestige drama that won Gaga Oscar nominations as both an actress and a musician.

A Star is Born is, of course, an elaborate act of pop mythology lovingly crafted to establish its first-time film star as a figure of unimpeachable authenticity and talent, a woman who needs nothing more than THAT voice to have the world spellbound. By eschewing the shock tactics and pop-art provocation of her earlier image, she proved that she didn't need attention-grabbing stunts to be successful.

A Star is Born is about how Gaga has the goods, how she's the real deal, how she can she sit at a piano in regular people clothes and still have you spellbound. Similarly, The Ridiculously Self-Indulgent, Ill-Advised Vanity Tour incontrovertibly proved that Al didn't need props, costumes, screens or extras to captivate audiences. He didn't even need his parodies.

Like Lady Gaga, Al is a brilliant musician and songwriter, as well as a world-class live performer who feels at home in any number of disguises. In 2018, with the Ridiculously Self-Indulgent, Ill-Advised Vanity Tour and *A Star is Born*, Al and Gaga respectively performed for their adoring public in decidedly different ways than ever before. In the process, they incontrovertibly illustrated that, without the glitter and the dazzle, they were, if anything, even more impressive and authentic than their biggest fans imagined.

2.
CNR

Introducing "CNR" on the Self-Indulgent Vanity Tour, Al explained that he called the late Charles Nelson Reilly's widower for permission to release a song about the 1970s game show staple, who requested only that the song not make him out to be too much of a sissy. Alec Baldwin had apparently played Reilly as something of a cartoon on *Saturday Night Live*; as both Reilly's partner and the keeper of his flame, Reilly's significant other was obviously a little hurt.

Luckily, with Al he had nothing to worry about. Instead of stereotyping Reilly as a lisping, stereotypical queen, "CNR" deifies him as a modern-day folk hero, a strapping, two-fisted slab of man meat capable of superhuman feats of badassery. The song is based on the curious, annoying afterlife of Chuck Norris as a human meme whose outsized feats have been disseminated throughout the internet and compiled in books with titles like *The Truth About Chuck Norris: 400 Facts About the World's Greatest Human*.

There is nothing remotely interesting about Chuck Norris, but an eternally inventive internet took a shine to him all the same. He was a blank, bearded cipher that online wisenheimers elevated to faux-god status as a culture-wide inside joke that was never particularly funny.

Yet Al has a way of turning trash into treasure, mold into gold and slime into shine. In "CNR" he makes a hoary online

trope into a righteous rocker by transforming a hackneyed meme into a dual tribute to the awesomeness of Charles Nelson Reilly and the blues-rock thunder of the White Stripes.

It's a testament to the versatility of Al's band that being able to perform *exactly* like Jack White and Meg White represents *maybe* one two-hundredth of guitarist Jim West and drummer Jon "Bermuda" Schwartz's skill set.

West isn't just forceful in an inimitably Jack White-like fashion; he's earth-shaking in his fury. Schwartz's drums are equally atomic in impact. Al howls the absurdist *Match Game* blues at similarly ear-splitting volume and with an equivalent level of pounding intensity.

Reilly is a comically unlikely subject for a tribute, but through sheer force of will Al makes the camp icon seem legitimately badass. Part of what made Al's anecdote about Reilly's partner not wanting him ridiculed so poignant is that there's an underlying sincerity underneath the absurdity here. There's a sense that Reilly is one of our guys – the weirdoes, the oddballs, the kids that never quite fit in. Consequently, he's more worthy of homage (ironic or not) than a macho drip like Chuck Norris.

The concept might be a little iffy, but "CNR" kills in execution. It's a very worthy tribute to men who represent vastly different breeds of offbeat masculinity – Jack White and Charles Nelson Reilly – from the only dude weird and wise enough to know they'd be the perfect combination for sonic and lyrical inspiration.

3.
TMZ

Taylor Swift's "You Belong with Me" was an absolute commercial monster (it went six times Platinum, which is good). But more importantly, it lends itself suspiciously well to alteration into a warning to B, C and D-listers of the dangers of allowing yourself and your transgressions to end up on TMZ.

Swift was still a teenager when she recorded "You Belong with Me," but she already possessed a precocious gift for writing infectious pop songs. "TMZ" builds on the shiny perfection of Swift's hit, from its monster chorus to the banjo and selectively deployed pedal steel guitar that gives it just enough of a country edge. Al borrows the breathless conviction of Swift's delivery as he conjures up a seedy TMZ tabloid tableau, involving someone who is only "sort of famous," a "minor celebrity" at most, committing the unforgivable transgression of looking like a human being in public, instead of an airbrushed, plucked and polished red carpet pro.

"TMZ" references a series of real-life celebrity scandals and meltdowns involving Britney Spears (the head-shaving incident), Mel Gibson (DUI and racist rant), and Eddie Murphy/Hugh Grant (picking up a transvestite for reasons beyond being good Samaritans). But many, if not most, celebrities are guilty of other exceedingly minor transgressions outlined in the song, from bad hair days to sweat-stained tee-shirts to wardrobe fails and embarrassing cellulite.

Swift's original is clean to the point of being antiseptic, and coltishly wholesome in that inimitable early Taylor Swift fashion. But Al's parody is sleazy and voyeuristic, albeit just as musically tidy.

My favorite part of the song is Tom Kenny (*Mr. Show* alum and the voice of SpongeBob SquarePants) channeling the insufferable cadences of a *TMZ* carnival barker and hyping soul-crushing "exclusives" like "We caught this Oscar nominee picking up DOG POOP," "Is that a BABY BUMP?," "I pronounce her guilty... of leaving the house while FAT," "Look who's drinking COFFEE," and finally, "Everything celebrities do is FASCINATING," which is more or less TMZ's mission statement and *raison d'être*.

The celebrity who would benefit most directly from the warning about "TMZ" is not ultimately future tabloid fixture Swift – who, rumor has it, has had a bit of a tumultuous romantic history – but rather Swift's arch-nemesis Kanye West, who inexplicably *chose* to go on TMZ to argue that, among other things, slavery was a choice. Al doesn't counsel celebrities here not to go on TMZ and argue that slavery was a choice, because understandably he didn't feel that he needed to. I mean, who in their right mind would do something like that?

It's another case of the real world being crazier and more far-fetched than even Al's imagination.

4.
SKIPPER DAN

During the Ridiculously Self-Indulgent, Ill-Advised Vanity Tour, we got a fascinating glimpse at what Al's shows might be like if he'd never become the most successful parody artist in the history of American pop music. We got to experience what a "Weird Al" Yankovic show looks and feels like without the props, costumes, bit players, screens and stagecraft Al employs to closely reproduce the look and feel of his music videos.

For one sublime tour, Al cast off the shackles and expectations of pop stardom and was a musician, a cult artist, a veteran troubadour taking his songs from town to town, catering to a more explicitly adult audience than he'd ever entertained before.

There's only one "Weird Al" Yankovic but Al isn't unique in writing and performing funny songs. The Ridiculously Self-Indulgent, Ill-Advised Vanity Tour gave Al an opportunity to tour like Loudon Wainwright III or Kinky Friedman, two fellow *Dr. Demento Show* favorites who can travel the world entertaining crowds with just an acoustic guitar, a deep catalog of great songs and a surplus of charisma. They didn't have to mount an elaborate multimedia extravaganza every time they hit the stage.

More pertinently to the song we're discussing, The Ridiculously Self-Indulgent, Ill-Advised Vanity Tour gave Al a chance to be like Fountains of Wayne's Adam Schlesinger, who writes funny, melancholy story songs for his band, other people and the stage and screen while remaining relatively anonymous. "Skipper Dan" was designed as a Weezer pastiche, but my brain refuses to see it as anything other than a tribute to Fountains of Wayne.

"Skipper Dan" is a fascinating anomaly in that it feels less like comedy music than a rock song that just happens to be funny. The song's humor is subtler and more bittersweet than Al's usual fare: instead of being rooted in harmless insanity or obsession, it's rooted in an unexpectedly life-sized sense of personal and professional disappointment.

"Skipper Dan" doesn't introduce its central comic conceit until over a minute in. We start off slowly, with the titular thespian radiating all the potential in the world as not just any aspiring actor but as a future giant of the stage and screen destined for great things – glamorous photo shoots and Tarantino movies and Broadway glory.

The under-employed thespian *kvetching* to us in song is full of hope, dreams and great expectations that die a slow, un-mourned death. The best he can manage as an actor is prostituting his talents for a payday as tour guide "Skipper Dan" on the Jungle Cruise Ride in a theme park prison known as Adventureland.

The gig's vague proximity to actual acting just makes everything worse. This is an artist whose suffering soul angrily demands to recite Shakespeare in front of rapt crowds. Yet he's stuck telling the same abysmal jokes over and over again, dying a little more inside with every canned wisecrack.

This late-period sleeper finds Al eschewing the usual trash and low-culture signifiers in favor of uncharacteristically middlebrow (even highbrow) references to actress/acting teacher/author Uta Hagen, David Mamet's *Speed the Plow* and celebrity photographer Annie Leibovitz.

"Skipper Dan" is just too good to be a pastiche of a second-rate band like Weezer. But it perfectly captures the literate sadness that makes Fountains of Wayne so special, albeit to a cult a fraction the size of Al's audience.

5.
POLKA FACE

After the traditional polka opening (in this case Will Glahé's "Liechtensteiner Polka") "Polka Face" kicks off, appropriately enough, with Lady Gaga, whose "Poker Face" provides a punishingly punny sendoff.

Listening to Al and the boys' gleeful romp through "Poker Face" so soon after "Perform This Way" highlights a seeming contradiction in Gaga's persona: her image is, or was, borderline avant-garde, but she expresses herself through exceedingly commercial dance-pop songs.

Then again, it could be argued that Lady Gaga gets away with being such an art-pop exhibitionist weirdo precisely *because* she delivers the goods commercially.

"Polka Face" is all killer no filler, the catchiest parts of the era's biggest hits in polka form. We're talking "Baby," the irresistible slab of bubblegum pop that introduced an insufferable Canadian man-child named Justin Bieber to the world (with a co-sign/guest rap from Ludacris), Britney Spears' "Womanizer" and the melancholy pop-country glory of Lady Antebellum's "Need You Now."

One of the great joys of Al's polka medleys lies in hearing Al put on (and then quickly discard) so many musical personas wildly different to his own – like when Al the teetotaler gets busy with comical sound effects on Jamie Foxx and T-Pain's homage to drunken hook-ups, "Blame It."

On "I Kissed a Girl," Al delivers a gender-bending re-imagining of Katy Perry's calculating breakout hit, singing from the perspective of a girl who kisses a girl despite previously being a girl who only kissed guys. The sober Al sings the stoned chorus of "Day 'n' Nite," the intimate stoner breakout hit from Kid Cudi (who would eventually get sober and precede Al as the second bandleader/sidekick of *Comedy Bang! Bang!*).

When I was a kid, pop music felt like it was made in heaven specifically for me and kids like me, while simultaneously providing a voyeuristic glimpse into the hormone-crazed world of adults. Then, as a half-assed juvenile delinquent, pop music became my life, my identity, my escape, my joy. At a certain point, it became my job. Then it wasn't my job anymore, but something I chose to write about in idiosyncratic ways reflecting who I am and how I see the world. Every step of the way, Al has been there, like a Hawaiian shirt-wearing, mustachioed version of *The Giving Tree*.

These days, new pop music is what I hear when I'm riding in Lyfts or shopping in stores. That's not a bad way to experience recent pop hits, but it's not the best way. That's through the "Weird Al" Yankovic polka medley, that unique spin through the ephemeral excitement of some of pop's greatest (or at least catchiest) recent hits.

6.
CRAIGSLIST

The saga of "Weird Al" Yankovic is overwhelmingly happy. It's the story of a nice guy who finished first.

Yet even a career as triumphant as Al's is bound to have disappointments. Al is a terrific director, for example, who frustratingly hasn't had an opportunity to direct a major motion picture, whereas Michael Bay has directed many.

Al is also a terrific comic actor and in-demand voiceover artist, who hasn't had many opportunities to showcase his gifts as a thespian on film, television or the stage.

That's one of the reasons I dug Al on *Comedy Bang! Bang!*. Since Al was as important to the show as Scott Aukerman, he got an opportunity to not just appear in sketches, but to actually act in pretty much every episode while still ostensibly playing himself.

When I write that Al is a good actor, I'm only partially talking about *UHF, Comedy Bang! Bang!* or the cameos he's contributed to classics like *The Naked Gun* and *Popstar: Never Stop Never Stopping*. A lot of Al's best (and certainly most-seen) acting is done in videos and on stage.

During his Ridiculously Self-Indulgent, Ill-Advised Vanity Tour, Al did not merely sing songs like his appropriately

psychedelic Doors tribute "Craigslist." No, Al *performed* them with his whole body. Even that is selling Al short. Al didn't just perform "Craigslist" as if overtaken by Jim Morrison's peyote-addled wandering spirit: he channeled the man in a way that bordered on spooky.

Jim Morrison was the anti-"Weird Al" Yankovic, a debauched libertine and the personification of bloated rock pretension. Morrison took himself so seriously that it's hard not to laugh derisively at him. Morrison didn't just croon pop songs and occasionally expose his penis in concert settings: he sang about Important Things, like sex and death and war and freedom and transcendence.

"Craigslist" re-imagines Jim Morrison not as the poet/rock star/philosopher of the public imagination, but as a lunatic Craigslist obsessive subjecting other users, and the public at large, to their eccentricities and oddball demands.

Replacing the Lizard King's bloated presence with Al's satirical, funhouse mirror version of Morrison can only be an upgrade. To paraphrase the title of a single by U2 (another rock group known for their pretentiousness), Al's perversely petty take on the Doors' frontman is even better than the real thing.

7.
PARTY IN THE CIA

Miley Cyrus' "Party in the USA" is pure sonic sugar, a girlish celebration of being young and American, innocent and alive. Al's black ops-themed parody "Party in the CIA" boasts an eviscerating darkness and body count he usually reserves for songs about Christmas or romantic relationships. "Party in the CIA" is the story of a new CIA agent with a head full of innocent dreams of assassinating foreign leaders, undermining legitimate governments, and performing what Patrick Bateman would lovingly refer to as "Murders and Executions."

"Party in the CIA" is political in a way Al's music generally isn't. There's satire and social commentary in Al's music about consumerism, consumption and the way first television and then the internet colonized and corrupted our brains. But this might mark the first time in Al's auspicious career where he wrote about the sinister side of American foreign policy and the many evil, illegal things the CIA does in the name of the greater good.

"Party in the CIA" is an incongruous mash-up of state-of-the-art girl pop and international intrigue. It's Jason Bourne meets Katy Perry: Al, ever the chameleon, borrows Cyrus' giddy, guileless enthusiasm to sing about the United States' intelligence agencies as a rogue arm of our government, one that ignores niceties like the Geneva Convention and international law when they get in the way of achieving their ominous objectives.

It's a jam, y'all, and a party, albeit one where the festivities are more likely to involve waterboarding and assassinations than Pin the Tail on the Donkey.

The upbeat, youthful optimism of "Party in the USA" becomes hilarious when applied not to Jay-Z jams and L.A. weather but executions, brainwashing and black ops drudgery. The encouraging cries of "like yeah" here refer specifically to "tapping the phones," "shredding the files," "staging a coup" and finally "brainwashing moles."

"Party in the CIA" subverts the ebullience of Cyrus' original by taking it in a bracingly dark direction, while simultaneously underlining the song's enduring strengths.

Al's parodies are almost never as dark, violent, satirical or political as this, nor as brutally funny and maddeningly infectious.

8.
RINGTONE

The ringtone is like so much modern technology. In theory, it radiates promise. The ringtone pointlessly empowers consumers to take control over their cell phone experience by purchasing nuggets of pop music that, to paraphrase Nicolas Cage in *Wild at Heart,* reflect their individuality and belief in personal expression.

When ringtones became a ubiquitous staple of American life, ringtone owners were liberated from having the same boring ring as everyone else. This proved another instance of technology managing to collectively make our lives worse (and more annoying) rather than better.

The singer of the Queen pastiche "Ringtone" begins the song in a place of prominence. "Once, not very long ago, I was respected, I was popular," he crows, before lamenting the schlocky instrument of his destruction – a ringtone so infuriating that it unites every human being on the planet Earth in their hatred of it.

Like "Bohemian Rhapsody," "Ringtone" was not written so much as it was lovingly, meticulously composed as a snack-sized musical suite, featuring a series of distinct components that add up to something symphonic, achingly ambitious and perversely banal.

The singer never specifies which ringtone led to his downfall. He doesn't have to. To call a ringtone annoying is redundant and unnecessary, since the much-maligned form of music is inherently irritating.

There's something inspired about making an epic suite about something so slight and meaningless. But I also dig the comic hyperbole, particularly the call and response where Al surveys the world and discerns that the one thing that brings us all together is hatred of this cursed ringtone. He sings, "Chinese factory workers (they hate my ringtone)/Muslim women in burqas (really hate my ringtone)/Starvin' kids in Angola (they hate my ringtone)/Even folks with Ebola (just hate my ringtone)/All the nuns and nannies (all the welfare mothers)/All the Pakistanis (all the Wayans brothers)/Everyone on the land, everyone on the sea/Every single person everywhere unanimously."

"Ringtone" is wonderfully consistent with Al's other portrayals of internet-era technology making our lives better, and worse, and many times more irritating, all at the same time.

9.
ANOTHER TATTOO

"Another Tattoo" hijacks B.o.B and Bruno Mars' "Nothin' on You"'s dreamy, yearning texture and swooning romanticism for a character study of a tattoo-obsessed American Jackass hopelessly in love with poor life choices and body art that is an insult to good taste.

"Another Tattoo" is part social satire about an idiot man-child whose body art tells a story all right, albeit of stupidity, vulgarity and cluelessness, but it is also rooted in the comedy of randomness.

The humor in "Another Tattoo" is also grounded in the irritatingly busy production on the obnoxious song it's parodying. "Nothin' on You" is a duet between B.o.B and then-rising pop star Bruno Mars, but it'd sound like a collaboration even if Mars was not singing the hook. B.o.B's vocals are double-tracked so relentlessly he acts as his own idiot hype man. He chatters at the end of seemingly every line, pointlessly repeats words with a slightly different inflection, cheers himself on, and laughs for no discernible reason.

Al picked up on the way B.o.B and his producers have the rapper/singer/flat-earth-proponent constantly responding

to himself in the most asinine possible way and ramp it up to comic extremes.

This may not be the most dignified parody in Al's catalog, but that doesn't make it any less infectious. It's tattooed on my brain – inscribed on it indelibly, as it were – in a way its lackluster inspiration simply isn't.

10.
IF THAT ISN'T LOVE

"If That Isn't Love" is Al's tribute to Hanson, whom he counts as friends and collaborators. Most people know Hanson mainly as the adorable trio of godly young brothers who exploded onto the pop culture consciousness with their Dust Brothers-produced bubblegum smash "MMMBop."

To most of the American public, that was the beginning and end of Hanson. They had their giant smash, and then a few lesser hits, and then they quietly went away forever. Except that Hanson didn't go anywhere: they continued to make music and tour and release albums for a devoted, loyal fanbase.

"If That Isn't Love" sounds nice. If it were a person, it'd be clean and presentable with a winning smile. It's upbeat, feel-good, squeaky-clean pop rock about a boyfriend who is anything but nice.

The singer of "If That Isn't Love" has a deluded conception of romance. In the song's chorus, the creepy Casanova sings of the many terrible things he does, "If that isn't love/I don't know what love is." But he could remove the "if" from that sentiment, and it would instantly become several thousand times more accurate.

This dirtbag's conception of *l'amour fou* involves being moderately less terrible than he could be. The singer's vows of devotion look suspiciously like insults, like when he promises his ostensible beloved, "I totally support every idiotic thing you do" and "When you're tellin' me about your feelings, I try not to yawn."

My favorite moment in "If That Isn't Love" is also its most exquisitely random. It's when Al humblebrags of his devotion, "I'll kiss you even if you've had omelets for breakfast/And I can't stand omelets!"

The misplaced passion and intensity Al brings to the words, "I can't stand omelets!" cracks me up, as does the singer's apparent belief that kissing someone with omelet breath represents the highest form of selflessness.

"If That Isn't Love" is modest in scope, a deceptively chirpy anti-love song from a major artist.

11.
WHATEVER YOU LIKE

Timeliness has always been important to Al. That was particularly true of "Whatever You Like," a parody of T.I.'s number one smash of the same name, which Al parodied while the original was still riding high on the pop charts.

But the song was timely in other ways as well: as the opening line acknowledges, the song's cheapskate aesthetic is rooted in the economic uncertainty of the Great Recession of 2007 and 2008.

The music industry was changing dramatically when "Whatever You Like" was released as a digital single in 2008, and the perpetually tech-savvy Al changed with it. In the Darwinian world of pop music, you either evolve or die.

"Whatever You Like" was released digitally on October 8th, 2008, just a few months after the original's release on July 29th the same year. As with "Trapped in the Drive-Thru," it's a very Caucasian take on R&B.

In this case, Al transforms T.I.'s tribute to conspicuous consumption into a cheapskate's uniquely unappealing spiel. Where T.I. played the big shot treating the lady of his dreams to a never-ending shopping spree, Al substitutes one of his trademark creepy Casanovas, albeit one who is excessively, even perversely thrifty rather than violently insane.

It's all about the Washingtons, as Al subverts Hip Hop and R&B's materialism with a downscale offer to share a life devoted primarily to pinching pennies. As with the materialistic rap songs it spoofs, "Whatever You Like" is all about the details. So instead of bragging about Bentleys and Rolexes and popping Cristal, the incongruously cocky tightwad substitutes staples of life near the bottom of the socio-economic ladder: ramen, government cheese, homemade haircuts, Minute Rice, White Castle and Goodwill.

Splurging – or rather "splurging," since Al's version has little in common with how the phrase is generally understood – has seldom been quite so pathetic or as deeply amusing as it is here.

Both versions of "Whatever You Like" are about money. But Al makes rapping/singing about saving money a whole lot more fun than bragging about wasting it, and much more relatable to boot.

12.
STOP FORWARDING THAT CRAP TO ME

As a songwriter, Jim Steinman has always written about what really matters in American life: love, sex, being young and free and the wrestler Hulk Hogan. Steinman is a master of musical melodrama. His songs are tacky drive-in movies in song form, cornball slices of pop Americana most famously interpreted by Meat Loaf.

Steinman writes big songs about huge subjects. On the transcendently prickly "Stop Forwarding That Crap to Me," Al adopts Steinman's musical theater bombast as the roaring, incongruously symphonic background for an all-too relatable gripe session about one of the preeminent irritations of an internet age that has provided fodder for many of Al's best late-period songs: the unwanted email.

Al almost invariably sings from the perspective of characters of varying degrees of outrageousness and/or insanity. He's putting on musical costumes in his parodies and pastiches. But on "Stop Forwarding That Crap to Me," it feels like we're getting a glimpse at Al's inner misanthrope. For a little under six minutes, Al unleashes the crank within. It is a thing of beauty.

"Stop Forwarding That Crap to Me" may be "Weird Al" Yankovic's sanest song. There's not an irrational sentiment expressed on it.

Technology has empowered us and made our lives better and easier, but it's also empowered friends and acquaintances to irritate us in new and aggravatingly easy ways, such as the unsolicited email forward.

Email forwards are like gifts. Ideally, they strengthen our bonds with our loved ones by illustrating just how well we know them by giving them something we know they'll like and appreciate. But the "gifts" the righteously enraged singer here receives in email forward form are more like curses. Instead of reaffirming relationships, they make the singer wonder what made them think he could possibly be interested in anything they have to offer in the cute cat video/conspiracy theory/viral YouTube clips/fake George Carlin "wisdom" department.

"Stop Forwarding That Crap to Me" works itself into a righteous fervor railing against a broad cross section of obnoxious online *faux pas*, some of them uncannily prescient. Over a half decade before Facebook began using Snopes as a fact-checking tool in an admirable attempt to be less of a toxic force for evil and disinformation, Al was singing to the folks bothering him with unwanted emails, "I have high hopes someone will point you toward Snopes/And debunk that crazy junk you're spewing constantly."

Al makes particularly deft use of a choir to give the song the spirit and moral authority of the church while delivering a decidedly secular message about the necessity of boundaries and discretion.

Despite the occasional, exquisite prickliness, there's a sort of cumulative joy to Al's oddball catalog that reaches a glorious crescendo with "Stop Forwarding That Crap to Me." It's a brilliant illustration of Al's genius as a singer, songwriter, producer and musician from an original at the height of his powers.

MANDATORY
FUN
(2014)

1.
HANDY

When I was hired to write *Weird Al: The Book* around the time of *Alpocalypse*'s completion, my job, as I saw it, was to present the strongest case for Al as an artist, musician and satirist.

By the time *Mandatory Fun* debuted at number one in 2014, I felt like that argument no longer needed to be made, and not because I did such an amazing job with *Weird Al: The Book*.

By his fourteenth studio album Al's longevity was self-evident. Al was never supposed to last, let alone endure for the 35-year stretch separating the release of the "My Bologna" single on Capitol and *Mandatory Fun*. Yet here Al was, as relevant, funny and popular as ever.

Part of it was generational: people who grew up on Al as a quintessential geek hero rose to places of prominence in society, musical theater, film and podcasting. They were doing things like writing *Hamilton*, directing *The Last Jedi*, and turning an absurdist podcast rich in in-jokes and weird conceptual humor called *Comedy Bang! Bang!* into an unlikely empire, with Al eventually playing an important role.

These powerful figures helped give *Mandatory Fun* a launch befitting Al's status. Al was received as a conquering hero, a living legend, a national treasure. But the hero's welcome the album received was also attributable to Al maintaining such a high level of quality control three and a half decades into his recording career.

Deep into middle-age, Al was still on top of the perpetually youth-obsessed world of pop music. For him, pop is a fountain of youth. As long as he tries on the guises of the teens and twenty-somethings that rule the pop charts, he never seems to age, let alone grow old.

Iggy Azalea's monster hit "Fancy" was the work of a woman in her early twenties, but it felt even younger. When

I first listened to "Handy," Al's parody, I'd read about Azalea without ever actually hearing the ubiquitous smash that made her simultaneously famous and infamous, envied and reviled.

Azalea was treated by the music press as a Vanilla Ice figure, a cultural parasite who stole from black culture without showing respect for Hip Hop or acknowledging her status as a cultural outsider.

The humor in "Handy" comes from the incongruity of using a snotty rap anthem (one overflowing with sneering, deliberately obnoxious adolescent braggadocio) to boast about something as dorky and dad-friendly as your skills as a handyman.

As with "Another Tattoo," Al captures the annoyingly busy nature of contemporary Hip Hop and R&B production, particularly the way vocals are double-tracked so that rappers serve as their own hype men (or women, in Iggy's instance), mindlessly cheering the most banal sentiments.

"Handy" is particularly sly with pop culture references – whether Al is bragging that he's got "99 problems but a switch ain't one" or boasting, "Still rocking my screwdriver/Got the whole world thinking I'm MacGyver." Al's technique on the mic is nothing short of amazing.

From the "Plumbing Song" to "Hardware Store" to "Handy," no one has gotten more comedically out of the Home Depot lifestyle than Al.

"First things first, I'm a craftsman!" sneers Al defiantly at the beginning of "Handy." In the most literal sense, he's referring to the kind of craftsman who'll fix your clogged toilet. But on this, his fourteenth and last studio album to date, he could also be talking about himself.

By the time *Mandatory Fun* rocketed to the top of the charts, no one could deny Al's status as a preeminent comic and musical craftsman. With "Handy," blame the hackneyed, familiar subject matter on the drain and the song's inspired execution to Al's big, flexible brain.

2.
LAME CLAIM TO FAME

Al has experienced fame from the inside out. He's famous. His friends are famous. Everywhere he goes, he's recognized by fans spurred to approach him by his reputation as the nicest man in show business. But Al is also fascinated by the subject of fame itself.

The Southern Culture on the Skids homage "Lame Claim to Fame" is a little like "TMZ" in its depiction of our culture's pathological obsession with fame and celebrity, no matter how tacky or unmerited. Tom Kenny's cry of "Everything celebrities do is fascinating!" from "TMZ" could double as the wonky thesis of "Lame Claim to Fame."

Al yowls the song from the perspective of a Southern yokel so obsessed with the A-list, as well as well as the B, C and D-list that he clings desperately to the flimsiest quasi-encounters with celebrity, which run the gamut from super-famous (Jack Nicholson, Kim Kardashian, Steven Seagal) to extremely non-famous (an extra in *Wayne's World 2,* an acquaintance of Brad Pitt's, Ralph Nader's second cousin).

The point of name-dropping is to make the name-dropper seem more impressive by association. In dropping a name, one transfers some of the famous person's magical glow onto the person who just so happens to be a close personal friend (something Al has a LOT of), or a cousin, or former acquaintance of a bona fide celebrity. The farther removed from actual fame, the less impressive the claim. In the case of the star-struck hick of "Lame Claim to Fame," he's so far removed from legitimate fame that he might as well be living on another planet from the superstars whose star power he hopes will rub off on him.

"Lame Claim to Fame" is a modest tribute to a modest band that Al sells with rowdy redneck energy. Al's own claim to fame is extraordinary, but this isn't the best illustration of why

Al deserves every bit of the success he's accrued. Al also deserves to be in the otherwise lame Rock and Roll Hall of Fame, of course, but that's an argument (and injustice) for another time.

3.
FOIL

Al is a master of brevity. He's gifted at cramming ideas, jokes, music and craziness into tiny songs as short on length as they are long on inspiration. Take, for instance, the lunatic brilliance of "Foil," his conceptually bonkers parody of Lorde's breakthrough underdog smash "Royals." The ingenious parody is barely longer than two minutes, but it changes tone and subject matter so unexpectedly that it's essentially two songs in one.

If "Foil" is one of Al's best late-period parodies, that's partially because he's riffing on yet another perfect pop song. "Royals" is a masterpiece of icy electronic minimalism which finds the New Zealand teenager forcefully rejecting the pop world's materialistic excess while acknowledging its glossy allure.

"Royals" is about something substantive. In its own weird way, "Foil" is too – though that's not apparent from its first verse, which finds Al once again venturing back into the grocery store to find inspiration.

Nobody sounds more excited or comfortable singing college words than Al, so it's a delight to hear him tear into scientific jargon: "I never seem to finish all my food/I always get a doggie bag from the waiter/So I just keep what's still un-chewed/And I take it home, save it for later/But then I deal with fungal rot, bacterial formation/Microbes, enzymes, mold and oxidation."

"Foil" wraps together a thrillingly banal first verse with an exhilaratingly deep second verse in one shiny package. After playing musical pitchman for aluminum, Al follows an audible sip of Earl Grey tea with a wonderfully off-handed, "Oh, by the way, I've cracked the code."

Al goes from 0 to 60 espousing crackpot conspiracy theories that paint a dark vision of a world spiraling out of control, with sinister forces furtively pulling the strings and a brainwashed populace none the wiser. Thankfully, our paranoia-crazed crooner has advice for thwarting monsters from space: "Wear a hat that's foil-lined/In case an alien's inclined/To probe your butt or read your mind."

It's not just aliens and moon fakers that our conspiracy theorist is worried about. He's worried about everything. As he warns hypnotically, "I've figured out these shadow organizations/

And the Illuminati know/That they're finally primed for world domination." Gaining in momentum, he warns of "black helicopters comin' 'cross the border, puppet masters for the New World Order."

Musically, "Foil" is all about cool, calm control. Al is as artfully measured as Lorde in his delivery; his tone never changes, even when he goes from selling the mundane virtues of aluminum wrap to warning of the dangers posed by the Illuminati, the New World Order and anal probe-hungry space aliens.

There is not a wasted moment here: it's one hundred and forty-three seconds of sonic and lyrical perfection. Everything from the sound effect of Al sipping tea to the hypnotically sinister groove adds to the winning juxtaposition of the soothingly mundane and deliciously insane.

4.
SPORTS SONG

Al and his band are wonderfully eclectic. Their discography is filled with glorious one-offs. Al seems to have challenged himself to make a song in just about every genre and style, from the zydeco of "My Baby's in Love with Eddie Vedder" to the college fight song parody "Sports Song."

The college fight song is not just a celebration of victory, but a promise. The arrogance of the college fight song is overbearing, but masked by grandiose verbiage.

"Sports Song" sounds at once timeless and old-fashioned; after all, most college sports songs sound like they were written in the Jazz Age by an F. Scott Fitzgerald type, wearing a raccoon fur coat to impress flappers.

The vibe of "Sports Song" is less Jock Jam than *Harvard Lampoon* satire. It starts off by rhyming "clearly inferior" with "collective posterior" and maintains that level of lyrical complexity throughout. Al sounds downright scientific when he taunts, "Your sports team will soon suffer swift defeat/ That theory's backed up by empirical evidence" before waxing metaphorical when he insists, "We're gonna grind up your guys into burger meat/Again, of course, we're speaking in the figurative sense."

After spending two glorious verses elucidating his team's greatness in increasingly insulting ways, Al gets to the heart of his argument when he chants during an infectious chorus, "We're great (We're great!)/And you suck (You suck!)/We're great (We're great!)/And you suck (You suck!)/We're great (We're great!)/And you suck (You suck!)/You see there's us (We're great!)/And then there's you (You suck!)/We're really, really great (Really great!) In contrast, you really suck (Really suck)."

Then Al makes a concession that changes the meaning of the song dramatically when he confesses, "Okay, full disclosure, we're not that great/But nevertheless, you suck."

The seminal 1974 political documentary *Hearts & Minds* drew a direct line between the rah-rah boosterism of college and high school football and the madness of the Vietnam War. There's a sense of that in "Sports Song" as well. Its arrogance is unmistakably American; when Al boils the essence of sports fandom down to a primal chant of "We're great, and you suck," he could just as easily be Donald Trump discussing our country's relationship with every other nation on earth.

Like the belligerent athletic supporter Al channels in the song, Trump's need to repeat as often as possible that we're great and that everyone else sucks is a product not of genuine confidence but insecurity. It's a desperate need to cover for the fact that, when it comes down to it, maybe *we're* the ones who suck, and our opponents are the ones who're great.

"Sports Song" is a one-size-fits-all wisenheimer sports satire directed less to tailgaters than the kind of high-I.Q. geeks who bring a book to college football games so they don't get bored. It's my all-time favorite college fight song because it doesn't have much competition. (I'm not much of a sports fan.) But I know enough to confidently assert that "Sports Song" is great, and all other college fight songs suck.

5.
WORD CRIMES

Al generally writes from the perspective of outsiders of varying degrees of insanity. Occasionally, however, we get a glimpse at Al Yankovic, the man behind the weirdness. "Stop Forwarding That Crap to Me," for example, is full of uncharacteristically reasonable sentiments.

"Word Crimes" is similarly rife with atypically sane beliefs and opinions it's easy to imagine Al having, being as good and precise at grammar as he is at everything else. I should know: when I was co-writing *Weird Al: The Book,* he was my editor and copy-editor as well, and he's as good at understanding and obeying the rules of grammar as I am terrible at them.

As a prolific longtime word criminal, I felt implicated by "Word Crimes" as well as Al's introduction to this book. The parody finds Al trading in the club/bedroom vibe of Robin Thicke, Pharrell and T.I.'s "original" – insomuch as the United States court system legally deemed "Blurred Lines" a trademark-violating knock-off of Marvin Gaye's "Got to Give It Up" – for the classroom.

A word-nerd subversion of Robin Thicke's controversial smash hit, "Word Crimes" has an unmistakable party groove. Unfortunately for Thicke, his accountant and his bank account, it's the party groove of a shindig where the Marvin Gaye song "Got to Give It Up" is blasting on the stereo.

Perhaps because it's spoofing such a controversial song, "Word Crimes" contains several of the most controversial lyrics in Al's catalog. When Al advised listeners, "You should never write words using numbers/Unless you're seven, or your name is Prince," fans speculated as to whether Al was sending shots in the direction of a certain purple-loving Minnesota eccentric with a long, public record of turning down his parody requests.

Was Al comparing the artist formerly known as The Artist Formerly Known as Prince to a bratty seven-year-old?

Al would never be petty enough to lash out in song at Prince. He's not that kind of guy. Al instead chose to express his displeasure with Prince killing potential parodies the only way he knows how: by seducing Prince's lovers/protégés. Apollonia. Vanity. Shelia E. A young Carmen Electra. All came to know Al's amorous charms intimately. But what began as mere revenge grew into an erotic obsession that would change all their lives forever. But that's ultimately not a story for me to tell.

The tone might be sharp and sarcastic, but Al pays tribute to Prince here by positing (correctly) that he is (or rather was) the only person who could get away with indulging that particular linguistic quirk without seeming obnoxious. "Word Crimes" echoes the sordidness of its source material with one of Al's biggest double entendres, when he advises listeners to procure the services of a "cunning linguist" to "help you distinguish what's proper English."

"Word Crimes" isn't just built on an obnoxiously infectious pop smash: it's based on two insanely catchy pop hits so it's only fitting that Al's cerebral subversion of Robin Thicke's creepy, controversial smash became his fourth biggest all-time chart hit, peaking at 39.

"Word Crimes" hits particularly close to home for me. When Al taunts the grammar-impaired, "You really need a full-time proofreader/You dumb mouth-breather," he's pretty much just offering me straightforward feedback on my website, the Weird Accordion to Al column and this book. Even more impressively, he's offering it years before the site and column even launched.

Al was ultimately so horrified by the word crimes I committed in the process of writing this book that he offered his services as a cunning linguist who could help me distinguish what's proper English by volunteering to copy-edit my book for free.

"Word Crimes" is such an undeniable monster of a parody that I'm a little surprised it wasn't *Mandatory Fun*'s kick-off track. But its spot halfway through the album gives *Mandatory Fun* a wonderful blast of energy that's pointedly smart and silly, as opposed to deeply problematic like Thicke's quasi-original.

6.
MY OWN EYES

In 2019 Al picked up his fifth Grammy, defeating Guns N' Roses, The Decemberists, The Grateful Dead and Johnny Nicholas. Even more impressively, the Grammy is for Al's 15-volume, career-spanning box set *Squeeze Box: The Complete Works of "Weird Al" Yankovic.*

Five Grammys is good. That's *real* good. That fifth Grammy separates the real from the fake. If you only have four Grammys, you might still suck. You may still be terrible at what you do and an embarrassment to your family. You can fake your way to four Grammys. *Easily.*

But *five* Grammys? That means you're legit. That means you're good at what you do and people like you. Five Grammys and you can throw away those Uber brochures, because you are officially successful at music and no longer need to contemplate a side-gig in the ride-share community.

Al didn't just win in the usual comedy or music video categories, either, where his competition are literally clowns who invite the world to laugh at them and their many failings. No, Al triumphed in a prestigious archival category that found him squaring off against legends. Once titans of the industry, Guns n' Roses and the Grateful Dead will now exclusively be seen as losers that Al beat like a misbehaving mule.

It was "Gotta Boogie" versus "Welcome to the Jungle" and "Box of Rain" for the big prize, and Al handed these doped-up rock posers the kind of whipping outsider artist Wesley Willis (himself a five-time Grammy winner) sang passionately about.

The box set is a testament to Al's status as more than just the "Eat It" guy. The consistency of the albums as cohesive entities, as well as the originals and the album cuts, illustrate how much more there is to Al than just the hits.

The aggressively goofy, goofily aggressive Foo Fighters pastiche "My Own Eyes" is a quintessential album cut. It's about a man afflicted with an intense case of Post-Traumatic Silliness Disorder. A series of unlikely (if not downright impossible) images are burned indelibly into his frazzled brain, each more ridiculous than the last.

This is as straightforward as Al gets. The choruses are fundamentally serious, but the verses are like little one-panel gag strips from *National Lampoon*, centered on a series of absurd conceits. A man's guinea pig commits *harakiri*, a Japanese ritualistic suicide by self-disembowelment, but finds a ghoulish second life as a hacky sack. The next door neighbor's children sell lemonade and weapons-grade plutonium, accepting payment in MasterCard (and sometimes human organs).

That might seem peculiar, if not the kind of thing that would drive a normal man insane. But we are assured that this is *really* good lemonade. In a wonderfully Al-esque subversion, the impassioned singer brings up human organs, children selling radioactive chemicals and a lemonade stand, then focuses monomaniacally on one aspect of the lemonade stand: the lemon drink's irrefutable quality.

Like Bieber fever and the danger posed by a mime's imaginary cleavers, Post-Traumatic Stress Disorder is no laughing matter. Post-Traumatic Silliness Disorder, on the other hand, is very much so, especially with Al and the gang rocking this hard.

7.
NOW THAT'S WHAT I CALL POLKA!

Al's history with the Cyrus family is deep, in a shallow way. His mock-hatred of Billy Ray Cyrus' "Achy Breaky Heart" inspired him to write "Achy Breaky Song," Al's first single to get airplay on country stations. Al next revisited the recorded output of the Cyrus clan when he parodied Miley's "Party in the USA" as "Party in the CIA."

Miley's number one hit "Wrecking Ball" is a product of her Hip Hop period, but there's nothing particularly Hip Hop about it. It's a string-laden ballad so raw that it retains some of its shattering emotional power even in tongue-in-cheek polka medley form. Al's polka medleys allow us to see and hear groaningly familiar smashes in new and sometimes revelatory ways. Consequently, "Wrecking Ball" doesn't need a full orchestra or Miley's wildly emotive vocals to pack a punch. Even as a joke, it's a monster.

"Wrecking Ball" is followed by "Pumped Up Kicks," an infectious pop song about a school shooting that derives its novelty from the ironic gulf between its grim subject matter and its mall-ready sound. In Al and the gang's hands, however, there's nothing subtle about the bloody nature of the subject matter: the gunshot sound effect prominently featured in the medley gives the game away.

From there, it's a dizzy spin through the most infectious jams of the early teens, from Psy's "Gangnam Style" to Pitbull (featuring Ke$ha)'s "Timber" to Carly Rae Jepsen's "Call Me Maybe."

A polka version of "Gangnam Style" is always going to be fun, especially with Al giving the "Sexy Lady" part of Psy's international novelty smash a Jerry Lewis by way of Professor Frink inflection, but I always prefer serious songs to disposable pop in medleys.

"NOW That's What I Call Polka!" ends on a satisfyingly familiar note with a polka-fied burst of Daft Punk's Pharrell Williams-assisted "Get Lucky" that focuses on a recurring theme in Al's medleys: the repetitive excess of hit pop songs. If the chorus of "Get Lucky"got stuck in our collective mind, that's probably because Pharrell repeats the title of Daft Punk's smash over and over and over and over and over and over and over and over and over again.

These pleasingly familiar mashups of monster hits afford Al the opportunity to simultaneously play the roles of crowd-pleasing party musician and covert music critic. By radically re-conceiving the top hits of the day, Al is commenting on these songs and the role they play in our culture, while exploiting the hypnotic power they hold over the music-buying public.

8.
MISSION STATEMENT

Al doesn't get much more conceptual than on "Mission Statement," which cross-pollinates the exquisite textures of Crosby, Stills & Nash's spacey, transcendentally sad "Suite: Judy Blue Eyes" with semi-impenetrable business jargon so technical it feels like another language.

That's fitting, since the joyous final portion of "Suite: Judy Blue Eyes" finds Stephen Stills trading the romantic ennui of the suite's early sections for something more optimistic, and English for Spanish.

"Suite: Judy Blue Eyes" quivers with passionate intensity. But there's also a desperate, poignant yearning for release from a world of suffering. Breaking up is agony, but there is life on the other side. "Mission Statement" features some of the most beautiful music of Al's career, wedded to some of the driest sentiments. "Suite: Judy Blue Eyes" consists of a series of movements that take listeners through a twisting, winding cavalcade of moods and tones and emotions – from harmony-laden, acoustic guitar-driven aggressive folk rock to trippy, moody, 3-AM-the-morning-after-a-hashish-fueled-orgy decadence, and finally to a place of fragile hope.

"Mission Statement" is exclusively about the sonic ride. Lyrically, it's deliberately impenetrable, a collection of buzz words and business school terminology that has a strangely propulsive rhythm all its own. Al chose his words here for how they sound rather than what they mean – although the point seems to be that these obnoxious phrases don't really mean anything at all, at least to people without MBAs.

The phrase "It's a paradigm shift!" has never been delivered with the child-like excitement Al brings to it here. Like the oddball protagonist of "Dog Eat Dog," he's deriving a kooky, counter-intuitive spiritual bliss from the soul-killing details of office life. Al sings of monetizing assets with the same passion Stephen Stills sang about heartbreak and folk-rockers sang of their hopes for a more just society.

The singer of "Mission Statement" nurses no such idealism. The song is strictly business, a groovy sonic be-in that mashes up the psychedelic sound of the 1960s with the naked money-lust of the 1980s and, who are we kidding, every decade before and after the '80s as well.

Americans didn't just decide to love money once Reagan was in office: that's always been our thing, as "Mission Statement" attests. We are a nation of consumers and TV addicts and furious masticators. But we're also a nation of capitalists hopelessly locked into the system whether we like it or not, at least until a long-overdue political and economic paradigm shift comes along.

9.
INACTIVE

Throughout the '80s, Al sang about consumers consuming';. The "Eat It" guy rose to fame singing about food. But he also sang about other forms of consumption, and other forms of being a consumer as well. He's sung from the perspective of couch potatoes, obsessives whose lives have been transformed by comically oversized television sets and their exposure to cable television and individual shows/performers like Ed McMahon, Bob Denver and *I Dream of Jeannie*.

"Inactive," Al's parody of Imagine Dragons' monster hit "Radioactive," puts these two different conceptions of consumption together into a scathing depiction of apathy, American style.

Our sloth-like protagonist is covered in evidence of his habitual over-eating: his apartment has become a museum of laziness, where exercise machines purchased in a delusional burst of optimism lie unoccupied.

This corpulent crooner has everything he needs to avoid leading a healthy life. Everything he requires (food, pretty much, but also soda) is within arm's reach (with the notable exception of his remote control) because he's not one of those fitness freaks who think nothing of "standing up" and "walking" or "breathing without considerable effort."

For lack of a better word, this man has allowed himself to get fat. Whether it's Spam, or Oreos, or Rocky Road ice cream, or even lasagna, this round mound of apathy is most assuredly going to eat it. For this exemplar of American laziness, inactivity isn't a weakness as much as a way of life. He's chosen the Way of the Couch Potato willfully, or because he just kind of fell into it.

If "Radioactive" is about a man waking up to his own power and agency, "Inactive" is about a big, crumb-laden puddle of "Who cares?" and "Why bother?" realizing his ultimate powerlessness, or rather his ultimate power in choosing to give up.

The singer is sliding into a 600-pound life, but "Inactive" isn't about fat-shaming. It's not about being morbidly obese so much as it is about not trying. It's about the sedentary, passive existence as the only life worth barely leading.

"Inactive" is a busy-sounding song about doing nothing, a satire of over-consumption and apathy taken to extreme ends. But it gets an additional kick from its roots in a maddeningly infectious pop song so popular and brazenly commercial that it qualifies as a tacky consumer product in its own right. As products go, "Radioactive" belongs in a supermarket bin alongside all the Cheetos, frozen pizza and other staples of the lazy life Al lovingly references.

10.
FIRST WORLD PROBLEMS

The concept of "First World Problems" is not terribly dissimilar from Harris Wittels' concept of the "humblebrag." In both cases, the exemplar of unexamined cultural privilege "complains" about something in a way that only reinforces what a charmed life they lead. "First World Problems" were originally called "White People Problems" before, ironically, people figured out that it's racist to act as if only Caucasians are rich and spoiled. Of course white people don't have a monopoly on being monstrously self-involved. Everybody can be terrible. Many people are!

So the concept of "White People Problems" was re-branded as "First World Problems" to make it less #problematic, while still taking aim at privileged people and their non-problems.

"First World Problems" is a Pixies pastiche that finds Al inhabiting the persona of a raging Black Francis to guest vocalist Amanda Palmer's Kim Deal. Over buzzsaw guitars, Al whines about the minor inconveniences of the over-privileged and under-self-aware. The complaints begin with "My maid is cleaning the bathroom, so I can't take a shower/When I do, the water starts getting cold after an hour."

Some of these not-so-fine whines are more relatable than others. You don't have to be a Kardashian to have experienced the very minor trauma of trying to fast-forward through commercials like a civilized human being, only to realize that you're watching what in olden times was known as "live TV."

You don't have to be rich to experience First World Problems, although it helps. As "First World Problems" illustrates, the titular phenomenon is a state of mind. You don't have to be wealthy to have it, just terrible.

Al's timely satire nails the underlying phenomenon of First World Problems – cursing a tiny element of your life that is somehow imperfect rather than appreciating your privileged existence. Yet these creature comforts are somehow never enough to ensure happiness for brats with a mindset of entitlement, guaranteeing that true contentment will remain forever outside their grasp.

11.
TACKY

Wikipedia describes American pop parodist "Weird Al" Yankovic as an American singer-songwriter, record producer, satirist, film producer and author. All that is true, of course. But for me, what Al does for a living is make people happy. And not just a little bit happy. No, Al makes people at his live shows deliriously happy. Ridiculously happy. Happy to an uncool, unhip extent.

Al's work made me happy when I was a boy. It makes me happy now. Joy is an essential but often overlooked component of Al's music and Al's world. Some of that joy comes secondhand from the songs Al is spoofing.

Songs don't get happier than Pharrell's "Happy." Being a canny hit-maker, the Neptunes frontman recorded a song for the *Despicable Me 2* soundtrack that might actually be *too* upbeat for a shiny CGI children's cartoon. "Happy" is the title, the vibe, the subject matter. And happy is what the song makes you, unless you've got the heart of a pre-transformation Grinch.

Pharrell is a phenomenally talented writer, producer, multi-instrumentalist and pop icon who has written, produced and guested on roughly four thousand songs that sound pretty much the same. "Blurred Lines," "Get Lucky" and "Happy" sound like all of Pharrell's other songs, only way better. Al adroitly cherry-picked the Virginia hit-maker's biggest, most ubiquitous smashes, preserving the elements that spark joy and cutting out the problematic Robin Thicke element.

"Tacky" is a satire of vulgarity American-style, but it's also a tongue-in-cheek celebration of vulgarity as well. The song captures how liberating it can be to purposefully disregard the dreary rules of propriety, even if that entails doing things that would fill most people with shame.

What makes "Tacky" so joyous is the immense pleasure Al takes in outlining his character's crimes against decorum. He's just as giddy singing about his collection of used liquor bottles as Pharrell is when he croons about pure bliss.

With references to practicing twerking moves in line at the DMV, a YOLO license plate, live tweeting a funeral and taking a selfie with the deceased, "Tacky" is incontrovertibly

alfredyankovic #yolo

a product of a very specific cultural moment. It's dated in the best possible way. Of course the raging hurricane of bad taste singing it is going to glom onto the most ephemeral of fads, right around the time they lose what little cultural currency they once possessed.

Appropriately, the Ed Hardy shirt worn with fluorescent orange pants in "Tacky" was already a dated reference in 2014. But that's fitting, since to be truly tacky you need to be deeply disinterested in keeping up with the times. Tackiness requires an astonishing level of obliviousness in terms of how you see yourself and the world. On "Tacky," Al makes shameless vulgarity feel like freedom – from rules, from elitism, from excessive self-consciousness.

About two years after the release of "Tacky" the American people elected a deplorable vulgarian who ran on a platform that posited tackiness as an essential, necessary rebuke to the cultural over-sensitivity of the elites. In Donald Trump's hands, tackiness doesn't seem quite so innocuous.

But on "Tacky," tackiness is just good, dumb, liberating fun – as long as you're not the one stuck behind a drunk guy taking off his shirt at the bank or the waiter being threatened with a bad Yelp review.

12.
JACKSON PARK EXPRESS

"Jackson Park Express" is the *Gone with the Wind* of Al's songs about creepy Casanovas. It's bigger, longer and more involved than any of Al's previous anti-love songs about *l'amour fou* at its most foolish.

"Jackson Park Express" is huge, an epic that stretches out over nine leisurely minutes. On a lyrical level, on the other hand, "Jackson Park Express" is about virtually nothing.

In the mind of the cracked romantic singing it, however, "Jackson Park Express" is about everything. It's about love at first sight. It's about destiny. It's about chemistry. It's about romantic obsession so outsized that it becomes a form of madness. To the listener, however, it's about something much more modest: the romantic fantasies of a bus passenger during the ride to work.

"Jackson Park Express" is about unrequited love at its most one-sided and delusional. Our insane antihero's life changes completely when the unfortunate object of his desire takes a seat opposite him on the bus to work, and the two exchange glances that give the singer a delusional sense of hope.

It's not unusual to read too much into body language – to interpret a warm smile as an invitation to flirt, or angrily crossed arms as a defensive gesture. "Jackson Park Express" opens on a comparatively sane note, with the lovestruck bus passenger thinking he and his oblivious would-be soulmate share a special connection based on her smile and their relative proximity. In a fit of optimism, our narrator interprets his fellow passenger's smile as an implicit "Hello, haven't seen you on this bus before."

The situation escalates from there: at first, the public transportation Romeo imagines weird flirtation involving nose jobs, Hewlett-Packard printers and baggies full of deer ticks, the unlikely *accoutrements* of romance.

In his feverish imagination, the singer and the woman he's mentally courting are experiencing all of the phases of a romantic relationship – from the big bang of love at first sight to the giddy intoxication of young love, and finally to the weary disillusionment of breaking up.

Our singer's conception of love more closely resembles Cronenbergian body horror. Through facial expressions, our creepy crooner tells the luckily oblivious object of his desire/madness, "I'd like to rip you wide open/And French kiss every single one of your internal organs/Oh, I'd like to remove all your skin/And wear your skin over my own skin/But not in a creepy way."

The song's narrator imagines a sweeping narrative of flirtation, infatuation, love and heartbreak. But the only gestures that can be understood by others are an unmistakable glance at his imaginary partner's shirt in a way that can only be interpreted as "I like your boobs," and another look that says, "Hey, I think you've got something on the side of your mouth."

"Jackson Park Express" begins in a place of delusional hope and closes in one of delusional resignation. Our antihero reconciles himself to a stoic ending to something that never actually existed in the first place, making this a very big song about a weird little man and his poignantly pathetic imagination.

MEDIUM
RARITIES
(2017)

1.
TAKE ME DOWN

Medium Rarities **functions as** an alternate-universe chronological ramble through Al's career, where the big hits and milestones are either available in mutated form (an instrumental "Dare to Be Stupid," a Japanese "Jurassic Park") or replaced with fascinating obscurities.

Medium Rarities begins on a dazzlingly obscure note with 1978's "Take Me Down," the first song of Al's career to appear on vinyl. "Take Me Down" appeared on *SLO Grown,* a charity compilation of songs from artists in and around San Luis Obispo (or SLO Town, as it is colloquially known by locals and referenced by Al in this song).

"Take Me Down" marks the first-ever appearance of a curious cowpoke known as "Country Al" Yankovic. On "Take Me Down," Al's accordion has a high, lonesome quality unique to this early track, a glimpse at an unformed Al as a teenaged collegiate wisenheimer paying ironic tribute to the area where he went to school. It's funny and irreverent without necessarily being a comedy song.

"Take Me Down" sounds like the earnest product of someone who performs in coffeehouses – as Al did with bongo player Joel Miller, who performs on the song along with guitarist and bassist Jon Iverson and Tom Walters, who contributes mandolin. This gives the song a strikingly different texture than Al's other early work, which would be characterized more by percussive flatulent noises than bluegrass instrumentation.

Al's voice sounds markedly different than it ever would again. Al sounds fascinatingly unfinished, without the nasal edge of angry nerd aggression that would distinguish *"Weird Al" Yankovic.*

There are lyrical turns of phrase about time shifting into neutral and wanting to go a place where "sentimental feelings arouse" you'd expect from a Greenwich Village folkie. But there's also literal toilet humor and poop jokes executed with a sly intelligence that belies their scatological nature. Even at the inception of his career, Al was adept at combining the highbrow with the lowbrow, at singing about dumb stuff in a smart way.

When Al suggests that tourists take a gander at "the toilets at Madonna Inn," among other attractions of questionable taste like Bubblegum Alley and the local car rally, he's referencing actual tourist attractions.

Even the cow poop joke in "Take Me Down" has a gentlemanly quality to it, as Al pays sarcastic tribute to a place "where the grass is so green/And the air is so clean/That when the wind is right you can even smell the cows."

"Take Me Down" sounds like nothing Al would release as a more seasoned recording artist. It's a fascinating one-off, a catchy lost-and-found obscurity that is unmistakably Al yet bears few of the lyrical or musical trademarks of his later work.

The proto-"Weird Al" Yankovic of "Take Me Down" isn't so weird at all. Quirky? Yes. Comedic? Sure. Instead of being the weird and wacky Al we have come to know and love, the raw but obscenely talented teenager here is understated and melancholy in a way he seldom (if ever) would be again.

2.
MY BOLOGNA
(CAPITOL SINGLE VERSION)

Around the time of *Pulp Fiction*'s release, Quentin Tarantino told *Movieline* that he originally wanted to use The Knack's "My Sharona" for the Gimp scene because, in the cult auteur's mind, the naughty New Wave smash had a beat conducive to rigorous anal sex.

The sodomy groove of "My Sharona" isn't the only filthy aspect of the song. Like most rock songs, "My Sharona" is a hymn of sexual obsession about a pervert's erotic fixation with a teenaged girl. If a song could get #MeTooed, a whole bunch of pervy tracks from the '70s and '80s would get cancelled, including this sordid concoction.

Given the filthy nature of "My Sharona," you would naturally assume that, if an accordion-playing teen weirdo were to make a parody of it called "My Bologna," the parody might be, if anything, even dirtier than the original. You would imagine that the wisenheimer would talk about his bologna the same way a more ribald soul might discuss his trouser salami.

Not Al. When Al puts out a song about bologna, you better believe it's actually, literally about lunch meat.

The original version of "My Bologna" is raw, all right, but not in terms of lyrical content or sexuality. The young Al was a ferocious carnal beast, to be sure, but on wax he kept things PG.

When Al revisited this seminal early parody for his self-titled debut, legendary rock god Rick Derringer handled production and guitar, and Jon "Bermuda" Schwartz mastered its pounding rhythm. But on the Capitol version of "My Bologna," Al is a one-man band, and not of the busker-with-harmonica-acoustic-guitar-and-knee cymbals-in-the-subway variety.

Some artists can sound like a band all by themselves. That's not Al here. No, Al sounds exactly like what he was: a supremely talented kid trying to replicate the filthy fury of the Knack with just an accordion and his voice. Instead of a beat redolent of sweaty fornication, the song moves to the more leisurely rhythms of a solo squeezebox.

The low-profile Christmas Eve release of the "My Bologna" single marked the beginning and the end of Al's relationship with Capitol. The label understandably assumed that the young singer-songwriter's future would be brief and undistinguished. They never could have imagined that, four full decades after the release of "My Bologna," the kooky kid with the novelty song about lunch meat would be a national treasure whose accomplishments would dwarf those of the Knack as well as many of the artists he'd go on to lampoon.

Capitol thought Al would be a singles artist at best. They had no idea that he would go the distance – that he was not just an album artist, but a box set artist as well. And not just any box set: a Grammy-winning fifteen-volume anthology that stands as an enduring testament to the incredible legacy of one of the most overachieving musicians in the history of American music.

3.
YODA
(DEMO)

"Yoda" missed the window to capitalize on the popularity of *The Empire Strikes Back* and its funny-talking breakout character not by a month or a few months but rather by a half-decade.

The demo version of "Yoda," recorded in 1980 when *The Empire Strikes Back* was still in theaters, would take five years to go from *Dr. Demento Show* favorite to a standout track on 1985's *Dare to Be Stupid*. Five years is a *long* time for a song to be in development, but once the general public and Al fans got a hold of "Yoda" they refused to let it go.

Even in its primordial form, the enduring brilliance of "Yoda" is evident. The demo consists of Al and his accordion (once again pressed into lead instrument duty by default), Joel Miller on Yoda noises, and the hands of "Musical Mike" Kieffer.

Miller's Yoda sounds don't sound much like "Yoda," and Kieffer's contributions sound less like the burbling swamp described in the song than a strange attempt at beatboxing with hands. But if the sound is primitive, the lyrics showcase Al at his incisive early best.

For all its irreverence about show-business, "Yoda" is, in its own strange way, extremely faithful. From the beginning, Al cared enough to get the details perfect; he was a geek creating pop art for an audience of geeks who would be unsparing if Al got even a tiny detail wrong.

I've thought a lot about the "Yoda" lines, "But I know that I'll be coming back some day/I'll be playing this part till I'm old and gray" and "The long-term contract that I had to sign/Says I'll be making these movies till the end of time," both delivered from the perspective of a young Mark Hamill. They're among the most important and incisive of Al's career.

When I listened to those lyrics before, I associated them indelibly with Luke Skywalker and Mark Hamill – the actor who, as a very young man, took on a role that he would indeed continue to play until he's old and gray.

Listening to this adorably homemade version of one of Al's most beloved early songs, I found myself thinking for the first time about Al himself. Not all contracts are literal. Some are more abstract. When a musician creates a song that catches on with fans and the general public the way Al's *Star Wars* songs have, it creates certain expectations. When fans take to a song like that, you have to play it for them, even in a context devoted to usurping expectations and giving audiences precisely what they're not expecting to hear, like the 2018 Ridiculously Self-Indulgent, Ill-Advised Vanity Tour. At all seven shows I saw, Al nonetheless ended his originals-only slate with a straightforward performance of either "Yoda" or "The Saga Begins."

If you're going to be permanently tethered to a song, *and* a movie, *and* a character for life, as Al is to "Yoda," *The Empire Strikes Back,* and the little green dude who sounds suspiciously like Grover, respectively, this particular trio is tough to beat.

4.
DR. DEMENTO
SHOW JINGLE

It is difficult to overstate the importance of Dr. Demento in Al's life and career. The good doctor didn't just give the talented young accordionist a sandbox to play in and a supportive home to refine his gifts; he gave Al a new way of looking at the world, one that was kind and inclusive as well as demented. He lovingly embraced geekiness and eccentricity instead of shunning it.

In *The Dr. Demento Show*, the young Al found a clubhouse where being uncool was cool, where the inmates ran the asylum, where being weird and demented was celebrated. Al is famously a creature of television but he was raised on the radio, specifically the *Dr. Demento Show*.

Before Al made the miraculous leap from watching television and singing about television to actually being on television, he made a similar leap with radio. Al went from consuming the zany ditties of the Funny Five to being a countdown king.

Al and the Doctor enjoy a wonderfully symbiotic relationship: Dr. Demento helped make Al a star, a household name, an unlikely hit-maker. In return, Al has done more to raise Dr. Demento's national profile than anyone else.

By the time Al and Jon "Bermuda" Schwartz recorded the eleven-second *Dr. Demento Show Show* jingle included on *Medium Rarities* in 1981, his association with the Good Doctor was already long and fruitful. Not long after making a quiet debut on Capitol with the "My Bologna" single in late 1979, Al repaid Dr. Demento for making his career happen by recording a jingle for his radio show that he still uses to this day.

There isn't a whole lot to the quickly recorded audio nugget – just Demento's name enthusiastically chanted three times, a spare, martial beat courtesy of Schwartz and some demented cackling. The jingle has an endearing homemade quality that comes from being recorded on primitive technology.

It didn't matter to Dr. Demento or his listeners that Al was raw and unpolished. He was one of them, but he was also an outlier – someone who would break into the mainstream and MTV and movies and the Top 40 charts in a big way.

Demento obviously knew Al had something special, or he wouldn't have lovingly mentored him when he was just a scarily smart kid. But even he couldn't have foreseen just how unique Al would ultimately prove to be.

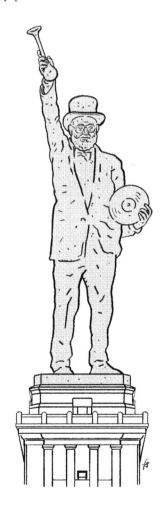

5.
PAC-MAN

With drummer Jon "Bermuda" Schwartz, guitarist Joe Nipper and bassist Tim Matta, Al parodied the Beatles' "Tax Man" as "Pac-Man" in the pre-album phase of his career and sent the ensuing magic to Dr. Demento. Al's mentor was happy to play the timely parody on his show, until he was hit with a cease and desist letter that instilled in the young, impressionable Al the notion that it might be a good idea to receive clear permission before recording or releasing parodies.

So while the monsters in Buckner & Garcia had astonishing success with their musical tribute to Pac-Man, it was back to the drawing board for Al, who would not be able to release the would-be single until decades later as one of the main attractions of *Medium Rarities.*

In hindsight, it's miraculous that Al managed (like Buckner & Garcia) to break out of the novelty ghetto and conquer the mainstream. If "Pac-Man" had been released, and hit the charts, it would have been harder for Al to prove himself as a recording artist with a future. Pac-Mania was undoubtedly a passing fad; being permanently associated with it could easily have pigeon-holed Al as a wacky opportunist. He wouldn't be someone we'd be reverently discussing four decades later.

"Pac-Man" is yet another early tongue-in-cheek ode to obsession, this time sung from the perspective of a reformed pinball maniac pathologically obsessed with Pac-Man. The humor in Al's hymns to consumer obsession often comes from the incongruity of someone experiencing life-changing enthusiasm for something unlikely. But I'm old enough to attest that kids and teenagers went absolutely insane for Pac-Man when it first came out. It became a preeminent fad of the early '80s, with addicted video game players pumping quarter after quarter into the slots in a mad frenzy to get the high score.

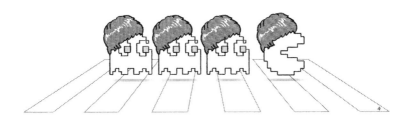

With "Pac-Man," Al was taking something very real in the culture – a wild mania for video games in general and Pac-Man in particular – and exaggerating it for comic effect.

Al sure sounds hazily, happily hypnotized by his new god here as he sings about quitting his job, selling his house and having all his mail forwarded to his new, permanent home in front of a Pac-Man arcade game.

"Pac-Man" finds Al on the familiar, fertile ground of pop culture obsession. Musically, "PacMan" boasts a confidence and swagger understandably missing from homemade recordings of just Al and his accordion. There's nothing tentative about the performances here: "Pac-Man" just plain *rocks*, possibly because the Beatles were a *really* good band.

"Pac-Man" may very well have marked the first time that Al took an idea that looks lazy on paper – a timely Pac-Man themed parody based on a classic song with a very similar name – and made something special out of it. It certainly wouldn't be the last.

Al might have lost the "Pac-Man" battle to Buckner & Garcia; "Pac-Man Fever" was such a hit that the album of the same name went gold despite every song being video-game based. But if Al lost that battle, he ended up winning the war. Buckner & Garcia might have scored their own hit song, but Al went on to have a hit career, and with *Medium Rarities*, the long-delayed eventual release of a sadistically catchy rocker that is as close to essential as a song about Pac-Man can possibly be.

6.
DARE TO BE STUPID
(INSTRUMENTAL)

Not many songs in the canon of Western music meet the impossible standard of perfection, but "Dare to Be Stupid" is one of them. It's one of those miraculous songs where everything goes right. Devo wasn't just the perfect act for Al to pay reverent homage to at that stage of his career; they're kindred spirits, Dadaistic comic geniuses who also happen to be musical visionaries.

With "Dare to Be Stupid," Al captured the essence of Devo's concept of "De-evolution" in a four-word challenge to American consumers. "Dare to Be Stupid" isn't just one of Al's best, most important singles: it's practically his signature song.

In this respect, it doesn't really matter that "Dare to Be Stupid" never charted. When assessing Al's legacy, the charts only tell a small part of the story. Heck, "The Saga Begins" never broke the top 100. Very few of Al's songs made the top 40, but a lot of them made a huge impact on fans and pop culture as a whole. This is particularly true of "Dare to Be Stupid," a transcendent ode to stupidity by an intimidatingly smart young man.

On the Ridiculously Self-Indulgent, Ill-Advised Vanity Tour, Al performed "Dare to Be Stupid" in most of the shows, but in a radical new context. Instead of being the greatest non-Devo Devo song imaginable, "Dare to Be Stupid" was re-contextualized as a Grateful Dead homage, a bluesy jam-band tribute to a forgotten number from the '60s.

Al had to give the people "Dare to Be Stupid," but he and the band changed it so thoroughly that it took on a whole new life. It almost felt as if Al and the band were covering someone else's song, instead of playing one of their defining classics. So when the "Dare to Be Stupid" instrumental appeared on the

B-side of 1996's "Amish Paradise," it was weird, but in a good, on-brand kind of way.

Unfortunately, in the decades since "Dare to Be Stupid" rampaged across pop culture, the masses have seemingly embraced the song's challenge in a non-ironic way. Al's music has chronicled, with wit and no small level of mortification, how technology continually improves in a way that empowers mankind to become their worst, stupidest selves.

When "Dare to Be Stupid" was released, Ronald Reagan was the grinning, blow-dried embodiment of De-evolution. Now we wish we were led by a leader with the intellectual gravity and fundamental seriousness of the Gipper. As a culture and a society, we dare to be stupid in a way that's no longer funny, but sad bordering on tragic.

7.
JURASHIKU PARK

Japan has always had a special affinity for Al. Why wouldn't it? Al is pretty much the Platonic ideal of the perfect American: an outsized cartoon character from Southern California who parodies icons like Madonna and Michael Jackson and makes outrageous songs about television and food and computers.

Al referenced the land of the rising sun in his breakout hit "Eat It" when he famously implored, "Don't you know that other kids are starving in Japan?"

In 1984, when "Eat It" mania was at its apex, Al's label released a pair of compilations for the Japanese market: *The Official Music of "Weird Al" Yankovic – Al Hits Tokyo,* which contained mostly originals from Al's first two albums, and *Eat It,* which focused on parodies. Al was even invited to perform on what he was told was Japan's version of *Saturday Night Live,* an experience that would have proven surreal even if Al had spoken Japanese.

Al's longtime love affair with Japan led him to record a Japanese language version of "Jurassic Park," a tribute to the film of the same name based on the blockbuster novel Michael Crichton published in 1990, a mere two years before his astonishingly racist anti-Japanese manifesto *Rising Sun,* which was also turned into a hit film.

Given Al's popularity in Japan, and the international popularity of *Jurassic Park,* the "suits" decided it couldn't hurt Al's popularity in the East for him to release "Jurassic Park" in Japanese.

Al might have watched over a hundred episodes of *The Flintstones* to research "Bedrock Anthem," but even he has his limits. So Al did not learn Japanese specifically for this one song; instead he delivered his vocals phonetically – and while the song didn't chart in Japan, that doesn't necessarily make it a failure. "Jurassic Park" didn't chart in the United States either, but that didn't keep it from becoming a fan favorite.

"Jurassic Park" may not have cracked the top 100 in Al's home country but it still feels like a T. Rex-sized success. Kids are starving in Japan, all right – starving for sweet, sweet, "Weird Al" Yankovic musical mischief created just for them. That's exactly what "Jurashiku Park" delivered.

8.
HEADLINE NEWS

The past doesn't change; it can't. But our understanding of the past is constantly in flux: our individual and collective pasts are fluid, perpetually shifting to accommodate the attitudes and sensitivities of the present.

On "Headline News," for example, Al borrows the weirdly infectious dirge-like melody and irritatingly catchy chorus of Crash Test Dummies' "Mmm Mmm Mmm Mmm," as well as its structure, to impishly chronicle three of the biggest tabloid scandals from the early 1990s.

The first is Michael Fay, a dumbass American tourist who made the unwise choice to engage in vandalism during a trip to Singapore, and who was punished by a vicious caning. Then there's Tonya Harding's descent into notoriety, which takes on new light after the Margot Robbie movie *I, Tonya*, which depicted the controversial skating champion as the troubled victim of abuse, first from her mother and then from husband Jeff Gillooly. Finally, there's Lorena Bobbitt, who was similarly the subject of a sympathetic film – the documentary *Lorena*, which portrayed her not as the tabloid cartoon of the public imagination but a passionate, dignified immigrant who was sexually terrorized by a dead-eyed sociopath until she was moved to take violent action against the instrument of her abuse.

We've changed in the quarter century since the release of "Headline News." We've evolved and de-evolved, made great social progress and regressed. Al's tongue-in-cheek spin through the top tabloid tales of the day is consequently the product of an earlier era.

"Mmm Mmm Mmm Mmm" is one of the goofier products of the Nirvana-fueled Alternative Rock boom of the early to mid-'90s, a borderline novelty song full of additional novelties. Crash Test Dummies frontman Brad Roberts sings in a bass-baritone so low that it almost sounds like he's doing a goofy fake voice to amuse friends.

Instead of words in its chorus, "Mmm Mmm Mmm Mmm" substitutes noises, namely strangely hypnotic humming. The same is true of "Headline News." It's one of the only songs in Al's oeuvre that has the same chorus as the song that Al is parodying, which finds Al singing in a register lower than he ever has before in a successful attempt to replicate the oceans-deep croon of Crash Test Dummies frontman Brad Roberts.

As "Headline News" draws to a close, Al pulls out all the stops. The kazoos employed to such delightful effect in "Smells Like Nirvana" return, along with the accordion that distinguished Al's self-titled debut, and with the musical hands of manualist Mike Kieffer.

When "Headline News" was released as a single from Al's first box set, the 24-hour news cycle had not quite attained the unstoppable velocity that defines it today. But this still feels unmistakably like old news.

9.
SINCE YOU'VE BEEN GONE
(KARAOKE VERSION)

An album cut from *Bad Hair Day*, "Since You've Been Gone" is eighty-two seconds of sublimely succinct sonic silliness, a bite-sized blast of *a cappella* romantic misery about one of Al's trademark toxic relationships.

Running under a minute and a half, "Since You've Been Gone" is over not long after it begins. It doesn't have time to wear out its welcome. It's too short a sonic snack to be conducive to the vocal gymnastics *a cappella* acts live for. But that didn't keep Al from puckishly including a karaoke version as one of seven tracks on the CD maxi-single for "Gump."

Do sweeter words exist than "CD maxi-single for 'Gump?'" Of course they do. But from a nostalgia angle, those are tough to beat.

An inveterate deconstructionist, Al likes to take songs apart and explore how they function. He does that with his own song here, removing the lead vocal but keeping the background crooning in a way that's impressive, disorienting, and full of bizarre, ghoulish imagery and phrases rendered even stranger in this new context.

The point of karaoke is to give the masses the instrumental version of a song, along with the lyrics so that they can add vocals themselves. Making a karaoke version of a song *without* any instruments is a stroke of warped genius.

The track feels unmistakably like a goof. But removing the lead vocal highlights how much craft, care and artistry went into making this genially bleak little number. The karaoke version of "Since You've Been Gone" also empowers fans to fill in for Al and assume his lead role, as they sing along to the fussily impressive backing track.

Even better, the "Since You Were Gone" karaoke version allows fans to realize their biggest dream– to be in an Ivy League *a cappella* group with "Weird Al" Yankovic called the Weirdenpoofs.

The karaoke version of "Since You've Been Gone" didn't make a whole lot of sense as a bonus track. It makes even less sense (and is even more wonderfully, perversely pointless) here; that could very well be the point.

10.
THE NIGHT SANTA WENT CRAZY
(EXTRA GORY VERSION)

The existence of two distinct versions of "The Night Santa Went Crazy" poses an unexpected philosophical question. It's surprising in that you don't expect Christmas songs *or* "Weird Al" Yankovic album-closers to make you think about the nature of punishment and rehabilitation.

Then again, "The Night Santa Went Crazy" is anomalous in other ways as well. Where most Christmas songs depict corpulent gift-giver Santa Claus as the twinkly-eyed embodiment of goodness and generosity, Al's song portrays him as a whiskey-soaked sociopath who finally snaps after centuries of unrelenting pressure, embarking on a blood-soaked rampage that leaves his trusty stable of flying reindeer brutally murdered and maimed.

In Al's evocative turn of phrase, not-so-jolly old Saint Nick is less every child's friend and benefactor than a "big fat drunk disgruntled Yuletide Rambo" who follows his traditional greeting of "Merry Christmas to all" with "Now you're all gonna die!"

In the album version of "The Night Santa Went Crazy," a psychotic Kris Kringle survives his massacre, is incarcerated and qualifies for parole in a mere 700 years. In the Extra Gory version of the song, the deranged spree killer isn't quite so lucky.

You can't turn Santa into a mass murderer and remain a beloved favorite of children and families the world over. What's more, you certainly can't violently end his cruel, tragic life in a flurry of bullets. But that's just what Al does on "The Night Santa Went Crazy" and its extra-gory version. Al got away with it because he's Al, a man who can go to incredibly ghoulish places and remain a figure of family-friendly fun. In the extra gory version of "The Night Santa Went Crazy," that ghoulishness extends to describing Santa's violent demise with a brutality as sadistic as the choice to kill Kris Kringle.

With child-traumatizing delight, Al takes malicious pleasure in singing, "Yes, Virginia, now Santa Claus is dead/ Some guy from the SWAT team blew a hole through his head/ Yes, little friend, now, that's his brain on the floor/I guess they won't have the fat guy to kick around anymore."

This is where the philosophical questions comes in. Is it crueler to use the power of the state to end a violent, irredeemable criminal's life? Or is it crueler to allow an immortal creature like Santa Claus to live forever in circumstances specifically designed to make him suffer?

Is a millennium-long sentence in a federal prison a fate worse than violent death? That's a question every Christmas music aficionado and "Weird Al" Yankovic fan ultimately has to answer for themselves. But there's no denying that this sick spin through North Pole mythology takes perhaps Al's darkest sick joke and makes it even sicker and darker. Or, depending on your perspective, a little kinder in its choice to terminate the jolly old elf with extreme prejudice.

"The Night Santa Went Crazy" makes a point of going way, way, way too far. The extra gory version of this Christmas perennial, God bless it, goes even further.

11.
SPY HARD

In the mid-'90s, Al got a chance to not only write and record the theme song to a major motion picture, but to direct its opening credit sequence as well. For an ambitious, visually-oriented aspiring filmmaker like Al, that was an offer he couldn't refuse. Unfortunately, the film in question was the little-loved 1996 Leslie Nielsen vehicle *Spy Hard*, a movie primarily known these days for Al's involvement.

The super spy spoof afforded Al an opportunity to do something new and challenging: create a lush, symphonic cinematic theme sexy and glamorous enough for an extended cinematic riff on James Bond, yet goofy enough for a "Weird Al" Yankovic theme song for a late-period Leslie Nielsen gag-fest.

Al corralled the costly services of an 85-piece orchestra to help him pay tribute to a man of mystery who always has "places to go and people to kill."

James Bond themes are not sung so much as they're belted out by singers with serious pipes like Tom Jones and Shirley Bassey. This challenges Al vocally, even before an ending where he holds a note for twenty seconds, causing his head to explode from the pressure *Scanners*-style in the opening credits.

Al has seldom sounded this sultry before. The movie he's shilling for might be a rinky-dink trifle from the unfortunate post-Zucker Brothers stage of the white-haired funnyman's career, but its theme sounds downright epic. As with the later espionage-themed "Party in the CIA," Al's take on the spy game is perversely health insurance-focused.

On "Party in the CIA," an overly enthusiastic secret agent chooses the Central Intelligence Agency over its domestic colleagues because they have "a better dental plan than the FBI's." On "Spy Hard" Al concedes that "facing death every day is a tough job for any man," but at least "his hours are flexible and he's got a great dental plan."

Why is a good dental plan important? Three words: Lisa needs braces.

As it nears the end, "Spy Hard" grows delightfully sentient, and becomes an opening credit song *about* being a song that accompanies the opening credits. Al sings helpfully, "By the way, if you walked in late/Allow me to reiterate/The name of this movie is *Spy Hard*/They call it *Spy Hard*." Later Al, ever the stickler for accuracy, returns to this theme when he croons over the end credits, "The name of this movie was *Spy Hard*/They called it *Spy Hard*/You just saw *Spy Hard*/It's the end of *Spy Hard!*"

Spy Hard's best jokes all come when Al is in control. That's only fitting, since this early Aaron Seltzer/Jason Friedberg (*Date Movie, Epic Movie, Scary Movie*) collaboration, directed by Jason's father Rick, finds the very best in musical parody working with some of the very worst in cinematic spoofery.

12.
LOUSY HAIRCUT

The second half of *Medium Rarities* is dominated by tracks that Al made for television in his capacity as a much sought-after voiceover artist, talk show guest, musical guest, guest star, one-man band/co-host and creator, head writer and star of a short-lived but much-loved children's television show.

It was in that last role (or roles) that Al recorded the thirty-second blast of cheeky aggression "Lousy Haircut" for his cult classic 1997 television vehicle *The Weird Al Show*. The "Firestarter" pastiche, put together by guitarist Jim West after

CBS nixed Al doing a full-on parody of the electronic smash, functioned as a fake music video within the gleefully absurd universe of *The Weird Al Show*.

During their brief late-'90s heyday, Prodigy was known primarily for the electronic attitude of hits like "Breathe," "Firestarter" and "Smack My B**** Up" and late frontman Keith Flint's spectacularly ugly hairstyle: shaved on top with follicular devil horns dyed unnatural colors like lime green and Ronald McDonald orange.

Keith Flint was infamous for his incoherent anger and egregiously lousy haircut. Al put these defining traits together and, for the purpose of this spoof, decided that Flint wasn't a big ball of rage *and* someone with a lousy haircut. Instead, he was someone who was apoplectic *because* he has such a terrible haircut.

"Lousy Haircut" came out just a year after the 1996 album *Bad Hair Day*. During this era, Al wasn't afraid to speak truth to power and tell pop stars like Coolio and Keith Flint, "The way you style your hair is comical to me."

"Lousy Haircut" takes aim at Keith Flint's iconic hairdo, but also his group's hypnotically lazy repetition. "Firestarter" wasn't a hit despite its lyrics consisting of little more than Keith Flint yelling "I'm a firestarter, twisted firestarter!" and then "You're a firestarter, twisted firestarter!" repeatedly; it was a hit *because* of the ferocious catchiness of its repetition.

Following suit, "Lousy Haircut" consists mostly of Al yelling about having a lousy haircut and being angry about his lousy haircut, and not knowing what to do with his lousy haircut.

When you do a project as immersive as this book, you begin to see things through an Al-centric lens. Consequently, when I saw that Keith Flint had committed suicide, this was the first thing that sprung to mind. I think it's safe to say that Al making a song poking fun at Flint's hairstyle in 1997 and him tragically ending his life twenty-two years later are wholly unrelated. Musicians are a famously sensitive lot, but they're not *that* sensitive.

13.
HOMER AND MARGE

Al is nothing if not consistent. This portion of *Medium Rarities*, for example, isn't just devoted to songs Al recorded specifically for the opening and end credits of *Spy Hard*, *The Simpsons* and *30 Rock*; that would be specific enough. But Al takes things a metatextual step further by making these tunes partially about our experience listening to Al sing at the start or end of a TV show or movie.

"Homer and Marge," a *Simpsons*-themed parody of John Mellencamp's "Jack and Diane" (which Al famously was barred from parodying as "Chuck and Diane" early in his career), is largely concerned with "Weird Al" Yankovic making a singing cameo at the close of a *Simpsons* episode.

Against the reassuring backdrop of *The Simpsons'* end credits, Al sings, "Weird Al sayin', 'Oh yeah, the credits go on/ Long after the viewers' interest is gone/Oh yeah, Weird Al had fun on this show/Even if it was just a brief cameo.'"

Yet "Homer and Marge" is also about everything else Al sings about, from overeating (Al praises Marge by saying her heart is as big as Homer's stomach is large) to food to television and rock star greed. In the spoken-word portion of the track, Al talks about taking a reasonably priced flight to Springfield after clearing the check Marge sent him for his services as a modestly priced singing Cupid. Later, he sings about Homer and Marge being "two folks I helped out for a nominal charge."

There's quite the mutual admiration society going on between Al and Matt Groening's satirical masterpiece. *The Simpsons* is referenced in three of Al's best songs – "Frank's 2000" TV," "Why Does This Always Happen to Me" and "Phony Calls" – while Al was invited to perform an extended version

of "Homer and Marge" during the show's big Hollywood Bowl show. He even has a figure commemorating his guest turn that hangs on the wall of my office, part of a modest, yet tasteful "Weird Al" Yankovic shrine.

The original version of "Homer and Marge" wasn't written by Al, but the highest praise I can give its songwriter is that it feels like one of Al's compositions, and not just because it manages to rhyme "After Homer went gay, they patched up their schism" with "dude never dealt with his alcoholism."

It ended up taking Al a *very* long time to make an officially sanctioned parody of "Jack and Diane." But it was worth the wait, as "Weird Al" Yankovic and *The Simpsons* predictably proved two great tastes that taste great together.

14.
THE BRAIN SONG

Nutty Professor Yankovic returns with a cerebral vengeance on "The Brain Song." The dense educational lecture in wacky comedy song form was originally created as the thrilling, largely animated climax of a 3-D movie entitled *Al's Brain: A 3-D Journey through the Human Brain with "Weird Al" Yankovic* that Al wrote, directed and starred in, which played the Orange County Fair and later Washington's Puyallup Fair in 2009.

It's a full-on musical extravaganza that sounds big and expensive, in no small part because Al and his band are joined by ringers like trumpeter Warren Luening, saxophonist Tom Evans, trombonist Bill Reichenbach, back-up vocalists including Lisa Popeil and even a children's choir featuring Al's daughter Nina.

With the exception of "Everything You Know Is Wrong," this is the closest Al has come to writing a They Might Be Giants song. The two Johns are never afraid to bring the classroom to the concert hall, to Trojan horse information inside catchy pop songs. Like Al's beloved TMBG pastiche, "The Brain Song" even features a reference to a disembodied head.

There's a subgroup of They Might Be Giants songs I categorize/dismiss as "scientific," but it's hard to get more science-tastic than Al does here. "The Brain Song" accomplishes the difficult feat of making a treatise on the functions of the brain fun, rather than eyeball-meltingly tedious. "The Brain Song" is so dense with information that it almost feels like understanding and processing it should give you a college credit or two at undiscriminating universities.

Al sets out to do nothing less than explain the inner workings of the human mind. That would be ambitious for an hour-long suite or an opera, let alone for a comedy song that

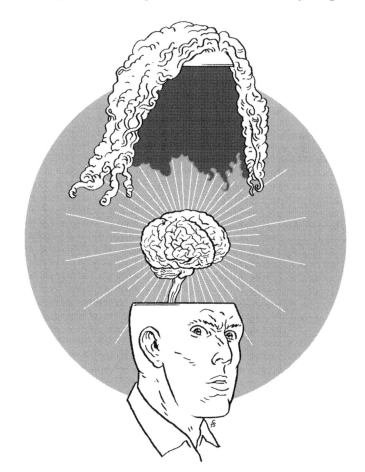

never even approaches the three-minute mark. But Al gets it done so quickly that he's able to devote the final twenty seconds of "The Brain Song" to its message: wear a helmet, for the love of God. That way, you can protect that unfathomably complex brain of yours from its most ferocious natural predator: the zombie.

It doesn't just take a big old brain like Al's to conceive of a song like this; it takes a sizable psyche to grasp it as well. One bigger and more science-adept, alas, than the one I happen to possess.

15.
30 ROCK THEME PARODY

As a subject for parody, the *30 Rock* theme offers unique challenges. How do you make fun of the lyrics of a song that has none? How do you change lyrics around if there are no lyrics to begin with? How do you mock *30 Rock* in a way that's both loving and biting, affectionate and cutting? Lastly, how do you do all these things in thirty seconds? The difficulty level for a *30 Rock* theme parody is so high that it's remarkable that Al's snarky spoof works at all.

The *30 Rock* theme song doesn't have the rhythms of a song with words. It's jazzy and peppy, all weird angles and overly caffeinated New York atmosphere. Yet Al somehow manages to transform this quintessential instrumental into a parody as satisfying as it is brief.

Al's *30 Rock* parody hit close to home for me. I reviewed *30 Rock* for The A.V. Club for much of its duration, an experience that came close to killing my love for the show. When Al sings, "That's right, the program is over/So now you can talk trash about it and vent your rage/On your Twitter and Facebook page," he could just as well be advising viewers to talk trash and vent their rage over at The A.V. Club, where "fans" of *30 Rock* expressed their love for the show by writing about how terrible it had become and also how I clearly knew so little about *30 Rock* that it was totally amazing that I got to review anything.

Al's spoof captures the weird duality at *30 Rock*'s core. On Twitter and Facebook and the comment sections of The A.V. Club, Tina Fey's inside-baseball television spoof was one of the most talked about and important comedies of the past twenty years. It *mattered*. Outside of that internet/media bubble, however, *30 Rock* was just a modestly-rated hipster comedy that was perpetually on the verge of cancellation.

Al's parody captures that ambivalent aspect of the show's fandom: it wasn't a popular favorite, but the people who loved it *really* loved it. Their opinions mattered more because they listened to NPR and read *The New York Times* and had post-graduate degrees and were just plain better than the mouth-breathers who love *Two and a Half Men*.

Al started singing about television as an outsider riffing on hokey reruns. By the time Al goofed on *30 Rock*'s theme he was an insider. He was a living legend the top comedy minds of the day grew up worshiping and leaped at the opportunity to collaborate with, if only for the sake of a brief cameo.

16.
SUPER DUPER PARTY PONY

Growing up in the '80s, Al was thought of as someone you fell in love with as a kid but eventually outgrew. Al's music has long been a rite of passage. But at a certain point you were supposed to move on to "serious," "adult" artists who sang about love instead of food and television.

That perception has changed dramatically with time. Part of that is attributable to Al's longevity: when you have endured the way Al has, it becomes impossible to write you off as kid's stuff or a phase.

Al has proven himself in every conceivable sense, but he's also benefited from seismic cultural shifts. Grownups are no longer expected to give up Al's music once they become adults any more than they're expected to give up superheroes or comic book movies. Heck, it's even become societally acceptable for adult men to love the My Little Pony series of toys and animated programs, specifically the beloved cult show *My Little Pony: Friendship is Magic*.

There is no shame in being a brony (as male fans of My Little Pony are called), only joy in not being made to feel guilty for the innocent things in life that give you pleasure and a sense of identity in an often brutal world. I can only imagine the joy that swept through Bronyland when Al lent his voice and ebullient essence to the scene-stealing role of Cheese Sandwich, a self-professed "super-duper party pony," super party planner and all-around party animal who sweeps into Equestria and challenges Pinkie Pie's dominance of the party-planning game.

On "Super Duper Party Pony," Al delivers a Harold Hill-like spiel about his Andrew W.K.-level mastery of partying as both a lifestyle and art form to a mesmerized crowd. It doubles as an origin story explaining just how he came to be.

"Fizzy drinks, Hawaiian shirts and brie fondue delight/ You know that with Cheese Sandwich, you'll be partying all night!" Al as Cheese Sandwich promises with irresistible brio, selling himself on the wonder of the Cheese Sandwich Party Experience as much as his ostensible audience.

"Super Duper Party Pony" sounds exactly like you'd imagine. It's a Pixie Stick in song form, a sprinkle-laden sonic cupcake just mischievous and tart enough to avoid being saccharine.

"Super Duper Party Pony" makes it easy to see why adults would become enamored of the sparkly world of *My Little Pony: Friendship is Magic*. It is almost disgustingly adorable, the kind of delight that prominently features a big-eyed, accordion-playing pony version of Al so cute he makes the real Al look like a big fat slobbering pig by comparison.

But "Super Duper Party Pony" is more than cute; it's clever and quirky and overflowing with sincerity and charm as well, the perfect fusion of Al and *My Little Pony*. Plus, should Al ever decide to become a furry, he's got a pretty nifty fursona just waiting for him.

17.
SIR ISAAC NEWTON
VS. BILL NYE

For YouTube phenomenon Epic Rap Battles' "Sir Isaac Newton vs. Bill Nye," nerdcore pioneer Al gets nerdier than ever before. Here, he straps on the perfumed wig and adopts the trademark angry, tight-lipped scowl of legendary scientist Isaac Newton to do lyrical battle with two fellow nerd icons/godfathers of geekdom, Bill Nye and Neil deGrasse Tyson.

Tyson is, of course, a gentleman who goes on the internet to complain that science fiction movies are not science factual movies and that many contain *numerous* factual errors and inaccuracies, thereby rendering them suspect. I get it, but I also just want to enjoy *Timecop* in peace.

Al-as-Isaac comes roaring out the gate, delivering scientifically engineered battle raps at a machine-gun clip against a poser he derides as "Beaker with a bow tie" and a lightweight who "wastes time debating creationists" while he created "the science you explain to kids."

Al rhymes with the kind of swagger that can only come with being one of the true fathers of science. He moves effortlessly from science to theology when he sneers at Nye, "I was born on Christmas, I'm God's gift/I unlocked the stars that you're dancing with."

Al/Isaac convincingly depicts Nye less as an essential popularizer of science than as a children's entertainer out of his league opposite one of the all-time greats.

Even though Nye promenades about in public like he has a PhD in Doing Science with a Minor in Being Smart, he only has a bachelor's degree in mechanical engineering – something the suspiciously knowledgeable Newton taunts him about.

For someone who died centuries ago, Newton knows a lot about Nye's weaknesses as a television performer, human being and scientific mind. Or, if this version of Newton can be trusted, less a real scientist than an entertainer who plays one on television.

Epic Rap Battles co-creator Peter Shukoff plays Nye as a cool geek with a sideward flow, while Chali 2Na of Jurassic 5 lends his cartoon baritone and old school swagger to the role of Tyson. Despite the prominent role Hip Hop plays in Al's career, it's still a delightful novelty to hear him share a track with another prominent rapper with a distinctive flow. I wish Al collaborated with other rappers more often. How sweet would a remix of "Isle Thing" or "Twister" with MF DOOM be? How awesome would it be to hear Ghostface or E-40 on new versions of "Word Crimes" or "Amish Paradise?"

With more than a little help from his friends at Epic Rap Battles, on "Sir Isaac Newton vs. Bill Nye" Al gives new meaning to "dropping science."

18.
LET THE PUN FIT THE CRIME

"Let the Pun Fit the Crime" from the cult cartoon *Wander Over Yonder* finds Al in character as Dr. Screwball Jones, a vaudeville villain who doubles as a sentient walking museum of terrible comedy tropes. He's got a head like a banana just waiting to be slipped on, a Dr. Demento-like top-hat, a multi-colored wig associating him with a nightmarish subsection of comedy known as "clowns," and a polka dot bow tie. And he plays the accordion, the only musical instrument zany enough for Al.

As the title of "Let the Pun Fit the Crime" betrays, he also has a horrible weakness for wordplay. Dr. Screwball Jones' sense of humor is a crime in and of itself, a form of comedic pun-ishment. Where Al uses his accordion and good time polka powers for good, the same can't be said of the bad guy he's voicing here, who wants to make the whole world laugh and have fun, but in a malevolent fashion.

Dr. Screwball Jones wields both his accordion and his terrible sense of humor as weapons in a duet with Jack McBrayer's heroic Yonder that doubles as a musical duel, a battle of instruments as well as ideologies.

The accordion is as synonymous with Al today as it once was universally associated with Lawrence Welk. But the angry, aggressive accordion of Dr. Screwball Jones was played by Andy Bean.

The more you know about *Wander Over Yonder* and "The Boy Wander," the episode that gave the world "Let the Pun Fit the Crime," the more you'll get out of this angry cartoon polka, which is unusually rooted in the episode's plot. There are lyrics that refer to sight gags that get lost in an all-audio medium, but on the whole this is a delightfully dark duet that illustrates Al's gifts as a voice actor as well as a musician.

"Let the Pun Fit the Crime" is far more reliant on context than "Super Duper Party Pony." But it's still a worthy addition to Al's treasure trove of TV tunes.

19.
HEY, HEY, WE'RE THE MONKS

The delightful doo-wop *a cappella* lark "Hey, Hey, We're the Monks," from the musical fantasy comedy television series *Galavant,* boasts the curious distinction of having a title spoofing the chorus but not the actual title of the Monkees' infectious introductory anthem "(Theme from) The Monkees." Despite its title, this is an original composition from the great Alan Menken (of *Little Shop of Horrors* and Disney fame) with eminently quotable lyrics from Menken's writing partner Glenn Slater.

Al flew to England and donned holy robes to play a Monk with Attitude alongside back-up singers/holy harmonizers Stephen Hill, Jeremy Budd, Stephen Weller, Michael Dore, James Spilling and Simon Grant, all of whom get a chance to shine despite "Hey, Hey, We're the Monks" lasting a mere seventy-six seconds.

Instead of the usual vow of silence, the Monks of the Order of Our Father of Perpetual Refrain have taken a vow of singing. They're a boy band in sacred garb whose members include "The Smart One," "The Cute One," "The Shy One" and finally "The Bad Boy," albeit "not so bad cause I'm a monk!"

"Hey, Hey, We're the Monks" is almost *too* clever. But what else would you expect from a Menken/Slater composition? That's one of the joys of *Medium Rarities*: getting to hear Al sing other people's songs outside of the context of a polka or a parody. On *Medium Rarities*, Al sings the compositions of Reggie Watts and Joey Ramone as well as Menken/Slater – a full spectrum to be sure.

"Hey, Hey, We're the Monks" and the guest spot that spawned it afforded Al a juicy opportunity to act as well as sing, to perform an infectious number in character as a man of the Lord with an unlikely excess of musical-theater razzamatazz.

Galavant only lasted eighteen episodes, but that's not because it wasn't smart or funny or original or good. If "Hey, Hey, We're the Monks" is any indication, it was probably excessively smart and funny and original and good, and consequently unfit for the American airwaves.

20.
COMEDY BANG!
BANG! THEME

Al and Reggie Watts each made for perfect *Comedy Bang! Bang!* co-hosts, one-man bands and comic foils for Scott Aukerman. They're both comic geniuses and utter originals, but otherwise they're a study in contrasts. Watts is a beatific, angel-headed hipster stoner god with jazz in his soul. He's so inveterately original and intuitively opposed to repeating himself that each breath is probably markedly different from the last. His blood probably circulates in a different way every day just to keep things interesting.

As with Al, nobody does what Reggie Watts does, let alone anywhere near as well. He's a pure spirit who seems to live in a world all his own, a blessed realm infinitely more colorful than the dreary universe the rest of us are stuck in.

Watts improvised what would become the *Comedy Bang! Bang!* theme song in studio during an episode of the podcast, along with a slew of other similarly inspired ad-libbed miniature make-em-ups. Watts was improvising loosely in the moment, but the result was so stellar that it was used not only as the theme for the podcast but for the television spin-off as well.

Like Watts himself, the hypnotic *Comedy Bang! Bang!* theme is at once organic and funkily retro-futuristic. Watts uses technology to transform himself into the ghost in the machine, layering and distorting his vocals as he repeats the words "Comedy Bang! Bang!" with different emphases over a beat that grows in momentum until a final, ecstatic release.

By reverently covering Watts' theme, Al was implicitly acknowledging that the future *Late Late Show with James Corden* fixture defined the role of *Comedy Bang! Bang!* bandleader/co-host. He was the gold standard, until Al slid easily into that role and proved equally ideal.

Just about the only element missing from Al's cover is the percussive beatboxing that gives Watts' original an old-school feel.

When Watts created what would become the *Comedy Bang! Bang!* theme song, he could not have anticipated that the inspired tomfoolery he created at Aukerman's request would provide the theme song to both one of the most influential and important comedy podcasts of all time, *and* the theme for a beloved cult television show that would run an impressive five seasons and one hundred and ten episodes.

He certainly couldn't have envisioned that a legend like Al would cover the tiny television tune on the final disc of a career-spanning, Grammy-winning box set. Not bad for less than forty seconds of inspired in-studio improvisation.

after
HORNSCHEMEIER

21.
IT'S MY WORLD
(AND WE'RE ALL
LIVING IN IT)"

When a cartoon employs "Weird Al" Yankovic as a voiceover artist, as many have over the years (including my personal favorites, *The Simpsons* and *BoJack Horseman*) it gets more than just the services of someone very good and experienced in the field. They also get the household name fame of the five-time Grammy winner – and, if they're very lucky, the music of "Weird Al" Yankovic as well, with or without accordion accompaniment.

If they're even luckier than that, they don't just get Al to pop in for an episode or two; instead they get Al to voice the main character and throw in a theme song for good measure. That was the case with Disney XD's *Milo Murphy's Law*, which hired Al to voice the title character, a descendent of Edward A. Murphy Jr., the real-life aerospace engineer and the man who came up with Murphy's Law, which states "Anything that *can* go wrong *will* go wrong."

Milo is a magnet for trouble as well, but that doesn't keep him from seeing the glass as perpetually half-full. "It's My World (And We're All Living in It)" sets up *Milo Murphy's Law* not by recounting its premise a la "The Brady Bunch," but rather by establishing Murphy's worldview.

Despite the habitual mishaps that befall him, Milo is a figure of irrepressible optimism. In "It's My World (And We're All Living in It)" Al conveys that sunniness through tone and inflection as much as through lyrics. The song follows suit: the music is as cheerful as the lyrics. It's a busy number with multiple catchy background chants, a sneaky ska/reggae rhythm and Al charming his way through two and a half minutes of sonic sunshine.

This Milo fellow is nothing if not a nice young man. And so polite! It's rare to find a young person who uses phrases like "please" and "thanks," let alone within the context of a peppy introductory song.

Al has been obsessed with television theme songs all the way back to the days of "Ricky" and "The Brady Bunch." Why wouldn't he be? Theme songs sell television shows as consumer products as well as entertainment. "It's My World (And We're All Living in It)" does a fine job on both counts.

22.
BEAT ON THE BRAT

The editing process for *Weird Al: The Book* went smoothly, but I will always remember an editor at Abrams Image, the book's publisher, complaining about a passage where I wrote that the famously primitive recording of "Another One Rides the Bus" and Al's hastily recorded debut album *"Weird Al" Yankovic* were *more* punk than Sid Vicious.

The editor stated that it would be inaccurate to describe Al's scruffy first album as *more* punk than the Sex Pistols, but it would be okay to describe *"Weird Al" Yankovic* as being *as* punk as the Clash.

I was engaging in breathless hyperbole when I compared Al's introduction to the record-buying public to the savage transgressions of the punk movement. When it comes to embodying the essence of punk, Al isn't exactly GG Allin. But I do think *"Weird Al" Yankovic* is only semi-secretly a punk provocation masquerading as a musical comedy album. Al had a real affinity for New Wave: they were his weirdoes – oddballs and outcasts with synthesizers, keyboards, questionable hairstyles, regrettable fashion and attitude.

Al's early output falls unmistakably on the New Wave side of the New Wave/punk divide. But having him cover the

Ramones for a Dr. Demento punk tribute album is inspired. The Ramones were essentially a comic book conception of a punk band, a gaggle of goofy-looking Neanderthal degenerates singing about being bored, sniffing glue and craving something to do.

The Ramones weren't just funny; they were hilarious. Dr. Demento understood the Ramones immediately and played songs from their groundbreaking debut album on his show, including "Beat on the Brat." If the Ramones weren't clearly human cartoons trafficking in rebellion, shock and transgression, then the subject matter of "Beat on the Brat" would be horrifying.

"Beat on the Brat" is singularly terrible parenting advice but a terrific punk song. Al's contribution to *Dr. Demento: Covered in Punk* is a reverent cover of a screamingly irreverent song. Osaka Popstar, whose frontman John Cafiero put together *Covered in Punk*, faithfully reproduces the punishing groove of the original, while Al's delivery is every bit as weirdly stylized as Joey Ramone's.

The lyrics for "Beat on the Brat" are as hypnotically repetitive as anything Al has lampooned for a polka parody. It's the same sneering words repeated over and over, before Al closes things out with the one thing desperately missing from the Ramones' original: an accordion.

When Al covered "Beat on the Brat" for the Dr. Demento compilation, there was an unmistakable element of novelty to Al performing a straightforward cover rather than a parody or polka. The same was true when I saw Al perform the song in concert in Chicago after being introduced by Dr. Demento. Yet by the time the Ridiculously Self-Indulgent, Ill-Advised Vanity Tour ended, Al and his crack band had performed no fewer than 77 covers, one per concert.

I wish my Abrams Image editor had been with me to see Al perform "Beat on the Brat" live. I'm pretty sure it would have convinced him that Al is not only *as* punk as Dee Dee Ramone prostituting himself to score money for heroin; he's considerably more punk than the Ramones, the Clash, the Stooges and the Sex Pistols put together. That's no small feat for a man who doesn't swear, or use drugs, or drink, or start fights, or do pretty much any of the things we associate with punk as not just a genre of music, but as a way of life.

23.
HAPPY BIRTHDAY

A re-recording of an album cut from the *Another One Rides the Bus* EP/ *"Weird Al Yankovic* feels like an inauspicious way to close out both *Medium Rarities* and a project as auspicious as Al's fifteen-disc career-spanning opus *Squeeze Box.* But Al is a methodical man, so there's a logic to his master plan.

Medium Rarities ends with a self-conscious return to the beginning that extends beyond the obscurities collection and box set to the outside world, where Al's hottest song right now is the album version of "My Bologna." That's thanks to its placement in the soundtrack to the third season of Netflix's *Stranger Things,* a pop culture phenomenon powerful enough to raise New Coke from the dead.

The end of *Medium Rarities* finds Al paying tribute to some of his favorite punks and the era that gave the world the Ramones' landmark 1976 debut album and "Beat on the Brat." "Happy Birthday" is built on the cracked foundation of Tonio K.'s 1978 masterpiece *Life in the Foodchain* and its giddily apocalyptic single "The Funky Western Civilization."

"Happy Birthday" was the first of Al's holiday songs – blood-splattered, corpse-strewn, sometimes post-apocalyptic ditties that depict Christmas, birthdays and Weasel Stomping Day as waking nightmares where the world's violent insanity is at its most glaring and appalling.

In the liner notes for *Medium Rarities,* Al says he was moved to re-record "Happy Birthday" for the soundtrack to the Ken Marino-directed sleeper hit *How to Be a Latin Lover* because he always regretted how quickly his debut album had been recorded.

But it's exactly that semi-primitive quality that makes *"Weird Al" Yankovic* so full of scruffy, underdog charm, and what makes "Happy Birthday" sound so punk. If any song in Al's discography benefits from sounding rushed and raw, it's this one.

Al's cover of "Beat on the Brat" added the accordion that alone kept the Ramones' original from becoming a chart-topping smash. For the re-recorded "Happy Birthday" Al went in the opposite direction, removing the accordion, no doubt out of a conviction that doing so would allow his birthday song to finally overtake the Hill Sisters' "Happy Birthday to You" in popularity.

I don't think he succeeded. Exposure in a hit movie is always nice, but the Hill Sisters' ubiquitous standard is one of the most famous songs of all time. Al's "Happy Birthday" isn't even one of the more famous songs on his scrappy debut album.

It seems poetically apt that this epic labor of love would close on a birthday song, however violently ironic. After all, what is the Weird Accordion to Al if not a celebration of a great American, the full extent of whose contributions to American music and pop culture are only now being recognized four decades after he released a nervy little parody of the Knack's "My Sharona"? The parody that began Al's career as a recording artist has boomeranged through time, becoming more popular, culturally relevant and iconic as the decades go by.

Against impossible odds, Al has endured. The Funny Five champion was supposed to have a silly song that did okay as a fluke. Instead, he's had a career for the ages. Al doesn't just sing about pop culture; when he steps onstage these days he is pop culture incarnate – four decades of living musical history that overlaps with the greatest artists of the day, the Madonnas and Nirvanas and Michael Jacksons.

Like birthdays, Al is perennial and cause for celebration. He's not going anywhere, and neither is his music.

Al doesn't sing "Happy Birthday" so much as he sneers it, tearing into imagery that wouldn't feel out of place on a self-released single from an L.A. punk band in the late 1970s. It's full of environmental devastation, poverty, violence and the promise of nuclear war. It's also one of Al's loudest, fastest, punkest songs, at once a howl of despair for a world that doesn't deserve to survive and a tongue-in-cheek embrace of our inevitable doom. It's a song that anticipates Armageddon with a smile, that raises a toast to our personal and collective destruction.

The voracious darkness found in songs like "Happy Birthday" is no small part of what makes Al such a source of joy and light for so many people. Al is sober and self-disciplined and rated PG onstage and off. But there's a persistent, perverse ghoulishness that undercuts the All-American wholesomeness.

Al's *weird* is what he is, a man with a uniquely powerful hold on our memories and our childhoods. And that's wonderful – then, now, and always.

ACKNOWLEDGMENTS

I would like to thank Al, first and foremost for giving me not just something to write about but *everything* to write about, and for helping me along throughout the process. I'd also like to thank my agent Daniel Greenberg for the nifty career as an author and Keith Phipps for giving me permission to write *Weird Al: The Book* as well as Stephen Thompson for everything.

I'd like to thank Al's manager Jay Levey and Al's extraordinary band: Jon "Bermuda" Schwartz, as well as Jim West, Steve Jay and Rubén Valtierra. I promise to do justice to you and your contributions to Al's career in the next book I write about Al. Or the one after that.

Felipe Sobreiro did an absolutely amazing job with illustrations. Your brilliance made this book ten times better. I am in genuine awe of you and your talent. Thanks for introducing me to Mariana Rausch Chuquer, who did an amazing job making this book look beautiful. I'd like to thank the We Hate Movies gang for all of their support me, Felipe and our overlapping endeavors:Andrew Jupin, Stephen Sajdak, Eric Szyszka and Chris Cabin.

Thanks also to the Long Shot Podcast: the enchanting Jamie Flam, Sean Conroy, Amber Kenny and Joe Wagner, Andy Greene and *Rolling Stone,* Eric Rhodes and Ramona Peel for always sharing Weird Accordion to Al articles. Thanks to everyone who pre-ordered the book via Kickstarter, GoFundMe and Backerkit and a mad shout out to everyone at the Society for the Toleration of Nathan Rabin, the readers of Nathan Rabin's Happy Place, Travolta/Cage listeners and my Juggalo nation.

OTHER BOOKS BY NATHAN RABIN

- *The Big Rewind (2009) Scribner*
- *My Year of Flops (2010) Scribner*
- *Weird Al: The Book (2012) Abrams Image*
- *You Don't Know Me But You Don't Like Me (2013) Scribner*
- *Postal (2020) (Boss Fight)*
- *Praise for Nathan Rabin:*
- *"Smart and funny"-Mindy Kaling, The New Yorker*
- *"Brilliant"-John Green*
- *The Big Rewind*

"I'm not as interested in anything as much as Nathan Rabin is interested in everything."– **Chuck Klosterman**

"With his uncanny grasp of cultural zeitgeist, Rabin could unseat Chuck Klosterman as the slacker generation's vital critical voice." – **Heeb Magazine**

"Nathan Rabin's life reads like a fanboy's collision with Dostoyevsky. Hilarious, sad, truthful memoir is compulsively readable."– **Roger Ebert**

"[Rabin] has packed [The Big Rewind], like a cannon, full of caustic wit and bruised feelings. The result is a lo-fi, sometimes crude book that is nonetheless more effective (and affecting) than it has any right to be."– **The New York Times**

My World Of Flops

"Nathan Rabin's My Year of Flops is like watching a genius nurse a score of frightened, wounded baby birds back to life – a superhuman level of care and compassion lavished on That Which Never Had A Right To Exist. Truly brilliant." – **Patton Oswalt**

You Don't Know Me But You Don't Like Me

"An extremely funny and engaging book about how fandom provides people with surrogate families and a way to escape day-to-day banality." – **Rolling Stone (four-star review), 20 Best Music Books of 2013**

"I Love This Book"– **Harris Wittels**

PRAISE FOR
THE WEIRD
ACCORDION TO AL

"A brilliant, heartfelt cry of obsession and love for an already beloved and obsessed-over artist. Share Nathan's madness and be freed!" – **Patton Oswalt**

"This book is pop culture history, music dissertation, and comedic theory. Nathan has exemplified the qualities that make Weird Al an artist who is equal parts Frank Zappa, Mel Brooks, and Mark Twain." – **Jonah Ray**

"You don't have to be a fan of Weird Al to enjoy Rabin's raucous deep-dive into the complete discography. But if you're not a Weird Al fan there's clearly something wrong with you" – **Alex Winter**

"From A to Y (Al to Yankovic), this book, in great detail, captures what makes the oeuvre of Al ooze with oddness. A must read for anyone unemployed, childless, or with ninety spare hours to kill." – **Scott Aukerman**

"The Weird Accordion to Al is the definitive companion to the "Weird Al" catalogue. It's chock full of fascinating insights that left my head spinning like a Frankie Yankovic record (no relation). Nobody covers the Al canon in better depth than Nathan Rabin. It's a must-read for the weirdos in your life. I learned so much from this VERY SPECIFIC book." – **Thomas Lennon**

"Nathan Rabin is obsessive in the best sense of the word. He literally ALREADY wrote the book on Weird Al that Weird Al asked him to write. That wasn't enough for Nathan and that's why we are lucky to have this book. Al's contributions to pop culture deserve the kind of obsession that only Nathan Rabin can bring to the page and he brings it big time in this book. He dares to be very smart about "Dare To Be Stupid.'" – **Jake Fogelnest**